Advanced

Media

Studies

Philip Allan Updates, an imprint of Hodder Education, part of Hachette Livre UK, Market Place, Deddington, Oxfordshire OX15 0SE

Orders
Bookpoint Ltd, 130 Milton Park, Abingdon, Oxfordshire OX14 4SB
tel: 01235 827720
fax: 01235 400454
e-mail: uk.orders@bookpoint.co.uk

Lines are open 9.00 a.m.–5.00 p.m., Monday to Saturday, with a 24-hour message answering service. You can also order through the Philip Allan Updates website: www.philipallan.co.uk

© Philip Allan Updates 2008

ISBN 978-1-84489-418-5

First printed 2008
Impression number   5   4   3   2   1
Year   2013   2012   2011   2010   2009   2008

Designed by Neil Fozzard
All photographs are reproduced by permission of TopFoto, with the exception of those otherwise credited.

Printed in Italy

Hachette Livre UK's policy is to use papers that are natural, renewable and recyclable products and made from wood grown in sustainable forests. The logging and manufacturing processes are expected to conform to the environmental regulations of the country of origin.

P1189

Contents

Introduction

We live in a cultural environment shaped by media images. Large multi-national corporations have the power to monopolise entertainment and news sources, commercial interests lie behind almost all media products, media persuasion techniques are used either to raise or suppress concerns about global issues and even the future of our planet. Public opinion can be manipulated by media representations to serve corporate and political ends. Individual freedoms are increasingly threatened by ever more sophisticated means of documentation, surveillance and control, leading to a growing state and corporate intrusion into our private lives. At the same time, individuals have a new freedom and power to communicate with each other and to generate and distribute media artefacts of their own, via internet blogs and networking sites.

All these elements of the contemporary world make an understanding of the power and influence of the media more important than ever before. Media studies is at the centre of a curriculum designed to encourage independent, articulate, free-thinking individuals who are alert to the challenges posed by constantly emerging new media technologies, who use these technologies in their everyday lives, and who are able to express considered opinions about our society and the world as a whole.

The new specification

The revised AQA specification retains all the essential qualities of the original and, in particular, its emphasis on the need to develop critical thinking skills in the context of text analysis and personal consumption of media texts. However, there is a greater emphasis on emerging technologies and the recognition that young people are increasingly involved with e-media, both as consumers and producers of media texts.

Advanced **Media Studies**

You, as a media studies student, should familiarise yourself with all new-media technologies. In particular, you should use the internet to find information and up-to-date statistics, such as newspaper/magazine circulations and ownership, film reviews, dates, directors, and media theory. Although this textbook contains some charts and figures, you are encouraged to research your own figures and also to use internet versions of newspapers, magazines, news and current affairs programmes to keep up with current events.

The more you engage with new technology, the easier you will find it to discuss issues raised during your media studies course. If you find that an issue or topic is not covered in sufficient detail in this text, or if you want more background on a subject, just enter the relevant details into a search engine like Google and the topic will come up. You could also use Wikipedia (with some caution, as entries are not always soundly checked and edited). There is so much information available on the internet that we have not given you many web addresses in this book — you can easily find these for yourself and learn from the experience.

The new specification has four equally balanced assessment units: two at AS and two at A2. Two of the four units (one at AS and one at A2) involve practical production. This textbook is designed to follow the AQA course closely while providing a structured academic underpinning of important media studies concepts and theories.

The AQA AS/A2 specification:
- provides comprehensive coverage of media theory and practice, emphasising the importance of new technologies
- focuses on the audience as both consumers and producers of media texts
- gives candidates the chance to develop and investigate their personal interests in the media, including cross-media studies
- provides a programme of production briefs and pre-set topics

The units are:
- Unit 1 Investigating Media (MEST1)
- Unit 2 Creating Media (MEST2) — this involves practical production
- Unit 3 Media: Critical Perspectives (MEST3)
- Unit 4 Media: Research and Production (MEST4) — this involves practical production

The specification identifies three central **media platforms**:
- broadcast
- print
- e-media

All **media texts** studied should be assessed across these three platforms.

Also important in Unit 1 and throughout the course are the key **media concepts** of:

- genre and narrative
- audience
- representation
- institution

All texts studied for Unit 1 should also be assessed for their use of **media language**. The above concepts will be explored in detail throughout this book.

How to use this book

This textbook covers all the media theory and terminology you will need to tackle the Assessments in Units 1 and 3, together with many examples of media texts and analytical techniques.

The subject matter for media studies is similar for both AS and A2; the difference between them is a matter of depth. Chapters 1–8 are essential reading for AS students. Chapters 9–13 go into a greater depth that is appropriate to A2 work.

Most media studies students beginning an AS course will not have taken the subject at GCSE and will have mixed motives and expectations when they sign up for the course. The obvious appeal of the subject, with its emphasis on film, television and popular magazine content, makes it attractive to many who have not really considered the demanding nature of media theory and the emphasis on critical and written analytical skills.

Students of English literature will be familiar with critical techniques and terminology, and all media students should be prepared to write deconstructive analyses of media texts and to construct and evaluate their own original media artefacts. At A2, you are also expected to show an understanding of the cultural, historical and economic contexts that affect the production and content of media texts. At both AS and A2, the production of your own media artefact and your personal research topic should be based on sound media principles.

The following features occur throughout this book:

- ideas for discussion and development
- case studies
- tasks
- key terms

Chapters 7, 8, 12 and 13 are called Unit Focus, and in these you will find a detailed explanation of the contents of each of the four Assessment Units, together with sample questions, model answers and mark schemes. Overall, you will find plenty of information, guidance and stimulation in the following pages. These have been designed to help you succeed in your A-level course and, at the same time, make your media studies course an enjoyable and rewarding experience.

Media concepts

How do you begin to study a topic as broad and wide-ranging as the media? AQA's key media concepts provide terminology and a framework for your work, and these can be used as a checklist of aspects to consider when discussing and evaluating a media text.

The following key concepts form the acronym GARI — a useful way to remember them:

- **G**enre and narrative
- **A**udience
- **R**epresentation
- **I**nstitutions

Also important in the study of the media are the concepts of:

- media language
- values and ideology

Genre and narrative

The **genre** of a text is its type. A Western is a type of film text, as are science fiction, romantic comedy, horror and action movies. In television, soap operas, police series, documentaries and game shows are all genres.

Genre is important because it helps to create expectations in an audience, and it allows media producers to use certain conventions of **iconography** and **narrative** to meet these audience expectations. Genre conventions and iconography allow an audience to identify the nature of the genre and to feel comfortable with a generally predictable narrative.

Children as young as 5 or 6 years old can identify television genres and define their viewing experience by referring to them. Genres assist in differentiating between what people like and dislike. In this way, they help to individualise the audience's consumption of media texts and also reflect lifestyle decisions and personal identity.

A note on terminology: it is important to learn and use media terminology as you progress through the course. To help you, key terms are emboldened in this textbook. All key terms are defined either in the main text or in a nearby key terms box.

Some examples of texts, genres and audiences

Bliss is a type of girls' lifestyle magazine. *Hollyoaks* is a soap opera television programme. *Harry Potter* is an example of a cross-genre text — starting out as books and later becoming a series of films. The *Guardian,* the *Sun* and the *Manchester Evening News* are different types of newspaper, written for different audiences and having different news agendas.

Bliss is unlikely to be read by teenage boys or adults. *Guardian* readers are unlikely to read the *Sun*. *Harry Potter* is aimed at children and adolescents but is also read and viewed by a much wider audience of adults. All these media products have a keen sense of who their audience is and what their expectations of the product are. These need to be met if the audience's loyalty is to be retained.

Key terms

iconography: the distinguishing elements, in terms of props and visual details, which characterise a genre. For example, Westerns have horses, desert locations, clapboard houses and men in hats.

narrative: the storyline and structure of a media text.

Ideas for discussion and development
• **Do you ever read magazines intended for the opposite sex? If so, why?**

Audience

The concept of an **audience** is fundamental to the exploration of the media. Consider, for a moment, what the purpose of media texts would be without an audience. Perhaps the gratification of the producers — a text for its own sake? This would be similar to an artist painting pictures no one will ever see. Media texts as we understand them are about communication. The creators, or senders, of the text target an audience and usually allow the audience to provide feedback on how the text has been received. This communication loop is the basis of an interactive media culture.

Audiences are the intended and sometimes unintended consumers of media texts, and we are all part of many different audiences for media products. All media texts are constructed with a specific target audience in mind. Market and audience research is carried out to evaluate the expected responses to the media product.

Feedback (see below) provides further information about audience reactions and allows the product to be developed accordingly. Being part of an audience for a media product can be a way of sharing attitudes, beliefs and values with other audience members, which in turn helps to construct a sense of personal identity. This can be particularly true with soap operas, where following the lives of characters creates a parallel experience to real life, and in some cases can replace real experience and actual relationships.

Feedback and audiences

In media terminology, **feedback** is any mechanism or communication that is designed to reduce the gap between actual and intended performance. In other words, feedback tells you how you are doing — well, not so well, badly — and by taking note of it you can adjust your performance to do better. Using feedback in the form of audience comments, e-mails, and even audience numbers, media producers can assess what aspects of a product are successful in meeting audience needs and expectations, and what aspects need changing. These changes in response to audience feedback are designed to improve the product's appeal and ultimately its success in terms of audience numbers and satisfaction. Media products that do not allow for feedback are unlikely to be successful.

Assessing a sample of target audience members' responses to proposed new film releases has become increasingly important in testing the popularity of a film before its general release. The target audience members' responses can influence the way a film is finally released. Scenes, or even endings, that prove unpopular can be changed to maximise the film's popularity and box office success.

> ### Ideas for discussion and development
> - **Discuss examples of where you have received feedback on your behaviour or performance and made adjustments.**

Representation

Representation is at the heart of media products and is one of the most important concepts in media studies. It features prominently in the AS/A2 specification and is referred to throughout this textbook (see especially Chapter 6).

Why is representation so important?

Apart from our immediate sensory experience, everything we know about our world comes to us by a process of **representation**. Representation is the means by which the media present different aspects of the world to us. Places are represented, as are people — individuals and social groups, institutions, races and religions. The media operate by selecting elements of the world and combining them to create recognisable versions of our experienced reality. However, it is important always to remember that representations are *not* reality.

By using audio, visual and print technology, the **mass media** construct versions of the world we live in. As it is impossible to recreate this actual world of events and experience, media products are constructed around versions of this world. However, these representations are often accepted by audiences as realistic versions of the actual world, despite the fact that they are often built around **stereotypes**. Some websites have taken this process even further, by creating artificial realities that substitute for actual experiences and social contact between people.

Key terms

mass media: the newspaper, magazine, advertising, television, music, radio, cinema and internet industries responsible for the transmission of messages to mass audiences. Mass media content is designed to inform, educate, entertain or persuade members of a target audience.

stereotype: the social classification of a group of people by identifying common characteristics and universally applying them in an often over-simplified way, such that the classification reflects value judgements and assumptions about the group concerned. For example: the 'dumb' blonde, the 'mean' Yorkshireman.

Example of representation of a social group: the police

In the UK, the police are a large social group with a clearly defined role. This group is made up of a wide range of people from different backgrounds who have a variety of attitudes, beliefs and values.

In representing the police in television series like *The Bill*, media producers select elements of character and situation. These fictional constructions can never encompass the whole reality of being in the police, but the way in which selections are made will affect how we, the audience, see the police and our expectations of their attitudes and behaviour.

British audiences will have different expectations of the behaviour of British police in situations they feel are familiar, as compared to the US police who live in a different, and for the audience more escapist, world. The 'realism' associated with the representation of everyday policing in the

UK is very different from the escapism of series set in foreign locations, with serious crime and hardened criminals.

If we encounter the real police, our experience and expectations will be affected by our exposure to fictional versions of police activity. It could also be argued that the behaviour of the police themselves will be affected by how they see themselves represented in the media.

Task

Look through your local newspaper and identify all the articles that refer to the police. Discuss the different ways in which they are represented. On the whole, are these representations positive or negative?

Media institutions

Media institutions are the organisations that produce and disseminate media products. The majority of media products are developed by such institutions rather than individuals working alone. They are structured along corporate lines, with hierarchies of authority — departments run by line managers, with directors and chief executives having overall responsibility. Individual departments are based on the division of labour, purpose and expertise, and they have devolved authority to manage their own areas. However, these departments are responsible to senior management for outcomes and general performance.

Companies have their own ethos, goals, targets and declared mission — in effect, their own ideology (see pages 8–12) — and this has an important influence on the products they create and how they conduct themselves in a competitive marketplace. For example, a correspondent reporting on the war in Iraq may be interpreting events in his or her own individual style and giving a point of view, but the report will be mediated by the organisation for which he or she works and without which the report would be unable to reach an audience. If the organisation edits or censors the report in some way — for commercial, political or ideological reasons — there is little he or she can do about it. Therefore, media organisations have the ultimate **gatekeeping** power in deciding what we see and hear through the media.

Key term

gatekeeping: the blocking or altering of a media text or message by someone controlling access to a media outlet, for example a newspaper or television news bulletin. Editors who make decisions on whether or not to run a story are gatekeepers. The term is often used negatively to criticise the power of large media organisations to set media agendas.

Examples of media institutions

The largest institutions are the size of the BBC or News Corporation, the smallest are an **independent** production company (or 'indie') like Hat Trick Productions.

The six core values of the BBC, as defined by the corporation itself, are:

- trust
- quality
- respect
- audiences
- creativity
- teamwork

BBC organisational structure

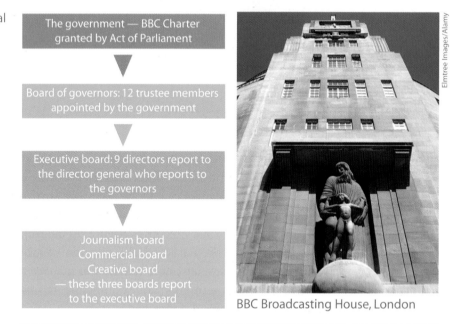

The government — BBC Charter granted by Act of Parliament

▼

Board of governors: 12 trustee members appointed by the government

▼

Executive board: 9 directors report to the director general who reports to the governors

▼

Journalism board
Commercial board
Creative board
— these three boards report to the executive board

Elmtree Images/Alamy

BBC Broadcasting House, London

Ideas for discussion and development

Trouble at the BBC

In late 2007, the BBC was engulfed with problems relating to fake phone-in programmes when it emerged that the winner in a *Blue Peter* 'name the cat' competition was fixed. The actual winning name, Cookie, was dumped in favour of the pre-chosen name, Socks. As many as 25 junior staff faced discipline or the sack while senior staff were not affected.

At the same time, the BBC was in trouble over a programme made for it by production company RDF Media. Pictures of the Queen were edited in such a way as to suggest that she had stormed out of a meeting after a row about removing her crown. The images were in fact of her arriving at the meeting. As a result of this, Peter Fincham, controller of BBC1, resigned.

A further issue emerged when it was alleged that BBC creative director, Alan Yentob, a senior figure who earns £300,000 a year, had allowed images of himself apparently nodding in response to answers to be inserted in interviews that he did not conduct, because of his busy schedule. For a while, Yentob was not sure whether this allegation was true, because editing could have taken place without his knowledge, but he eventually decided it was not and that he really had conducted the interviews. This conclusion was only reached after damaging media coverage of the allegation.

• **How successful would you judge the BBC to be in meeting its own institutional core values in the light of these events?**

Why do we need media concepts?

These concepts give us a procedural approach for analysing and discussing media products. By applying them systematically to the media text being considered, we can be sure that we cover all angles when we deconstruct it and draw conclusions. All the concepts outlined in this chapter are important in the study of any media text, and they will be referred to and developed throughout this book. You should familiarise yourself with them and use them when deconstructing media texts, whether you are acting as a consumer or a producer of these texts.

Media language

Media language refers to the particular codes used within different media forms to convey messages to audiences. It therefore includes not only the written word but also the audiovisual, photographic or digital code used to convey meanings and construct a text. Media products are created using a specific language appropriate to their form. The language of film, newspapers, television, advertising, e-mails, websites and even text messages all reflect the constraints of the form chosen.

For example, tabloid newspapers like the *Sun* and the *Mirror* rely on photographic images for the impact of their front pages. This means that if a particularly sensational picture became available — e.g. of a famous person punching a photographer in a nightclub — this photograph would probably be chosen for the front page and would dominate the news, forcing all other stories off the front page.

Examples of media language

The press

Newspapers use a combination of written language and photographs to construct stories. The language used is directed at different audiences. For example, if you compare the front pages of the *Sun*, the *Daily Mail*, the *Daily Telegraph* and the *Guardian*, you will see a diverse range of stories designed to appeal to the interests of their different readership groups.

Film

Films are sequences of visual images joined together and overlaid with sound and dialogue to form a narrative. Reading a film is a complex skill that we learn from an early age through exposure to visual images. We come to identify a film's genre and understand the conventions of film structure, and we learn to recognise such techniques as voice-over narration, flashback sequences and non-linear narrative structures. Visual literacy is an acquired skill, although none of us remembers how we learned it.

New technologies

The language of the website has developed a specific form linked to the technology. For example, terms like 'thumbnails', 'portal', 'bookmark', 'favourites', 'links', 'scrolling' and 'pop-ups' have specific meanings related to internet use. E-mails tend to use a more familiar form of language that would not be acceptable in traditional written correspondence. Text messages are often incomprehensible to those unfamiliar with the shorthand involved.

Ideas for discussion and development
- **Identify and discuss ways in which text messaging and e-mail have changed the conventions of written English.**

Values and ideology

All media texts are constructed within a framework of **values** and **ideology**. All media products are produced by individuals or groups working within an ideological or values framework, so they reproduce the beliefs we use to govern our lives.

Attitudes, beliefs and values can be explored in media products, particularly in soap operas and the parallel universe they contain. Sensitive issues such as abortion, rape and domestic violence are represented through the characters, and audience members form judgements about the acceptability of the behaviour shown. In this way, social values are tested and, with the help of the tabloid press, heroes and villains are created and consensuses formed.

The values of those producing media texts are also important, as are the ethos and aims of the organisations for which these people work. Such values will be reflected in all media products, whether by accident or design. Equally, the values of the audience will affect the way in which media texts are interpreted (see preferred, negotiated and oppositional readings of media texts on pages 22–23).

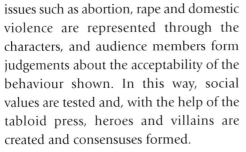

Key terms

attitudes, beliefs and values (ABV): terms commonly used when discussing the audience for media products and the factors influencing the reception of media messages.

attitudes: the positions people adopt in relation to a particular issue, for example being for or against fox hunting.

beliefs: deeply held views, like a belief in human equality or a belief in God.

ideology: a set of attitudes, beliefs and values held in common by a group of people and culturally reproduced within that community to sustain its particular way of life.

values: the things we consider important in conducting ourselves, e.g. about how we should behave and how we should conduct our relationships with others. For many people, values include binary opposites such as right and wrong, and good and evil.

Examples of ideology

Religion and secularism

Religion is an example of ideology because different religions contain structured belief systems relating to all aspects of life. Religious value systems are directed by divine revelation and guidance. For example, the Ten Commandments of the Old Testament are a value system adopted by Jews because they are believed to come from God via Moses; the Qur'ran is believed by the faithful to be the actual word of God as dictated to the Prophet Mohammed, and structures a way of life accepted and followed by all Muslims.

Secularism, by contrast, is the belief that human conduct should be directed by logic, reason, debate and moral intuition. In a practical sense, secularism argues that certain social institutions — such as the education system, the government and the legal system — should exist separately from religious institutions and that religion should not influence political judgement. In secular societies, religion is seen as a personal matter: all religions are tolerated and accepted as the choice of individuals and communities, but these communities are not allowed to impose their beliefs on others.

Traditionally, both the religious or secular values of a community are passed on from generation to generation through the family and the wider social environment.

Consumerism and ecology

Free market capitalism (which forms the basis of the economic and social world in which we live) is an ideology based on the belief that society is best served by encouraging individual enterprise and fulfilment. It finds expression in the accumulation of wealth or capital and in the consumption of consumer goods. The welfare of the many is seen as being best served by allowing the few to generate a prosperous, ever-expanding economy. This value system is clearly at odds with 'green' or ecology-based value systems that see never-ending economic growth as a recipe for disaster in a world threatened by climate change and environmental pollution.

Ideas for discussion and development

In 2004, a law was passed in France banning the wearing in state schools of conspicuous religious symbols, including the Muslim headscarf. In the UK, moderate Muslim dress (the hijab) is allowed in most schools but clothing that covers the entire face is considered inappropriate.

- **How far do you think that secular institutions should go in accommodating the beliefs, customs and special requirements of different religious groups?**

The media's role in reflecting values and ideologies

The changing nature of society and the ever-increasing role of the media in people's everyday lives mean that the media now play an important part in identifying, reflecting, evaluating, modifying and even imposing the value systems and ideologies of the modern world.

This is made more complex by the co-existence of different and sometimes conflicting value systems in the same multicultural society. For example, images of women in bikinis are perfectly acceptable to the majority of people in Western societies but are regarded as offensive by Muslims, who — when living in the same cultural and media environment — will also be exposed to them.

Ideas for discussion and development

Controversy about Danish and Swedish cartoons

In September 2005, the Danish newspaper *Jyllands-Posten* published 12 cartoons depicting the Prophet Mohammed. The cartoons were reprinted in many other newspapers around the world, and some Muslim leaders claimed that the cartoons insulted Islam. Violent demonstrations followed in Muslim countries, with the deaths of at least 139 people. Danish flags were burned and death threats were issued against the editors and journalists responsible. Danish goods were boycotted in some Muslim countries, and the Danish prime minister described the controversy as the worst international crisis for Denmark since the Second World War. In August 2007, death threats were issued against Swedish journalists following the publication of another caricature of Mohammed in the *Nerikes Allehanda* newspaper. The Swedish prime minister gave his support to the journalists involved and emphasised Sweden's commitment to freedom of speech.

• **Are journalists right to insist that the publication of cartoons of this kind is in the interest of freedom of speech?**

Protest about the Danish cartoons in the UK, 2006

Assessing values and ideology in media texts

When assessing a media text, ask yourself what assumptions are being made about the attitudes, beliefs and values of the audience and how these are embedded in the product, for example:

- How does the text represent relations between men and women?
- Does the text show heterosexuality as the norm?
- Is the text homophobic?
- Does the text show violent solutions to disagreements as the norm?
- Does the text assume that people live in nuclear families (man, woman and children)?
- If older people are represented, are they treated with respect or ridicule?
- Does the text assume that acquiring and spending money are the principal goals of life?
- Which **cultures** and ethnicities are represented?
- Does the text ridicule any culture or group?
- Who and what are not represented?
- What assumptions are made about the right or wrong way to behave?
- Are the values **mainstream** or **alternative**?
- Is there any evidence of **dominant ideology**?

Key terms

alternative: describes any media product that challenges dominant or mainstream values and ideology.

culture: the social practices of a group of people, usually involving shared language, history, values, beliefs, lifestyle, appearance, dress and entertainment.

dominant ideology: the belief system that serves the interests of the dominant ruling elite within a society, generally accepted as common sense by the majority and reproduced in mainstream media texts.

mainstream: the uncontroversial, generally accepted attitudes, beliefs and values of the majority population. Mainstreamers are individuals who feel comfortable with the status quo and threatened by change. Mainstream entertainment and media products tend to be family-orientated and unchallenging in terms of representation and content.

Ideas for discussion and development

Theories of ideology owe much to the work of Antonio Gramsci (1871–1937), the Italian Communist party leader who was imprisoned by the dictator, Mussolini. Gramsci used the term 'hegemony' to describe the way in which dominant elites can maintain power over the economic, political and cultural direction of a society. The values that sustain dominant elites are reproduced every day by the media and are made to seem like the 'common sense' views of the majority, so that any challenge to them is marginalised. Common sense is difficult to challenge, since it is assumed to indicate the obvious way to behave — a belief shared by all but deviants and subversives.

- **Do you think that common sense works this way in the UK today? If so, which power elite is making use of it? How does it compare to political correctness?**

Analysing and deconstructing media texts

Chapter 2

Media texts are produced for one or more of the following purposes:

- to inform
- to instruct
- to persuade
- to entertain

They are also designed to generate revenue for the media organsiation, either directly through sales or sponsorship, or indirectly by delivering audiences to advertisers (advertisers pay for access to an audience).

When you are asked to analyse a media text, you should begin by asking yourself the following questions:

- What is the genre of the text? Which of the above purposes is it intended to meet?
- What media platform does it use? Visual images? Audiovisual? Print? New technologies?
- How are the various elements combined? For example, a television advertisement will be audiovisual, with images joined together in a linear sequence, and accompanied by a voice-over or dialogue and music. At the end there may be a caption or slogan and an image relating to the product being advertised.
- How does it relate to other media texts? Where is it placed? For example, advertisements in magazines are often positioned alongside similar content in written articles. The television news is often shown in specific time slots, although some channels show a rolling news programme, e.g. CNN and BBC News 24.

Having identified a text and placed it in the context of other media products, you are then in a position to deconstruct it and explore its meanings.

Construction and deconstruction

All media texts are **constructed**, i.e. put together by selecting and combining various elements to create a product with a specific purpose. (You will be constructing your own media texts as part of the course.) The **deconstruction** of a text is the reverse process — taking the text apart to examine its component elements and explore the choices made in its construction.

When you look at the front cover of a magazine — see, for example, the one on page 74 — your eyes initially range over the page. They are probably drawn to a photograph with a caption that interprets what you are seeing, and a range of information presented in a tantalising and eye-catching way to make you want to buy the magazine. In order to explore this process in a more thorough and disciplined way, we need a systematic methodology to isolate and describe all the elements of the cover.

Semiology and text analysis

Semiology, or **semiotics**, offers a structured method for deconstructing and analysing media texts. It is the study of signs (semiology takes its name from *sēmeion*, the Greek word for 'sign') and the way in which meaning is created in texts, by a process of selecting various elements and combining them into a meaningful whole.

Semiology was first developed by the Swiss linguist Ferdinand de Saussure (1857–1913) and the American Charles Pierce (1839–1914) in the early twentieth century. Saussure applied his system to the study of linguistics, while Pierce's interests were more broadly based on the cultural use of signs. Both approaches were adapted and more widely applied to cultural artefacts and media language by French sociologist Roland Barthes (1915–80) in the 1960s.

Media texts derive their meaning through the coming together of the producer and the audience. It is important to recognise that meaning is derived as much from what the audience brings to a text as from the text itself. When you look at a photograph in a magazine, what you already know about the images presented is essential for you to make any sense of it.

Signifier and signified

In semiotics, a text is made up of **signifiers** (the physical object) and **signifieds** (the mental concept or meaning that the signifier conveys). Together, these constitute signs that have meaning specific to a particular cultural frame of reference. For example, a photograph of a rose is made up of the photographic image of the flower (the signifier) and the actual flower (the signified). Thus the photograph is a 'sign' for the rose.

This photograph of the rose operates on a **denotational** level — the image represents or denotes the flower; it shows us simply how it looks. However, in human cultures objects often represent things other than themselves. So, on a **connotational** or metaphorical level, a photograph of a red rose could represent Lancashire (it is the county's symbol), or it could represent romantic love on a Valentine's Day card. Princess Diana was described by Elton John as 'England's Rose', so a photograph of a rose could be used to denote her (see the case study on page 20). The rose has also been used to represent socialist political parties in France and the UK, although it has no particular historical connection with these movements. The Tudor rose, as a heraldic symbol of England, combined the white rose of York and the red rose of Lancashire in symbolic unity at the end of the Wars of the Roses in 1487.

Signs can be iconic, indexical or symbolic, depending on how they relate to the object or idea being signified. An **iconic** sign looks like what it represents, for example a photograph of a car looks like the car. An **indexical** sign points to what it represents, for example a photograph of the Eiffel Tower makes us think of Paris. A **symbolic** sign is chosen at random to represent something by association.

Semiology: summary of terminology and principles

Shared cultural meaning is derived from the construction of signs. These consist of the idea or object (the signified) and the means used to represent that object (the signifier). For example, a drawing (signifier) of a tree denotes or signifies the real tree (signified).

- The signified and signifier together constitute a sign.
- The first or simplest level of meaning is that of denotation where, for example, a photograph of a rose denotes or stands for the flower.
- The second, more complex level of meaning is one of connotation, where cultural knowledge and values add metaphorical meaning to the

sign. For example, a stylised photograph of a red rose can mean New Labour or England.

- Complex connotations can form cultural myths. For example, pictures of the English countryside can mean healthy life, clean air, tradition, heritage.

Signs can be classified as follows:

- Iconic signs look like what they refer to, for example a photograph of a car.
- Indexical signs are those where the meaning is pointed to, for example the Eiffel Tower standing for Paris.
- Symbolic signs have no obvious relationship with an object, for example the three-point star badge standing for Mercedes Benz.

Symbolic signs can develop fixed cultural meanings, which make it difficult to use them in other contexts. For example, although the swastika is an ancient Greek design and a Hindu sign for the sun, with connotations of good luck and happiness, its use by Hitler as the symbol of Nazi Germany and its associated anti-Semitism has made it impossible to use it in other contexts, except perhaps in India.

Similarly, the cross is so associated with Christianity and in Muslim countries with the Crusaders that it is impossible to use it as a sign of neutral medical help. Muslim states use the red crescent symbol as an alternative to the cross. The international Red Cross organisation has now devised a totally neutral symbol to replace the cross in some cultural contexts.

> ## Ideas for discussion and development
>
> - **Can you think of other signs that have become locked into a particular culture?**

Organisation and combination of signs

Signs are organised into **codes** from which selections are made to construct meaningful combinations — in much the same way as words are chosen to construct sentences. These combinations can be in visual media (paintings, advertisements and posters of films) and also in any other cultural medium, from architecture to dress and appearance.

Sign systems involve selecting and combining various elements involved in the different codes. These selections involve **paradigmatic** choices (the selection element) to make up **syntagmatic** chains of meaning (the combination element).

Choices from particular codes are called **paradigms**, where one unit is chosen to fit into a chain (or **syntagm**) to form a whole. For example, in a woman's wardrobe a choice can be made from hats, shirts, T-shirts, skirts, trousers and shoes to form the look of an outfit, but she can only wear one of each element at any time. If you change the hat or shoes, you change the look or meaning of the whole outfit.

Application of semiology to cultural artefacts

All cultural codes and media texts involve the rules of paradigmatic selection and syntagmatic combination. Here are some further examples of how this works:

- **Architecture** — paradigmatic choices from different styles of windows, roofs, doors, arches, flooring, building materials, decoration and styles (e.g. gothic, classical, modern, postmodern). The syntagm is the finished building.
- **Food** — paradigmatic choices from a menu of starters, main courses, desserts and drinks. The syntagm is the complete meal.
- **Gardening** — paradigmatic choices from different plants, trees, shrubs and flowers. The syntagm is the completed garden.

Task

Cultural myths become embedded — sometimes on a subconscious level — in a society over time, and can be used as a framework for advertisements. For example, the countryside as a wholesome, traditional and healthy environment is a useful backdrop for Anchor Butter, Baxters Soups and wholemeal bread, all of which are actually the products of a factory conveyor belt. The myth of the English countryside was seriously challenged by images of burning mounds of dead cattle during the 2001 foot and mouth epidemic.

Collect images of the English countryside.

Discuss how it is being represented.

Application of semiology to the visual image

Semiotic terms can be used when analysing print material, such as magazine advertisements, posters or moving images:

- **Advertisement** — the whole advertisement is a syntagm made up of the paradigmatic choices of elements, e.g. the subject being advertised, the location, setting and context, the colour palette, iconography and captions.
- **Film posters** — the poster is a syntagm. Paradigmatic choices are made accordingly and might include images of celebrity stars, awards from film festivals, quotations from favourable critics, and a scene that acts as a **metonym**. These scenes are sometimes accompanied by an anchoring strapline, for example 'In space no-one can hear you scream', from *Alien* (Ridley Scott, 1979).
- **Film** — paradigmatic choices are made from type of shot, location, lighting technique, character, overall setting, the mise-en-scène and editing choices of shot sequence. The syntagm is the completed film.

Key term

metonym: part of a representational image used to stand for a whole. Metonyms are an essential part of media texts, which can only ever provide a partial representation of a complex and ever-changing reality. As we read media texts metonymically, the choice of single images used to represent larger events or concepts will have a crucial and powerful effect on our understanding.

Task

Apply the principles of semiology to analyse the DVD cover below.

Analysing and deconstructing media texts

Case study

The cultural myth of Diana, Princess of Wales

Cultural myths are developed when images become firmly fixed in people's minds and represent more than just symbolic or connotational values. The life of Princess Diana has become a myth in British culture. Newspapers only have to print her picture on the front page to sell more copies, and it is in their interests to keep the myth alive. This explains the endless speculation that continues about the circumstances leading to her death.

Diana has come to represent a combination of emotional accessibility and openness (she showed empathy towards people and sought it from them by revealing her feelings) and celebrity (she was a glamour icon). The sudden and shocking nature of her death somehow completed the myth — it was horrific, dramatic, tragic, tinged with scandal and surrounded by rumour.

Task

Explain in your own words what the 'myth' of Princess Diana tells us about attitudes, beliefs and values in our society. Among other factors, you could consider attitudes towards the royal family and public displays of emotion.

More than 10 years later, her image seems as vivid as ever. Her whole life story has become a folk tale ending in tragedy and now serves as a modern myth. She went from being a fairytale princess at the time of her spectacular wedding to a vulnerable and tragic prisoner of her unhappy marriage, only to re-emerge as a glamorous world celebrity, and ultimately to meet her fate as a tragic sacrificial victim and become deified as 'the people's princess'. She is fixed forever in the popular imagination by the constant reproduction of her photographic image.

Task

You have to choose a photograph of a bridge to use as part of a design on a European Union poster with the theme: 'European countries are working together to bridge the differences between them and form a closer union.'

You have collected photographs of the following:

- The Pont de St Nazaire, a suspension bridge over the mouth of the river Loire, France (1974).

- The Humber Bridge in Yorkshire over the Humber, the fourth longest single-span suspension bridge in the world (1981).

- The Forth Road Bridge in Scotland (1964).

- Tower Bridge over the River Thames, a famous London landmark (1894).

- The Millennium Bridge, a pedestrian footbridge in London over the River Thames (2000).

- The Clifton Suspension Bridge, Bristol, by famous Victorian engineer I. K. Brunel (1864).

- The Ponte Vecchio bridge in Florence, Italy (1594).

Choose **one or more** photographs to illustrate the theme.

Explain in 250 words your choices and your reasons for not selecting the other photographs.

Provide a caption to anchor the image and reinforce the theme of the poster.

How would the choice of a different bridge or bridges affect the meaning of the poster?

Different ways to read a text

While semiotic techniques and analysis can be applied to any cultural artefact, from a film to a dinner menu, the meaning of the combinations or syntagms is culturally determined and subject to variation and change. Understanding of syntagms is **subjective** and dependent on the cultural background of individuals, and the contextual value system and codes of the culture from which they arise. The way an audience interprets a given image is dependent on each individual's background knowledge, beliefs and expectations, so the image is therefore open to a wide range of interpretations, unless it is **anchored** by a caption or in some other way, to limit the **field of interpretation**. The placing of images next to each other creates a syntagm for the viewer. For example, a photograph of a dead body followed by one of a man holding a gun suggests that the man is the killer. In this way, the **montage** of a series of signs creates a meaningful narrative, as in film-making.

There is no guarantee that texts will be read in the way intended by their creators. Once a text is in the public domain — available to anybody who chooses to access it — the creators lose control of what the text means.

Key terms

anchorage: the process whereby an image is explained or interpreted in such a way as to limit the possible meanings attributable to it, e.g. a photograph of diseased lungs can be anchored by the caption 'smoking kills'. A moving image can be anchored by use of techniques such as montage, lighting, camera angle and caption.

field of interpretation: the possible meanings of an image which differ from that intended by the image maker. This can be limited by anchorage.

montage: the selecting and piecing together of material for a film, composite photograph or artwork.

subjective: from the subject's point of view. A subjective response or opinion is one that is based on an individual's attitudes, beliefs and values rather than on any objective, detached criteria. According to semiologists, by consuming media texts, individuals are seen as bringing their own subjective experience to the construction of meaning, which is therefore both culturally determined and individually adjusted in line with each person's unique experience.

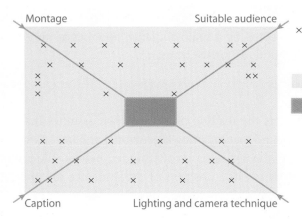

Anchorage

Montage

Suitable audience

Caption

Lighting and camera technique

× Possible meanings of the image that differ from the intended meaning

Field of interpretation

Intended meaning of image achieved by anchorage

(Diagram adapted from the work of Guy Gauthier as quoted in *The Semiology of the Image*, BFI Publications 1976)

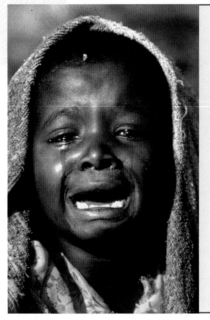

Ideas for discussion and development

• **Who is the boy? Where is he from? What is the location? Where are his family? Why is he crying?** Without a caption or explanation of the photograph, the answers to these questions are open and undetermined — anyone could have an opinion or an answer. How many variants did your group consider? For example, he could be crying because he has: lost his parents, been beaten up, cannot find his way home, had his money stolen, just watched his favourite football team lose, just seen his cat being run over etc.

• **The caption beneath the photograph is 'Hunger on the streets of Mogadishu'. Discuss the image again.** Even so, how can we be sure he is crying out of hunger?

The following terms are associated with the work of Stuart Hall and David Morley. They define the view that texts can have open, various meanings, or closed, restricted meanings depending on their origin, intention and complexity, but that readers can always interpret texts in line with their own attitudes, beliefs and values. For more on Hall's encoding/decoding model, see pages 238–39.

Preferred reading

The **preferred reading** is the meaning that is intended by the producers of the text. Preferred readings are often in line with dominant ideology. For example, a photograph of a topless female model in a tabloid newspaper might be accepted by a male audience member as an entertaining picture of a desirable, attractive woman.

Negotiated reading

The **negotiated reading** is the reading of a text which assumes that no absolute meaning exists, and that meaning is generated and negotiated by what the reader brings to the text in terms of attitudes, beliefs, values and experiences, i.e. it emphasises the position of the audience member. A photograph of a topless model might be viewed by the male reader's girlfriend with an attitude of disapproval but acceptance.

Oppositional reading

An **oppositional reading** of a text (also known as aberrant decoding or an alternative reading) is arrived at by an individual who challenges the preferred meaning and uses his or her own experiences, value system and cultural knowledge to decode the text in a different way. The same photograph of a topless model could be read by a feminist as being an unacceptable, degrading image involved in the exploitation of women as sex objects for male enjoyment.

Mixing up different sign systems to create new meanings

This approach is often called **bricolage**.

In the 1960s, the wearing of military-style jackets along with medals and other elements of military insignia by undisciplined and pacifist hippies subverted the codes of group membership, discipline and reward for wartime achievement originally conveyed by the uniforms. Punk, skinhead and chav dress codes all borrow clothing items from different periods/styles and mix them up to create new fashions.

Key term

bricolage: the mixing together of different elements (the French for 'do it yourself'), whether images, signs or physical objects, to create new cultural meanings. It is often associated with youth cultures, such as skinheads' use of Doc Martens boots, old fashioned braces, Ben Sherman shirts and military crew cuts to create a distinctive uniform and signal group membership.

Case study

Burberry versus the chavs

The use of their distinctive beige check, once associated with A-list celebrities, as the uniform of a very different social group — the chavs — has been a nightmare for top luxury fashion company, Burberry. With UK sales falling and fears of becoming a laughing stock, how does a top designer label repair a damaged image?

Burberry's relaunch several years ago was very successful. 'It really tapped into a sense of the early years of the millennium,' says Andrea Cockram of Verdict Research. But the brand soon became a victim of its own success. Fashion-conscious football hooligans began adopting the distinctive beige check. 'It was associated with people who did bad stuff, who went wild on the terraces,' says Peter York. 'Quite a lot of people thought that Burberry would be worn by the person who mugged them.'

Laughing stock

Burberry had worse to come. The brand became a national joke when photos of soap star Daniella Westbrook and her baby, dressed head to foot in Burberry check, appeared in all the papers. The look was adopted nationwide and was fed by the appearance of counterfeit Burberry products at market stalls all over the UK. Burberry and the chavs became the focus of a thousand national jokes.

Pub ban

In summer 2004, pubs and clubs across the UK banned customers who were wearing Burberry check.

Burberry took action. They removed checked baseball caps from sale and cut back on their use of the famous check, reducing it to appearing on only 5% of their products. The company also took action on counterfeit goods sold well below the price of the real thing.

However, this led to an incident with Welsh rap band, Goldie Lookin' Chain, who were given a Vauxhall Cavalier with a Burberry check paint job. Dubbed the 'Chavalier', the car was being auctioned on eBay until Burberry's lawyers intervened, demanding that the car be destroyed as it infringed copyright. Band member Eggsy said: 'I cried when they said you've got to destroy the car. What next? Taking Rupert the Bear to court for having trousers that looked like Burberry?'

Early in 2005, allegations of drug abuse leveled at Kate Moss, the face of Burberry at the time, caused more problems for the brand.

However, as most of Burberry's sales are overseas and the problem was essentially a UK phenomenon, the company's profitability worldwide has not been adversely affected.

Source: adapted from the BBC news website

Task

Read the article about Burberry and the chavs.

Describe from your own experience any current examples of bricolage where young people have borrowed and adapted styles and cultural artefacts to create new meanings.

Genres and narrative

A genre (French for 'type') is a category of media products classed as being similar in form and type. Film, magazine, newspaper and television programmes are all media genres. They allow audiences to express preferences and make choices on the basis of the known characteristics of genres. In this way, audiences can feel a degree of confidence in making choices, knowing that their expectations of content will be met.

Genres are used by media producers to segment audiences into categories and to create products that meet particular audience requirements. Genres are used by audiences to select from a wide range of media products those they wish to consume. Consider for a moment what media genres you consume and why. What are their characteristics and how do they meet your needs as a consumer? You might make a list that includes the following:

- local newspapers
- style magazines
- girls' or lads' magazines
- soap operas on television
- action, animation, blockbuster etc. films
- Facebook and MySpace

Assessing a text

Ask yourself the following questions when assessing a text.

- **What is the genre, sub-genre or type of media product?** Is it a magazine advertisement? A television commercial? A television sitcom? A slasher horror movie?
- **What key iconographic elements identify the genre?** For example, in the vampire horror genre these would be vampire teeth, Gothic settings, graveyards, bats, crucifixes, garlic, wooden stakes and coffins.

- **What are the narrative conventions of the genre?** For example: they all lived happily ever after — fairytale; the final girl unmasks the killer — teen slasher horror movie; the product is identified with a positive and desirable lifestyle — advertisement.
- **How does the genre meet or challenge the expectations of an audience?** Is the outcome predictable or does it have a twist? Can the audience members guess the ending or are they surprised?

It is certainly possible to challenge an audience's expectations of a genre. For example, the crime thriller *The Usual Suspects* (Bryan Singer, 1995) seems to follow a fairly predictable pattern during the prolonged police interview with key witness Verbal Kint (played by Kevin Spacey) about the identity of the mysterious gangster Keyser Söze. However, in the final moments of the film the audience is stunned by the sudden realisation that Verbal Kint is the elusive gangster. This narrative device has the effect of encouraging the audience to watch the film again to pick up the clues they missed about the gangster's identity.

Theories of genre

Genre theory is concerned with identifying the characteristics of genres and the relationship between audiences, media texts and media producers. Genres can be used by media producers to target specific audience groups. In a commercial world, this can help to assess the likely response to a media product (in terms of audience numbers and responses) and the financial return it is likely to achieve.

Key term

utopia: an idealised (often future) world where everything is perfect, derived from the title of a book by Sir Thomas More (1478–1535) which described an island where people live in social harmony ruled by a perfect government.

Ideas for discussion and development

Richard Dyer is an influential genre theorist who argues (1992) that genres are pleasurable because they offer escapist fantasies into fictional worlds that remove the boredom and pressures of reality. He sees these worlds as **utopian**, offering the audience an escape from everyday problems and routines, together with an abundance of energy, excitement, spontaneity and community — not all of which are present in their everyday lives.

- **How useful is this theory in explaining the appeal of different genres?**

Views of some genre theorists

- Genres are agents of ideological closure; they limit the meaning potential of a given text (John Hartley). This means that, for example, within a classic Western, the expected behaviour of stock characters in particular situations limits unexpected developments of the narrative. In fact, increasingly, genres have been adapted to allow alternative representations, as in *Dances With Wolves* (Jim Wilson, 1995) and *Brokeback Mountain* (Ang Lee, 2005).

- Genres are typical forms of texts that link kinds of producer, consumer, medium, manner and occasion (Hodge and Kress). For example, Disney creates a form that links classic cartoon fairytales, computer-generated animation films, general release in multiplexes, and DVD and internet availability.

- Genres rely on readers already having knowledge and expectations about particular texts (Fowler). This means that producers do not have to explain the conventions of a text and the nature of characters, as audiences are already familiar with them.

- To make sense of any text, audiences require what is sometimes called 'cultural capital' (Allen). This means that audiences bring their knowledge and experience of a genre to a particular text, and this enables them to understand it.

- The assignment of a text to a genre influences how the text is read (John Fiske). If audiences believe a text to be in a particular genre, they will interpret the text in accordance with their expectations of that genre. For example, the ups and downs of relationships in a romantic comedy such as *Bridget Jones's Diary* (Sharon Maguire, 2001) are not taken very seriously and the audience expects to see a happy ending.

- Genre may offer various emotional pleasures, such as empathy and escapism (Knight). In other words, we enjoy identifying with characters and imagining ourselves living out their experiences.

- Pleasure is derived from repetition and difference (Neale). This means that, while audiences like to feel secure with the familiarity of a genre, they also enjoy being surprised.

- Audiences take pleasure in observing how the conventions of a genre are manipulated (Abercrombie). Knowing what to expect makes audiences enjoy the unexpected.

- Enduring genres reflect universal dilemmas and moral conflicts, and also appeal to deep psychological needs (Konigsberg). Human experience is repeated in every generation, and the essential dilemmas of life always remain the same (e.g. questions about life, death and the hereafter; the search for love and personal fulfilment; relationships and the family; economic survival; questions of values and religion; war and conflict, and the disruption they cause; happiness and tragedy; fear of the unknown).

For a more detailed discussion of genre theory relevant to A2 work, see pages 242–44.

Genre variants

A **pastiche** is a media text made up of pieces from other texts or imitations of other styles. It can involve **homage**, where one text deliberately imitates the characteristics of another as an acknowledgement of that text's importance, e.g. *What Lies Beneath* (Robert Zemeckis, 2000) contains elements of homage to Alfred Hitchcock's *Psycho* (1960). It can also involve **parody**, where one text deliberately imitates another for comic effect, e.g. *Shaun of the Dead* (Edgar Wright, 2004) is a parody of *Dawn of the Dead* (George A. Romero, 1978); *Scary Movie* (Keenan Ivory Wayans, 2000) is a parody of slasher horror movies.

A **hybrid** is a cross between one genre and another. Examples are *From Dusk till Dawn* (Robert Rodriguez, 1996), which starts as a crime drama and becomes a vampire movie, and *The Matrix* (Wachowski Brothers, 1999), which is a cross between an action and sci-fi movie. Hybrids are becoming more popular because they allow film-makers to increase their potential audience by including elements that appeal to more than one group.

Scene from
The Matrix

Pictorial Press Ltd/Alamy

Genres and producers

Producers like genres because:

- They are constructed for a known audience with predictable responses.
- They allow for the repeated use of storylines and stock characters.
- They allow reuse of sets, props and actors, with consequent financial savings.
- They are tried and tested, and provide an element of security for investors.
- Budgets and financial returns are easier to predict.
- They allow for clear product and **audience segmentation**.

Genres and audiences

Audiences like genres because:

- They know what to expect from media products and can therefore make easier choices about entertainment.
- They can enjoy subtle variations within a predictable framework.
- They can find a consistent form of release and escapism.
- They can quickly engage with easily recognisable plots and characters.
- They can enjoy predicting outcomes.
- They can easily follow the narratives within genres.
- They can experience a sense of cultural and emotional security.

What happens if genres become too predictable and unimaginative?

Media products within particular genres must avoid being too predictable and unimaginative because:

- Audiences will fall away and investing institutions will lose money.
- Changes in social/cultural attitudes, values and expectations must be reflected, or audiences will find the product offensive and/or unrealistic.

Stale genres can be revived by being less predictable and unimaginative. For example, although the Western is generally out of favour for its limited mise-en-scène, iconography and narrative potential, *Brokeback Mountain* (Ang Lee, 2005), with its theme of homosexuality, was a great success because it reflected current attitudes towards gay relationships.

The underlying narrative structures of predictable genres can be present in films of different genres. For example, the narrative of *Black Hawk Down* (Ridley Scott, 2001) contains elements of a Western — it involves sending US air 'cavalry' into hostile territory controlled by 'savages', where they suffer a serious military setback and are trapped in enemy territory. This triggers a heroic self-sacrificing rescue attempt to 'leave no man behind', which fits easily into a classic US Western film like *She Wore a Yellow Ribbon* (John Ford, 1949).

As discussed earlier, audiences seek both familiarity and difference within genres. The conventions of a genre give an easy point of reference and allow film-makers to take short cuts by using stock characters and locations that are easily recognisable to the audience. However, audiences also want plot twists, variations and hybrid developments to keep them interested in the narrative. Modern films increasingly mix elements of several genres to appeal to a wider audience and to retain their interest.

Example of a classic film genre: gangster

A **gangster** film is based around the activities of a criminal gang or gangs. Gangster films are often in a drama-documentary style, with an emphasis on realism. Classic gangster films represent the conflict between good and evil, played out in the slums of the large US cities. The poor, city-dwelling cinema-goers of the early twentieth century could relate to the aspirational dreams of gangsters, who were faced with the conflict between the legitimate desire to achieve the 'American Dream' of wealth and happiness by the illegitimate use of crime. As a result, gangsters are usually morally ambivalent. The iconography of gangster films includes fast cars, guns, smart suits, desirable women and a glamorous lifestyle setting for the successful gangster.

The first identifiable gangster film, *The Musketeers of Pig Alley* (D. W. Griffiths, 1912), was based on gangs in New York and tackled themes of poverty, crime and retribution. *Regeneration* (Raoul Welsh, 1915) followed the rise to gangster status of Irish-American immigrants from the slums.

Representations of gangsters as 'folk heroes' troubled the Hays Office (the US film industry censorship body of the time), and after 1934, studios were forced to make moral pronouncements condemning the behaviour of the gangsters featured in the films. These pronouncements were even backdated to earlier films, such as *The Public Enemy* (William Wellman, 1931). However, gangsters continued to be folk heroes, in spite of attempts to portray the pursuers as saviours of society. This can be seen in *The G Men* (William Keighley, 1935).

The gangster genre is adaptable and can be transferred to any time, city and cultural environment. Contemporary examples of the genre include *City of God* (Fernando Meirelles and Kátia Lund, 2002) and *Kill Bill: Vol 1* (Quentin Tarantino, 2003). Ethnic variations on the theme can be found in Italian, Irish, Hispanic, British, Jewish, Black, Japanese, Russian and east European cinema.

Landmark gangster movies include: *Underworld* (Josef Von Sternberg, 1927), *City Streets* (Rouben Mamoulian, 1931), *Little Ceasar* (Mervyn Le Roy, 1931), *The Public Enemy* (William Wellman, 1931), *Scarface* (Howard Hawks, 1932), *Bonnie and Clyde* (Arthur Penn, 1967), *The Godfather* trilogy (Francis Ford Coppola, 1972–90), *Goodfellas* (Martin Scorsese, 1990), *Reservoir Dogs* (Quentin Tarantino, 1992), *Casino* (Martin Scorsese, 1995), and *Gangs of New York* (Martin Scorsese, 2002). This last film is 'retro-gangster', in that it traces the origins of gang violence in the early days of the city's foundation.

Variants on gangster films include the British black comedy *Lock Stock and Two Smoking Barrels* (Guy Ritchie, 1998) and *Snatch* (Guy Ritchie, 2000), and the psychodrama *Sexy Beast* (Jonathan Glazer, 2001).

Scene from *Goodfellas* (1990)

Everett Collection/Rex Features

Why are gangster films attractive to audiences?

The following narrative elements of gangster films are attractive to audiences:

- The rise of ordinary individuals to positions of power, fame and success means that characters are easy to relate to, providing escapist fantasy for the audience.
- Action scenes with extreme violence grab the audience's attention.
- Love stories and family relationships are used as background.
- The use of the classic 'rise and fall' narrative or 'nemesis' means that there is retribution for evil-doing.
- Gangsters have antihero status — bad guys are more interesting than good guys.
- The narrative can be transferred to any time, place and culture.
- The films seem realistic because storylines often run parallel to real-life events.

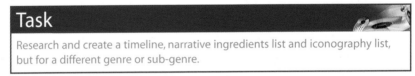

Task

Research and create a timeline, narrative ingredients list and iconography list, but for a different genre or sub-genre.

Other film genres and categories

The following is a list of the characteristics of some other film genres and categories:

- **Adventure film:** a film where characters are placed in an exciting and often dangerous location far from home. Characters often face physical and environmental challenges, e.g. human enemies, dangerous or exotic animals, difficult terrain, natural disasters and dangerous missions. Adventure films are usually produced as family entertainment, with a range of characters to appeal to all ages, genders and ethnicities. The genre is a broad one, and includes action movies, historical fantasy and even war movies. Examples include *Spy Kids 2: Island of Lost Dreams* (Robert Rodriguez, 2002) and *Mission Impossible* (Brian De Palma, 1996).
- **Art house:** a film produced for aesthetic, artistic or social reasons rather than as a means of generating large revenues. Art house directors include Michelangelo Antonioni and Ingmar Bergman.
- **Black comedy:** a film that deals with serious or disturbing subjects in a comic way. Subjects might include war, personal injury, murder, crime, gangsterism, violence, suffering or serious social issues like drug abuse.

Classic examples include *Dr Strangelove or: How I Learned to Stop Worrying and Love the Bomb* (Stanley Kubrick, 1964) and *A Clockwork Orange* (Stanley Kubrick, 1971). More recent examples include *Trainspotting* (Danny Boyle, 1996), *Lock, Stock and Two Smoking Barrels* (Guy Ritchie, 1998) and *Snatch* (Guy Ritchie, 2000).

- **Blockbuster:** a big-budget Hollywood film, e.g. *Spider-Man* (Sam Raimi, 2002). Blockbusters combine well-known film stars with fast-moving action narratives, spectacular sets and many special effects. Heavily marketed and promoted, they are designed to generate maximum revenues at the box-office to justify the large sums invested. The emphasis is on hype and spectacle, with huge set pieces and special effects rather than plot and character development. Blockbusters are part of an extensive merchandising operation designed to sell associated products. Ideologically, they are dominated by US cultural perspectives and values.

- **Chick flick:** a film targeted at a young female audience. Chick flicks are usually light, entertaining romances with contemporary music scores and comic undertones. Their narratives are directed at mainstream audiences and usually focus around the life experiences of their female protagonists, e.g. *Legally Blonde* (Robert Luketic, 2001) and *Bridget Jones's Diary* (Sharon Maguire, 2001).

- **Epic:** a film produced on a grand scale with a large cast, impressive settings and locations, and a powerful theme (often involving life-and-death power struggles, love, conflict and tragedy). Examples include *Gone with the Wind* (Victor Fleming, 1939), *Ben Hur* (William Wyler, 1959) and *Gladiator* (Ridley Scott, 2000).

- **Re-enactment:** a film that attempts to reproduce actual events as accurately as possible, e.g. *Downfall* (Oliver Hirschbiegel, 2005), about the last days of Hitler and Nazi Germany, and *Iris* (Richard Eyre, 2001), the story of the tragic illness of writer Iris Murdoch. Re-enactment sequences are often incorporated into fiction narratives, adding credibility and blurring the distinction between fiction and reality in the eyes of the audience.

- **Romantic comedy:** a film genre developed in the 1930s, where the two main protagonists are a man and a woman who seem to be at odds with each other but end up romantically involved. The genre was associated in the 1930s with such stars as Carey Grant and Katherine Hepburn and more recently, in its British version, with Hugh Grant in *Notting Hill* (Roger Michell, 1999) and *Love Actually* (Richard Curtis, 2003).

- **Science fiction:** a film involving a futuristic or alien world setting and technologies not available in the contemporary world. The first science fiction film was *Metropolis* (Fritz Lang, 1927). The futuristic writings of H. G. Wells provided screenplays for *Things to Come* (William Cameron Menzies, 1936) and *The War of the Worlds* (Byron Haskin, 1954). The imaginary future often has a dystopian setting or reflects current fears and phobias involving alien or foreign invasion, e.g. *Independence Day* (Roland Emmerich, 1996), technological nightmares, e.g. *Terminator* (James Cameron, 1984) or ecological disaster, e.g. *Waterworld* (Kevin Reynolds, 1995). The genre is equally adaptable to the mystical and mysterious *2001: A Space Odyssey* (Stanley Kubrick, 1968) and to fairy-tale fantasy narrative *Star Wars* (George Lucas, 1977).

Narrative

Narratives, or stories, help to shape and explain all aspects our lives from earliest infancy. They are part of the way in which we make sense of the world and seek reassurance in the face of the dangers and contradictions of everyday experience. It is obvious that all media texts tell stories or parts of stories. Theorists have constructed various models to explain how these stories work.

Classic theories of narrative

The following pages outline three classic theories of narrative. Remember that these theories will not apply to all media texts. Never try to force a narrative theory onto a structure or claim that it is proved by the structure. Use each theory as a tool, not a straightjacket.

Claude Lévi-Strauss (1908–)

Using the techniques devised by Ferdinand de Saussure to develop the principles of semiology, Claude Lévi-Strauss identified the underlying structures of all myths as being essentially the same.

His narrative theory of **binary opposition** is based on the essential difference between such concepts as culture and nature, and good and evil. Narratives are based on these oppositional forces and on the resolution of conflict. Audiences are positioned on the side that justifies their own cultural values, and the resolution reduces the underlying anxiety about threats to their way of life.

In contemporary media narratives, cowboys and Indians, and gangsters and the police represent oppositional forces. The audience is attracted by the dynamics of this conflict, and the narrative usually leads to the ultimate triumph of good. Audiences are rewarded by the success of the ('good') side they have identified with. In *Black Hawk Down* (Ridley Scott, 2001), the audience is positioned alongside the 'good' US forces in conflict with the 'bad' forces of Somali rebel leaders. The narrative structure of this particular film largely follows that of a classic Western, where US cavalry are pitched against Native Indians.

It is important to realise that binary narratives are also present in non-fiction texts like news reports and newspaper articles, where audiences are positioned on one side of an argument, for example security forces/terrorists, the police/criminals, and management/unions.

Vladimir Propp (1895–1970)

Russian formalist writer and folklorist Vladimir Propp analysed the structure of folk stories in his work *Morphology of the Folktale* (1958). His research refers to the types of character in folk tales and the events that involve them. He found that folk tales begin with an initial situation where the characters are introduced. This is followed up with 31 functions, not always present but always occurring in the same order.

His work emphasises the role of character in structuring narrative and is useful in helping to understand generic conventions, but it is rigid and of limited use in deconstructing complex contemporary narratives.

Propp's character types include:

- the **hero**, who seeks something
- the **villain**, who opposes the hero's quest
- the **donor**, who provides an object with magic property
- the **dispatcher**, who sends the hero on his way with a message
- the **false hero**, who disrupts the hero's hope of reward by making false claims
- the **helper**, who aids the hero
- the **princess** — the reward for the hero and an object of the villain's scheming
- her **father**, who rewards the hero for his efforts

Do not attempt to force narratives into Propp's structure. It is enough to remember that he focuses on character and the generic conventions of folk tale and argues for the similarity of structure behind all narratives. Contemporary narratives, while working within these conventions, often subvert the expectations of audiences rather than offering them comfortable and predictable characters and outcomes.

Tzvetan Todorov (1939–)

Originating from the Russian formalist school, Todorov is a Bulgarian intellectual who has been living and writing in France since the mid-1960s. He is the author of a wide range of political and philosophical works, but is particularly known for his work on 'narratology', or the structuring of narrative. His approach is founded on the belief in a common basis of human experience and the underlying narrative behind all human activity.

Todorov's sequence is made up of five propositions outlining a basic state of narration, which is disturbed and then re-established:

- a state of equilibrium, where everything is in order
- a disruption of the order by an event
- a recognition that a disruption has taken place
- an attempt to repair the damage of the disruption
- a return to some kind of equilibrium

We can apply this sequence to the narrative of the Second World War:

- equilibrium (stability or peace)
- disruption (Germany invades Poland)
- disequilibrium (climax: the war)
- attempt to repair the change (Germany is defeated)
- equilibrium (peace on new terms or a form of compromise)

It is easy to apply Todorov's pattern to mainstream film or television drama. For example, in a disaster movie:

- the opening scenes show life before the disaster and engage the audience's interest in the characters
- disaster occurs disrupting the characters' lives
- key character figures or 'heroes' recognise the disaster and rush to the rescue
- they struggle to repair the damage and save people's lives
- calm and harmony are restored as all the characters come to terms with the past events. Audiences are reassured by the harmonious ending

Task

Describe a specific James Bond film in terms of these three classic narrative theories.

Media platforms

The term **platform** comes from computer technology and is used to describe the hardware (the computer) and/or the software (operating system and application programs). In media studies, platforms are the technological means whereby the media communicate with an audience. The following media platforms are central to the AQA specification and your study of media texts should always be based on their dissemination across these platforms:

- **broadcasting** — television and radio (factual and fictional), films, advertisements, trailers and other audio/visual promotional material
- **print** — newspapers, magazines, advertising and marketing texts
- **e-media** — websites, blogs, podcasts; advertising and promotional material; radio, television, music and film downloads; games and emerging forms

Cross-media topic areas

Examples of media texts across the three platforms

In all cases, you need to consider the production and reception of the text:

- **broadcast or film fiction** — primarily found in broadcast or cinema platforms, but also on the internet and portable electronic devices (e.g. opening sequences available for download), in magazines and newspapers, and advertisements.
- **documentary and hybrid forms** — primarily found in broadcast or cinema platforms, but also in newspapers and magazines, the internet and portable electronic devices.
- **lifestyle** — broadcasting, the internet, newspapers and magazines.

- **music** — broadcasting, the internet and portable electronic devices, newspapers and specialist magazines.
- **news** — broadcasting, newspapers (including online newspapers), the internet and portable electronic devices.
- **sport** — broadcasting, the internet and portable electronic devices, newspapers and magazines.

Documentary and film fiction are discussed as examples of cross-media texts at the end of this chapter.

Although some texts are designed predominantly for one media platform, you must examine them across all three. The phrase 'production and reception' means considering the process of putting a text together and shaping it with an audience and platform in mind, and the response of the audience to that text.

Intertextuality

Intertextuality is the practice of making references to other media texts within a media text, with the intention that audiences recognise these references. By attaching their own product to already-established and successful media texts, media producers aim to achieve success by association and trigger a positive response in the audience. In marketing terms, this helps to ensure the success of the new text. Intertextuality can involve homage (respectful reference) to famous texts, parody (where the text referred to is mildly satirised), or pastiche (a simple imitation).

An example is Robert Zemeckis's film *What Lies Beneath* (2000), which pays homage to film-maker Alfred Hitchcock by using similar filming techniques to those in *Psycho* (1960) and *Rear Window* (1954). Audience enjoyment is enhanced by recognition of these references.

Another example is Robbie Williams' use of a sample from the James Bond film *You Only Live Twice* (Lewis Gilbert, 1967) as a backdrop to the track 'Millennium' on the album *I've Been Expecting You* (released 1998). The CD cover shows Williams dressed in white shirt with black tie and jacket, posing in a similar way to Sean Connery or Roger Moore as Bond. The title of the album is taken from dialogue spoken in the film *The Spy Who Loved Me* (Lewis Gilbert, 1977). The photographic images used on the CD cover, which include night-time cityscapes and a swimming pool with an attractive woman, also have echoes of the Bond films.

Ideas for discussion and development

- **How many examples of intertextuality can you find in texts known to you?**

Broadcasting

Audience access to television is changing dramatically. **Digital television** has developed rapidly and the British government plans to cut off the **analogue** signal entirely by 2012. This, together with satellite broadcasting from companies like BSkyB, means that audiences have access to far more television channels than ever before.

The quality of these new channels is variable, but some, like the Discovery Channel, the History Channel and various sports channels available with satellite subscription packages, have put pressure on the five terrestrial television channels. The BBC's digital television and terrestrial service require a considerable budget and some — notably veteran broadcaster John Humphrys of the BBC Radio 4 programme *Today* (a popular morning news programme that has seen severe budget cuts) — have argued that BBC funds are spread too thinly and the quality of traditional broadcasting is suffering as a result. It may well be true that the demands of finding sufficient material to broadcast across the greatly expanded digital services has led to a decline in the standard of programming.

Key terms

analogue: a method of recording visual and sound images. Analogue technology represents the shape or appearance of an object in an unbroken form. Traditional film is analogue, as it runs through a camera in an unbroken sequence.

digital: a communication system that is based on the storage and retrieval of numerical information.

digital television: sound and images that are converted to computerised digits for reception by aerials, satellites or cables and then decoded in a television set-top box. The system is faster, allows for multiple channels, and produces better-quality images than the analogue signal. Digital signals also allow for greater interaction with pay-per-view television, television shopping and choices of viewing angles already available to viewers.

Watching television in the 1940s

Television

Brief history of television

Television's early development took place before the Second World War, but the new service was closed down for the duration of the conflict. The BBC television service was reopened in 1946 and the audience was encouraged to 'look in' on a range of programmes in the evening. Since then, the following developments have occurred:

- ITV, the first commercial channel, arrived in 1954, with advertisements — famously described by show-business entrepreneur Lew Grade as 'a licence to print money'.
- BBC 2 arrived in 1962 after a report by the Pilkington Committee castigated ITV for US imports and 'sponsored' programming.
- In 1984, Channel 4 was launched, with a brief to cover film and sport, minority interests and the other gaps left by ITV coverage.
- The 1990s saw deregulation and the development of satellite broadcasting, as well as plans being made for digitalisation and the switch-off of the analogue signal in 2012.

Case study

Future of television?

Vinton Cerf, Vice President of Google, has said that television is dying. A founding father of the internet, Cerf said that television is facing 'an iPod moment', when viewers will soon be downloading most of their favourite programmes onto their computers. 85% of all video we watch is pre-recorded so you can set your system to download it all the time. 'Live television would only be for news sporting events and emergencies. Television will be like the iPod; you will download to watch later.'

Source: *Daily Telegraph*, 28 July 2007

Today, new technologies mean that traditional television reception will soon be part of a multi-faceted service, providing interactive links, the internet, multi-channel television and computer facilities all on the same screen.

Ideas for discussion and development

- **Do you agree with the ideas of Vinton Cerf? Do you spend more time in a week watching television or at your computer?**

Media institutions in British television

The following institutions dominate the British television industry:

- **BBC:** see pages 108–11 for an overview of the BBC.
- **Independent Television (ITV):** the commercial television network of companies franchised to provide regional independent television coverage. In spite of its commercial nature, ITV was constrained by a

public service requirement, monitored by the Independent Broadcasting Authority (IBA), to ensure that its programmes contained agreed percentages of news, current affairs and quality drama-based productions, together with programmes produced in the UK. In 1968, major changes in the franchises created five big ITV companies: Thames, London Weekend, Yorkshire, Granada and ATV. After the 1980 franchise review, new companies such as Meridian emerged. The progress of deregulation, begun in the 1990s, created further upheavals and changes of franchise and by 2000 Carlton, Granada, United MAI and the Scottish Media Group (together with few independent franchises) dominated the network, with ITV 1 in England and Wales being controlled entirely by Carlton and Granada. The overall tendency was towards merger, with a few large companies taking control and a consequent reduction in distinctive regional identity. The merger of Carlton and Granada in 2003 created one giant new company, ITV plc, which owns 40% of Independent Television News (ITN).

- **Channel 4:** an independent commercial television channel established in 1982 under the IBA, with a brief to cover minority interests, the arts, documentary and film, and to act as a complementary channel to both ITV and the two BBC channels. Channel 4 developed a reputation for cutting-edge and challenging programming, often drawing criticism from television watchdog groups such as Mediawatch. Its support of the British film industry through its Film 4 channel has been an important source of finance for independent producers. The high-status social profile of its audience has made the channel a favourite with advertisers and has helped secure its financial viability.

- **Five** (known as Channel 5 until September 2002): independent commercial terrestrial television station, launched in 1997 as a result of a requirement in the Broadcasting Act 1990 for the Independent Television Commission (ITC) to establish a fifth terrestrial channel in the UK. With difficulties involving uninspired programming and poor signal quality in many parts of the UK, the channel had a slow start with low viewing figures. An improvement in programmes has increased its share of the terrestrial market. The licence was awarded on the basis of competitive tender, with the aim of appealing to a 'modern mainstream' audience. Its owners were Pearson, United News and Media, CLT Ufa (a European TV company) and Warburg Pincus and Co. (a US company). Five agreed a partnership with Zip television, a specialist in interactive advertising, in 2004.

- **British Sky Broadcasting (BSkyB or Sky):** the company name of Rupert Murdoch's television satellite channel in the UK and Europe, and part of the News Corporation. BSkyB has become the largest and most successful of the satellite broadcasters.

Television genres

Traditional television schedules are made up of selections of programmes from a range of genres. Some of the main ones are discussed here.

Soap operas

A **soap opera** is a continuing, episodic serial on radio or television. The 'soap' portion of the term originates from US radio where, in the 1930s, soap powder companies sponsored continuous serials. The 'opera' element suggests the melodramatic and often fanciful nature of soap plots.

Soap operas choose known locations, with a focus — often a pub or a bar — around which the life of the local community revolves. They contain a range of characters who are easily recognisable to the audience from their own everyday experiences. Soap characterisation and plots — insofar as production schedules allow — attempt to cover topical matters, although of necessity in a very general way.

Ideas for discussion and development

Location	Soap	Pub/club
Manchester	*Coronation Street*	The Rovers Return
West Yorkshire	*Emmerdale*	The Woolpack
Chester	*Hollyoaks*	Max's club and Tony's restaurant
East London	*EastEnders*	The Queen Vic
Ambridge (rural England)	*The Archers* (Radio 4)	The Bull

- **Why do all these British soaps revolve around the pub/club?**

The time sequence of soap operas is parallel to that of real life, so Christmas episodes coincide with Christmas, summer holidays with summer holidays etc. Soaps have **cliffhanger** endings for every episode. A cliffhanger is a dramatic moment in the story where the audience is left guessing what will happen next and so is encouraged to watch the next episode.

Why do people watch soaps? The following reasons might apply:
- Something to talk about with friends.

- Assessing your own behaviour and opinions — following the life decisions of others may help you make decisions yourself.
- Substitute relationships — soap characters have more close relationships than many people have.
- Addiction — some viewers may become obsessed with characters' lives and behaviour. Soap audiences often have difficulty in separating the fictional lives of characters from the actors who portray them.
- Prediction — audience members enjoy guessing where the plot is going.
- Moral judgement — people enjoy moralising about the behaviour of others: 'he should be in prison; she shouldn't have the abortion; he's out of order' etc.
- Spin-off activities — e.g. reading about soap celebrities in magazines.

Crime fiction

Crime fiction is an important television genre dating from the 1950s. It encompasses a whole range of programmes, with narratives and representations being adapted to reflect changing social and cultural values and expectations.

Crime fiction drama exists in many varied forms, ranging from the traditional 'whodunnit' detective story (e.g. Agatha Christie's *Poirot* and Colin Dexter's *Inspector Morse*) to hard-hitting contemporary dramas (e.g. Jimmy McGovern's *Cracker*). Consequently, it appeals to many different audiences.

Representations of the police and criminals have varied considerably since the 1950s, with British mainstream series like *Dixon of Dock Green, Z Cars, The Sweeney* and *The Bill* attempting 'realistic' domestic representations of crime and law-and-order issues, and thus often reflecting the changing British social scene. Such series can act as vehicles for the airing of public concerns about crime and related issues, e.g. drug abuse, domestic violence, juvenile crime, alcohol-related crime, racism, and even police corruption. We can say that the genre has a **social action** agenda.

Imported US series, from *Dragnet* (1950s and contemporary remake) to *NYPD Blue* (1993–2005), have provided more escapist entertainment value, representing a different crime culture and distant locations.

Key term

social action broadcasting: television and radio programming that is designed both to analyse current social problems and issues and to encourage people to respond to what they have seen and heard. Social action programmes are a form of interactive television or radio. An example is the BBC's *Crimewatch UK*.

Ideas for discussion and development

If possible, watch an episode of *The Sweeney*. Try analysing the way the episode represents:

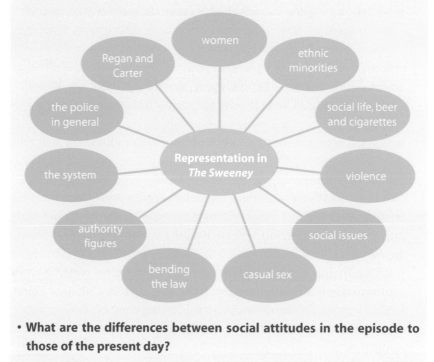

- **What are the differences between social attitudes in the episode to those of the present day?**

Situation comedy

Situation comedy (sitcom) refers to a television or radio comedy in which characters are located in a particular contained environment. This can be a house, a shop, a workplace, a prison or any other restricted location. Classic BBC examples from the 1970s include *Rising Damp* and *Porridge*.

Alternative comedy

Alternative comedy is a form of often experimental comedy that challenges mainstream values and expectations. First developed in radio programmes such as the *Goon Show* (1950s) and then on television, alternative comedy shocks the audience by extreme, unexpected or unorthodox representations, e.g. in *The League of Gentlemen* (1999–2002) one of the comic themes has suggestions of cannibalism. Other successful alternative comedy series include *Monty Python's Flying Circus* (1970s), *The Young Ones* (1980s), *The Fast Show* (1990s) and *Little Britain* (2003–06).

Hospital drama

This is a television genre centred around hospitals and the lives of hospital staff and patients. Hospitals have always been a popular setting for television drama and romance, the first British series being ITV's *Emergency Ward Ten* (1957–67). Currently popular are *Casualty* and its spin-off *Holby City*, and the US series *ER*.

Since the National Health Service is a sensitive subject politically, hospital dramas often contain a strong social action element. Issues are highlighted, such as funding, management styles, staff shortages, malpractices and a range of other political, social and economic concerns relating to hospitals and the medical profession, both for their entertainment value and also as a means of encouraging public debate.

> ### Ideas for discussion and development
>
> • **Watch an episode of *Holby City*. List all the issues relating to healthcare provision that you can identify.**

Reality television

This is a style of television that claims to represent real-life situations rather than scripted pre-recorded constructs. It has become extraordinarily popular in recent years. For television companies, reality shows are relatively cheap to make and they can bring in large audiences if successful. Reality shows have developed a variety of different sub-genres:

- Chosen participants (either celebrity or non-celebrity) are placed together in a setting and observed as they interact and manage their surroundings (which are manipulated by the programme makers) and each other.
- Ordinary people are assessed by 'experts' for such things as body shape, diet, house-decorating abilities, and marital and domestic lifestyle.

The first type has replaced the 'fly-on-the-wall' documentaries popular in the 1960s and 1970s, where hidden cameras observed people's everyday lives and behaviour. These programmes were based on the principles of subjectivist sociology, which argued that social studies should concentrate on analysing what people do rather than relying on any preconceived theories of behaviour. However, the more recent programmes are designed purely for entertainment and have little academic value.

Reality television was developed in the late 1990s, with programmes like *Castaway* and *Survivor* first airing in 2000 and 2001 respectively. In these examples, analysts comment on and discuss the participants' behaviour. The audience develops likes and dislikes for individuals and can vote participants off the show. Plain ordinariness and banality, forced

Eviction of Charley Uchea, *Big Brother* 8, 2007

sexual encounters and conflict all blend together to feed audience obsessions with these programmes.

The second type of reality shows are appealing because of the ordinariness of their participants and the everyday situations in which they are placed. The audience gains pleasure from criticising or sympathising with the participants and in judging the value of the expert's advice.

Very little is 'real' about reality shows. Recent evidence about the faking of scenes in the BBC's *Castaway* is a reminder of the artificial nature of these programmes.

Big Brother (Channel 4) is now a national institution. Named after the all-seeing leader in George Orwell's novel *1984*, *Big Brother* originated in Holland in 1999. The first UK series aired in 2000 and is famous for the character of 'Nasty' Nick Bateman. The show is now so well-known that any would-be celebrity invited to take part acts up to the cameras from the first moment.

It still seems amazing that an audience will watch ordinary people sleeping — as they do in the unedited versions of the show. The prime-time version is edited, with a voice-over giving details of time, place and character to bring out any drama involved. The power given to the audience is of spying on people — part of an increasingly voyeuristic culture encouraged by the internet — and being able to choose who to evict. Of course, the

Ideas for discussion and development

- **Is reality television 'dumbed down' television at its worst?**

characters in *Big Brother* want to be spied on and hopefully get 'discovered', as new 'celebrities' are guaranteed lucrative contracts with tabloids and advertisers.

Radio

Brief history of radio

Radio is the original broadcasting medium. It was developed between 1904 and 1922, and was officially established in the UK in 1927 with the founding of the BBC as a broadcasting monopoly offering, originally, three radio channels.

Radio was the predominant medium of news, entertainment and propaganda between 1927 and 1950. In the UK, radio was a public service, whereas the USA had a commercial radio system carrying advertising. In the UK, radio became the focus of national identity and resistance during the Second World War.

Radio faced strong competition from television in the 1950s and saw declining audiences. With only three (later four) radio stations offered by the BBC and with the challenge of 'pirate radio' in the early 1960s, the structure of radio broadcasting was adapted through legislation. The BBC's monopoly was broken after commercial stations were allowed to broadcast legally in 1974. In the 1990s, after deregulation, new commercial franchises encouraged the further expansion of national, local and community stations. The BBC launched Radio 5 (later renamed Radio Five Live) in 1990 with a mix of sport and lightweight news.

In the 1930s, radio was the first medium used to bring all the countries in the British Empire together to hear the King's Christmas message. Current expansion of radio services is on a narrowcast basis, with local and ethnic services developing to serve the needs of particular communities and interest groups.

Digital radio (Digital Audio Broadcasting, or DAB), with an enhanced digital signal, has been available in the UK since 1995 and the BBC launched five digital-only services in 2002.

Radio is regulated by Ofcom, which monitors and regulates programming and advertising on all independent (non-BBC) radio stations.

Music and radio

Music has been a major part of radio output from the early days of the BBC, with classical music being offered on the BBC's Third Programme

(1946–67), popular music on the Light Programme (1945–67), and dance band music on the Home Service (1939–67). The division reflected the distinction between 'highbrow' (classical) and 'lowbrow' (popular) music forms.

The popularity of US big band music during the Second World War and the development of swing, jive and the jitterbug paved the way for the postwar music scene. The postwar period also saw the development of 'pop' — short for 'popular' — and the subsequent emergence of rock and roll.

Rock and roll music culture became associated with teenage rebellion and the growth of subcultures (see the section on youth culture on pages 135–40). The BBC devoted only limited airtime to this new music, and its slow response to cultural change meant that Radio Luxembourg (broadcasting from Europe) and illegal 'pirate' radio stations (broadcasting from boats outside territorial waters, e.g. Radio Caroline, 1964–67) filled the gap until the advent of Radio 1 in 1967.

The establishment of commercial radio in 1974 greatly increased the number of stations available, and the deregulation of broadcasting in the 1990s further diversified the range of stations available, with an increasing emphasis on ethnic and local broadcasting.

Radio is important in the development and dissemination of music culture, as music not played on radio often goes unheard. Consequently, disc jockeys are under pressure from record companies to promote their products. Music downloads from the internet, and the growth of **iPods** and **MP3** players, are challenging the dominant role of radio in directing music tastes by controlling output. However, with the increased institutionalising of websites such as YouTube, this challenge may already be under threat. In recent years, the growth of 'talk radio' and the advent of deliberately controversial 'shock jocks' has helped refocus interest in radio output.

Ideas for discussion and development

• **Discuss the reasons for the continuing popularity of radio and explore ways in which new technologies have affected the medium.**

Key terms

iPod: a brand of portable music player produced by the Apple Corporation and launched in 2001. Apple iTunes software is used to transfer music to the devices. By 2007, 100 million units had been sold worldwide, and Apple were launching a more sophisticated device with internet download facilities for watching films and television programmes.

MP3: a computer software package that allows users to convert a music CD track into a computer file and post it on the internet for downloading by others.

Print

Newspapers

The British press is usually divided into three groups: the quality press, the **mid-market** and the tabloid. This distinction broadly coincides with the social class and employment status of the readership concerned. The UK has traditionally had one of the most socially classified newspaper cultures in the world. Advertising slogans from the 1970s and 1980s, such as 'Top people read *The Times*', 'No *FT*, no comment,' (the *Financial Times*) and 'Every woman needs her *Daily Mail*', typify a process of readership categorisation largely unfamiliar in Europe and the USA.

This culture, although undermined by many factors in recent years, is still in evidence in **newspaper readership** surveys using the **ABC1** classification system. In the most simplistic terms, this system suggests that the quality press is for managers and professional people, the middle market is for shop-assistants and clerks, and the tabloids are for the manual working classes. The old British class system still survives in this way.

Another way of looking at the differences is to see the quality press as presenting 'hard news' — a balance of reporting, comment and opinion, with an emphasis on news rather than entertainment. All the other newspapers could be seen as providing sensational and 'soft news', with an emphasis on entertainment rather than news. However, the increasing difficulty of attracting and holding readers — witnessed by the declining circulations of all national newspapers — and with strong competition from other news sources, such as rolling news television and the internet, means that the quality press is also now concerned with entertaining its readers.

The differentiation of the mid-market is difficult to explain. The *Daily Mail* is clearly a more serious and substantial newspaper than the *Sun*, with more hard news and comment. However, it does have a tabloid agenda in terms of sensational reporting. Does it deserve to be in a different category? The real distinction between the mid-market papers and the tabloid

Key terms

ABC1: a system of social classification based on an individual's occupation, used by advertisers and market researchers. The scale is used to classify media audiences and, in particular, to distinguish between the readership of quality and tabloid circulations. It is also used by advertisers as one method of identifying audience profiles and different market segments.

mid-market: demographic term applied to people, products, campaigns, services or media directed at or leaning towards the C1 or C2 social grade.

newspaper readership: the total number of people who read a newspaper rather than just the number who buy it. It provides vital information for advertisers and newspaper publishers, not only on the number of readers but also their social status and income level. Newspaper readership statistics are available from the Audit Bureau of Circulation (ABC) website.

'redtops' (so-called because the masthead of the tabloids concerned is on a red background) is in the readership profile rather than the content of the newspapers.

Financing newspapers

Newspapers deliver audiences to advertisers and depend on advertising revenue for their existence. Freesheet newspapers, like the *Metro* titles (owned by Associated Newspapers), can be given away to passers-by in the major cities because the advertising has already provided a profitable return for the producers. This does not always mean that volume sales guarantee a newspaper's survival. The *Guardian* (circulation 363,562) is healthier financially than the *Daily Express* (770,403). This is because the young professional readership of the *Guardian* is more attractive to advertisers than the readership of the *Daily Express*, and advertisers are prepared to pay more to reach this audience.

A current issue for newspapers is whether a distinctive Sunday version of a daily paper or a paper in the same ownership (e.g. the *Independent* and *Independent on Sunday*, *The Times* and *Sunday Times*, the *Guardian* and *Observer*) can survive a 24/7 online newspaper culture.

The resignation of *Observer* editor Roger Alton in October 2007, when his paper had achieved increased circulation and had won the coveted Newspaper of the Year award, highlighted tension and disagreement with its owners Guardian Media over whether the *Observer* could continue in its present form. Continuous news coverage on the internet challenges the distinctive once-a-week role of the Sunday papers, and it remains to be seen whether they will survive as independent entities. For the *Observer*, the prospect of becoming the *Guardian on Sunday* does not appeal to staff.

The quality press

The **quality press** is a distinguishing term applied to British broadsheet (now compact in some cases) newspapers to separate them from the popular tabloid or 'gutter' press. The quality press is seen to focus on hard news stories and responsible, balanced reporting and comment. Its readership profile shows high levels of A, B and C1 readers with employment in the professions and managerial roles.

The following newspapers make up the quality press in the UK:

- *The Times*: this is owned by News International, and has a circulation of 633,850 (July 2007). Its politics are right of centre, although it tends to support New Labour with reservations. The paper was viewed as the

elitist voice of the UK establishment, but is now more down-market and populist than it used to be. It became the flagship newspaper of Rupert Murdoch's News International in the UK after his acquisition of Times Newspapers (*The Times* and *The Sunday Times*) in 1981.

- The *Guardian*: this is owned by the Guardian Media Group (The Scott Trust), and has a circulation of 363,562 (July 2007). Its politics are centre-left, and the paper has become the mainstay of liberal-left opinion in the UK. Its readership of young professionals is attractive to advertisers.

- The *Daily Telegraph*: this is owned by the Barclay brothers, and has a circulation of 891,768 (July 2007). Its politics are centre-right, and it tends to support the Conservative Party. It is the highest selling quality daily newspaper, with a traditionally strong middle-class readership. However, the paper's circulation is not as healthy as it seems because its figures are boosted by discounted subscription sales. It also suffers from an ageing readership, which deters advertisers. The paper was acquired in 2004 by the Barclay Brothers following a protracted wrangle with the former owner Lord Black.

- The *Independent*: this is owned by Independent News and Media, and has a circulation of 238,291 (July 2007). Its politics are in the centre. The paper often uses its pioneering compact format to run a single issue on its front page, which makes it more distinctive than other papers. It was the only quality daily to stand firmly against the Iraq war. Despite having the lowest circulation of the quality newspapers, it has built up a loyal and growing readership.

- The *Financial Times*: this is owned by Pearson, and has a circulation of 444,763. Its politics are in the centre. As well as being required reading for people working in the financial world, the paper also carries excellent arts coverage and strong editorial leads.

Task

Choose one tabloid and one quality newspaper published on the same day. By analysing the front pages, discuss the differences in news values and agendas of the two publications. How do you account for these differences?

The tabloid press

The term **tabloid** is generally associated with the more popular, less intellectual newspapers and frequently has negative connotations. The tabloids are also known as the **gutter press** because of their tendency to build stories around the worst aspects of human behaviour, e.g. sexual infidelity or misconduct, betrayal, impropriety, corruption, homicide etc.

Tabloid newspapers are published in tabloid format (approximately 40 cm x 30 cm when folded), the smallest of the standard newspaper sizes. They have a readership profile of largely C2, D and E social class brackets.

Tabloid-sized newspapers in the quality press bracket are called 'compact', a term used to avoid the negative populist connotations associated with the term 'tabloid'. Some quality newspapers use the **Berliner** format.

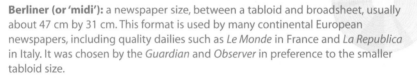

Key term

Berliner (or 'midi'): a newspaper size, between a tabloid and broadsheet, usually about 47 cm by 31 cm. This format is used by many continental European newspapers, including quality dailies such as *Le Monde* in France and *La Republica* in Italy. It was chosen by the *Guardian* and *Observer* in preference to the smaller tabloid size.

Mid-market

The following newspapers make up the mid-market tabloid press in the UK:

- **The *Daily Mail*:** this is owned by Associated Newspapers, and has a circulation of 2,303,438 (July 2007). Its politics are right of centre and it tends to support the Conservative Party. The paper was first published in 1896 and has a long tradition of supporting right-of-centre politics — in the late 1930s, it advocated avoiding war by appeasing Hitler. Strongly anti-European Union and supportive of the Thatcher government in the 1980s, the paper became the established voice of middle England and the aspiring middle classes. Its successful formula has seen off its rival *Daily Express,* and its circulation stands second only to the *Sun* in daily tabloid sales. It has a high percentage of female readers.

- **The *Daily Express*:** this is owned by Northern and Shell Media and has a circulation of 770,403 (July 2007). Its politics are right of centre. Founded in 1900, the *Daily Express* was once the biggest selling newspaper in the world and the first newspaper to carry news instead of adverts on the front page. However, in recent decades the paper has been unable to match the growing success of its long-term rival, the *Daily Mail*.

Popular

The following newspapers make up the popular tabloid press in the UK:

- **The *Daily Mirror*:** this is owned by the Trinity Mirror Group and has a circulation of 1,565,711 (July 2007). Its politics are centre-left, and it tends to support New Labour. The *Mirror* has a long tradition of supporting the Labour Party, going back to the Second World War when it even challenged Churchill's handling of the conflict. The paper faced strong competition from Rupert Murdoch's *Sun* during the 1970s and 1980s, and its circulation fell as a result. In 1984, the group was acquired by corrupt tycoon Robert Maxwell for what became a disastrous period in its history. Mirror Group Newspapers survived Maxwell's death and disgrace in 1991 to be taken over by Trinity, which became the Trinity Mirror Group in 1999.

- **The *Sun*:** this is owned by News International and has a circulation of 3,054,376 (July 2007) — the largest of any newspaper. Its politics are centre-right and it tends to support New Labour. The paper was acquired by Rupert Murdoch in 1969 and soon became a national institution. It combined eye-grabbing headlines, 'page three' topless models, sex and scandal, soap operas, sport and celebrity gossip, and right-wing, anti-European politics. During the 1980s and early 1990s, the paper claimed to have won election victories for the Conservative Party. In 1997 its switch in political allegiance, following a meeting between Murdoch and Tony Blair, was seen as an important factor in creating the bandwagon effect that helped to bring New Labour to power. Cultivating the support of the *Sun* has become an important feature of political parties seeking election success, and this has encouraged the 'tabloid-isation' and dumbing down of British politics.

- **The *Daily Star*:** this is owned by Express Newspapers, Northern and Shell Media, and has a circulation of 795,891 (July 2007). Its politics are populist with no obvious political leanings. Founded in 1978, the paper's celebrity gossip and sport appeals to readers bored with hard news and depressing storylines.

An analysis of the *Daily Mail*'s front page would address the following questions:

- How does the choice of lead article reflect the paper's readership and their interests/concerns? Is it good or bad news?
- Why is a David Attenborough DVD being plugged?
- Why has Felicity Kendal been chosen as the star/celebrity?
- Why have 'before' and 'after' photos been used of Felicity Kendal? How do these reflect the interests and concerns of the readership?

Example deconstruction of a mid-market tabloid: Daily Mail

The Sunday papers

Quality

The following newspapers make up the quality Sunday press in the UK:

- **The *Sunday Times*:** this is owned by News International, and has a circulation of 1,173,956 (July 2007). Its politics are centre-right and it tends to support New Labour. The paper styles itself 'the Sunday papers' because of its large circulation and the wide range of supplements it contains. It is clearly the market leader for the Sunday quality market.

- **The *Observer*:** this is owned by Guardian Newspapers Ltd, and has a circulation of 451,425 (July 2007). Its politics are centre-left and it tends to support New Labour. Seen by many as the *Guardian on Sunday*, the *Observer* has its own distinct identity but attracts the same readership as the *Guardian*. The paper has traditionally championed liberal causes and human rights issues. It was established in 1791 and is one of the oldest media publications in the UK.

- **The *Sunday Telegraph*:** this is owned by the Barclay brothers (Telegraph Group Ltd), and has a circulation of 652,497 (July 2007). Its politics are centre-right and it tends to support the Conservative Party. It is a solid right-wing Sunday quality newspaper, with much the same agenda as its daily namesake.

- **The *Independent on Sunday*:** this is owned by Independent Newspapers, and has a circulation of 245,952 (July 2007). Its politics are in the centre. It is the sister paper to the *Independent* and takes an equally strong line on environmental issues and the Iraq war.

Tabloid: mid-market

The following newspapers make up the tabloid mid-market Sunday press in the UK:

- **The *Mail on Sunday*:** this is owned by Associated Newspapers, and has a circulation of 2,276,107 (July 2007). Its politics are centre-right and it tends to support the Conservative Party. It is a highly successful sister paper to the *Daily Mail*, with the same readership base.

- **The *Sunday Express*:** this is owned by Northern and Shell Media, and has a circulation of 743,327 (July 2007). Its politics are centre-right. It is the sister paper of the *Daily Express*, with the same readership base.

Tabloid: popular

The following newspapers make up the tabloid popular Sunday press in the UK:

- **The *News of the World*:** this is owned by News International, and has a circulation of 3,269,483 (July 2007) — the largest Sunday circulation. Its politics are populist and it tends to support New Labour. It is the sister paper of the *Sun*. Sex, celebrity, scandal, wrong-doing by those in high places, and naming and shaming of paedophiles are all standard content in the *News of the World*. It attracts the largest readership of any UK newspaper.
- **The *Sunday Mirror*:** this is owned by Trinity Mirror, and its circulation is 1,411,428 (July 2007). Its politics are centre-left and it tends to support New Labour. It is the sister paper of the *Daily Mirror*.
- **The *People*** (previously *Sunday People*): this is owned by Trinity Mirror, and has a circulation of 736,438 (July 2007). Its politics are populist and it tends to support New Labour. It covers the same type of content as the *Sunday Mirror*.
- **The *Daily Star Sunday*:** this is owned by Express Newspapers, Northern and Shell, and has a circulation of 394,920 (July 2007). Its politics are populist, with no obvious political leanings. With a small circulation for a Sunday popular paper, the *Star* has yet to make any real impact on the market with this Sunday version of the daily paper.

Ideas for discussion and development

- **Are there too many Sunday newspapers? Will they all survive?**
- **Which newspapers do you think might be facing problems? What factors will influence whether they continue or not? Will the posting of all newspapers on the internet mean the gradual decline of all traditional newspapers?**

Media institutions: newspaper publishers

- **Associated Newspapers:** newspaper publishing company and subsidiary of the Daily Mail and General Trust Ltd, established in 1905 by Alfred Harmsworth (later Lord Northcliffe). It publishes the *Daily Mail*, the *Mail on Sunday*, the *Evening Standard* (London region), *Loot*, *Metro* (freesheet newspapers) and a large number of regional titles. Associated Newspapers is the only major British newspaper publisher still in the hands of the original founding family (Harmsworth/Rothermere).

- **Guardian Media Group (GMG):** a media organisation overseen by The Scott Trust, which owns the *Guardian, Observer* and *Manchester Evening News* newspapers, together with other print publications, radio and digital television companies.
- **Mirror Group Newspapers (MGN):** publishing group responsible for the *Daily Mirror*, the *Sunday Mirror* and the *Sunday People*. The group is part of Trinity Mirror.
- **News Corporation:** parent company of Rupert Murdoch's global media empire. News Corporation claims to be the only vertically integrated media company, producing and distributing television, cable, film, satellite and e-media productions on five continents.
- **News International:** subdivision of News Corporation, responsible for newspaper publication in the UK. Company titles include the *Sun, The Times*, the *Sunday Times* and the *News of the World*.
- **Northern and Shell:** media company, under the chairmanship of Richard Desmond, which owns of a wide range of lifestyle magazines, including *OK* and various soft pornography titles, together with Express Newspapers, publishers of the *Daily Express* and *Sunday Express*.
- **Trinity Mirror:** the UK's biggest newspaper publisher, which employs around 11,500 staff and produces some 250 titles. The company's varied media base includes national and regional newspapers, including the *Birmingham Post* and *Evening Mail*, along with websites and magazines. Nearly half the population reads one of their titles, which include the *Daily Mirror* newspaper (Mirror Group Newspapers) plus three of the top ten regional evening newspapers and three of the top ten regional Sunday newspapers.
- **United Business Media (formerly known as United Newspapers, United News and Media and United MAI):** a media company associated with Lord Hollick, with 35% holdings in Five (Channel 5) and ownership of other high-tech publishing and business services. The

Case study

Murdoch, Rupert (1931–) is chairman of the News Corporation and one of the most powerful figures in the media world. Australian by birth, Murdoch was born into a family with newspaper publishing interests. He arrived on the British media scene in 1969 with his purchase of the *Sun* newspaper from Reed International. He has expanded his newspaper holdings to cover one third of all daily and Sunday newspapers sold in the UK. Murdoch's companies, under the corporate title News Corporation, represent one of the three largest media holdings in the world.

Murdoch's company has worldwide media interests, from BSkyB and HarperCollins publishers in the UK to Fox TV, Fox News, Twentieth Century Fox film studios, numerous sports channels and the *New York Post* newspaper in the USA. The company also has significant holdings in Australia, with a large stake in regional newspaper ownership and publishing interests.

company was formerly a stakeholder in regional ITV franchises (e.g. Yorkshire, Tyne Tees and Anglia), part owner of Independent Television News (ITN) and also owner of Express Newspapers, which it sold to Richard Desmond's Northern and Shell company in 1997. United Business Media sold its ITV holdings to Granada in 2000 and has since consolidated its activities in the production of business information services.

National newspapers and politics

Traditionally, national newspapers support one of the major British political parties — the Labour Party, the Conservative Party or the Liberal Democrats — and recommend which party their readers should vote for at general elections. Changes in political alignment following New Labour's victory in 1997 have made redundant the old accusation by the left and the Labour Party that the press is 'Tory' (i.e. supports the Conservative Party).

The current government has had an easy time with the UK press since 1997, thanks to the broad consensus created by New Labour and the effective media management practised by Tony Blair's advisers. Confusion and disarray in the Conservative Party and changes of leader and policies have meant that even the *Daily Mail* has been a supporter of much government policy. On the controversial issue of the Iraq war in 2003, only the *Daily Mirror* (with Piers Morgan as editor) and the *Independent* actively campaigned against the war, and Morgan was later sacked partly because of this policy. All other papers tended to support the government.

The key feature of contemporary newspapers is their **populism** and this applies now as much to the quality as to the tabloid press. Populism means that newspapers are happy to go along with the non-intellectual instincts of their readers and meet the demand for light, easy to read journalism based on lifestyle trivia, entertainment, personalities, sex and relationships — all dressed with sensationalism. Even for the quality press, human-interest stories and soft news are becoming more important than hard news and politics in the battle to halt declining readership.

With so many other sources of news and entertainment available, including the internet versions of the papers themselves, the general trend in traditional print newspaper circulations is downwards. For the tabloids in particular, this creates even greater pressure to hold on to existing readers.

Political terminology

The following are explanations of many of the traditional terms used in UK politics.

- **centre politics:** a term used to describe the middle or common ground between left- and right-wing views, increasingly sought by politicians seeking electoral success. The crowding of this middle ground, with similar policies being produced by different parties, makes distinguishing between the parties increasingly difficult for the electorate, especially since the election in 2005 of David Cameron as leader of the Conservative Party.

- **communism:** belief in the views of Karl Marx (1818–83), principally that capitalist society involves the exploitation of the working class by the ruling class and that, through a process of class awareness, struggle and revolution, the more numerous working class will eventually seize the means of production and build a classless, socialist society. In the medium term, a dictatorship of the proletariat would involve the control of all the means of production and distribution by an authoritarian state. In the UK there is limited support for both the Communist Party and other extreme left-wing groups, such as the Socialist Workers Party. These have become little more than minority pressure groups.

- **Conservative:** the belief in the importance of the freedom of the individual to create wealth in a society for the benefit of all, and in the need to maintain existing institutions and traditions, such as the family and the monarchy, in the face of demands for radical change. These beliefs are usually expressed by support for the Conservative Party.
- **fascism:** a term derived from the militaristic, anti-communist right-wing Italian National Facist Party led by Benito Mussolini, who was in power in Italy from 1922 to 1943. The term was used to describe similar movements in Germany, Spain and elsewhere. It is now loosely applied to any nationalist, authoritarian, repressive, right-wing politics, sometimes with racist connotations. In the UK, the far-right British National Party is often described as 'fascist', although this term is rejected by its supporters.
- **fringe politics:** this is a term used to describe small groups outside the political mainstream and often without any clear left/right tradition. Extreme socialist and fascist groups could be described as fringe, as could single-issue groups like the Animal Liberation Front and supporters of Islamic revolutionary groups.
- **left wing:** in support of the socialist or Labour Party.
- **Liberal:** the term traditionally used for supporters of the Liberal Party (in Britain now called the Liberal Democrats). Liberal policies are not anchored to party dogma and tend to be more free-thinking and radical, particularly in social matters.
- **liberal (economic context):** implies opposition to state control and government regulation of national economies. Liberal economists, sometimes called free-market capitalists, are against the protection of national economies through trade barriers such as tariffs and import quotas, and believe that market forces alone should be left to determine the relationship between the supply, demand and price of goods and services in a globalised market.
- **New Labour:** the term coined by Labour Party election strategists to signal a move away from traditional socialist principles (like the public ownership of major industries) in pursuit of more populist policies, following an 18-year period in opposition. The so-called 'third way' associated with the party's 1997 election victory represented a continuation of many previous Conservative government policies, but with increased public expenditure on health and education services.

- **pressure groups:** groups that seek to exert pressure on the government to introduce particular measures or adopt particular policies. They include Greenpeace, War on Want, Age Concern, the League Against Cruel Sports, the Countryside Alliance, the Society for the Protection of Unborn Children and the Muslim Council of Britain. By focusing on a single issue or representing a specific minority, these groups can be highly influential as they target MPs and cultivate the media. At a time when individual involvement with mainstream political parties is in decline, these groups are exerting an increasing influence on government policy, decision-making and legislation.
- **progressive:** a view of society that sees social change and evolution as positive and desirable.
- **radical:** a belief in dramatic change and a break with tradition.
- **right wing:** resistant to social change and desiring the maintenance of traditional conservative values and beliefs.
- **socialism:** a belief that it is the duty of the state to take measures to break down social class barriers and ensure the provision of equal opportunities and the fair distribution of wealth for all in a society. This means that the state involves itself directly with the national economy and the means of production, through public ownership or nationalisation of major industries and public services, such as the health service. Unlike communism, which advocates change through revolution, democratic socialism advocates change on a gradual consensual basis through the ballot box. These beliefs were traditionally expressed by support for the Labour Party.

The use of political terminology has been made increasingly complicated by the many changes in the policies, positioning and ideology of the recognised political parties.

Some would argue that many of these traditional terms are no longer relevant to British politics for the following reasons:
- Politicians increasingly offer populist packages pitched at the public by media-friendly personalities, which have little or no ideological content and differ only in their presentation, not in their substance.
- Politicians are marketed as 'celebrities' who go in and out of favour with the media and are easily exchangeable for new faces when their popularity falters.
- Politicians who are physically unappealing and perform poorly for the media have little chance of sustaining or even reaching high office.

- Manipulating media presentation of policies and personalities through communication managers and 'spin doctors' has become a major aspect of any political party's effort to achieve power.

The 'feel-good' factor

When people are reasonably happy with their income, levels of taxation, service provision and their overall way of life, they are consequently reasonably happy with the government. This sense among the electorate is called the **'feel-good' factor** and is important for those wishing to retain power. However, people who feel that none of the mainstream political parties represents them are unlikely to vote. In the 2005 general election, just 60% of British voters actually voted and only 9.5 million out of an electorate of 44 million voted for the winning party.

The 'feel-good' factor can be easily upset by economic depression, shortages of key resources like food or fuel, excessive taxation levels, low income levels, inflation, unemployment, and disquieting factors such as war, terrorism or environmental disaster. In the UK, the increase in the value of property since the mid-1990s has been a major factor in creating a sense of economic wellbeing.

Newspapers will concentrate on the negative or positive aspects of life in accordance with their own political allegiances and overall philosophy, and their behaviour has an important influence on the 'feel-good' factor in a society.

The language of tabloid newspapers

The language used by tabloid newspapers is designed to grab the reader's attention and engage in an informal one-way conversation. It is **subjective** — it adopts a point of view on behalf of the reader — and assumes the reader's agreement with the position adopted. Tabloids use a range of rhetorical literary devices for this purpose:

- **alliteration** — often used in headlines to grab attention and create memorable phrases, such as 'Big BBC bung for Brucie' (generous BBC contract for Bruce Forsythe)
- **rhyme** — 'Islander Kate shuts the gate' (about *Big Brother* winner Kate Lawler signing up to *Love Island*)
- **metaphor** — 'Lions maul Russian bear' (England–Russia football match)
- **puns** — 'That's a fat lotto good' (on lottery cash for Manchester United)
- **hyperbole** — 'England massacred, fans gutted!'

Another feature of the language is the casual familiarity created by the use of:

- **slang and popular idiom** — hubby, babe, wasted, bender, cheater, boobs, footie, dosh, gutted, gotcha
- **misspelled words** — 'It was the Sun wot won it!' (1992 general election)
- **clichés** — 'I was over the moon'

Task

Analyse a copy of a 'red top' tabloid newspaper (*Sun*, *Mirror*, *Star*) using the information on pages 62–63 to identify examples of rhetorical language.

Tabloid news agendas

Tabloid newspapers cover a large number of political stories, but their overall news agenda is likely to be based on the following areas of interest:

- Public and private morality — financial affairs, sexual behaviour and relationships of those in the public eye.
- Perceived threats to the wellbeing of the community, whether physical, economic, cultural or social. This means an emphasis on crime and punishment, taxation, income and expenditure levels, issues involving asylum and immigration, and 'moral panic' issues involving paedophilia and threats to children, the family and traditional values.
- Crime and punishment — court reports with sensational treatments.
- Sport, particularly football and the careers of sporting heroes.
- Human interest stories involving individual triumphs and tragedies, illness and recovery, the loss of loved ones, acts of bravery and courage. This area also includes ordinary individuals as victims of bureaucracies, or the failings of government, the police or institutions such as the National Health Service.
- Health, beauty and diet-related subject matter aimed at female readers.
- Television soap operas — following the lives of the stars and celebrities involved.
- National lottery, competitions, prizes and other transformational processes that offer escapism to readers.
- Glamour and fashion in all titles, and glamour as soft pornography in the *Sun* and the *Star*.

Moral panics

This is a concept devised by Jock Young and developed by Stan Cohen to explain the way in which media-focus on the behaviour of a social group or an event — and inflated by sensational reporting and the repeated use of stereotypes — can result in a public over-reaction or panic at a perceived threat to society. The key element is the feeling that the situation is out of control in some way and therefore represents a threat to the moral order.

Classic moral panics

- **1960s:** mods and rockers fighting in the streets (fear of breakdown of law and order, with youth out of control).
- **1970s:** the obscenity trial of the *Oz* magazine 'School Kids Issue' (1970) (fear of pornography and subversive material corrupting the young, even when, as in this case, the magazine was produced by the young themselves).
- **1970s–1980s:** *The Exorcist* (William Friedkin, 1973) was controversial at the cinema and its video release was banned for 25 years (fear that blasphemy and satanism could lead to the undermining of moral values).
- **1980s:** video nasties i.e. films regarded as offensive and banned by the censors, including *I Spit on Your Grave* (Meir Zarchi, 1978), *Driller Killer* (Abel Ferrara, 1979) and *The Texas Chainsaw Massacre* (Tobe Hooper, 1974) (fear that viewing these films leads to uncontrolled copycat violence and moral degeneracy).
- **1990s:** murder of James Bulger and suggested link with the film *Child's Play 3* (Jack Bender, 1991) (fear that watching video nasties leads to copycat crime including murder).
- **2000s:** the lyrics of rap music and other alternative music (some music lyrics were thought to encourage gun crime. There were claims that the perpetrators of the Columbine High School massacre had been inspired by listening to Marilyn Manson songs. Garage band So Solid Crew were accused of glorifying violence by government minister Kim Howells after two girls were shot dead in Birmingham in a drive-by gang shooting on New Year's Eve 2002).
- **2000s:** paedophilia and child abduction (fears about known paedophiles being at large in the community. The obsession of the tabloid press with cases involving paedophilia followed a campaign of 'naming and shaming' launched by the *News of the World* in 2000, which came about after the abduction and murder of 8-year-old Sarah Payne. Sarah's killer was caught, convicted and imprisoned but it emerged that he was already a known sex offender. As a result of the emotion whipped up by the campaign, vigilante attacks on individuals occurred. The subject is kept in the public eye by ongoing coverage of concerns about internet child pornography).

Child abduction stories are not really a moral panic in themselves, but they are part of an exaggerated sense of the dangers facing children in the modern world. The unpleasant truth is that most harm inflicted on children is done by their parents or those close to them, often in their own home and not by lurking strangers. Stories about children in general, and harm done to children in particular, involve highly charged emotional content, so they have huge audience appeal and therefore help to sell newspapers.

Task

Madeleine McCann

The disappearance of 4-year-old Madeleine McCann in Portugal in the summer of 2007 received saturation media coverage in the UK over 3 months and continued to dominate the news agenda, particularly in the tabloid press, well into the autumn of 2007. All newspapers were involved in publicising the disappearance of the girl, and they were encouraged and orchestrated by her family in the hope that she would be found. However, the tabloids became obsessed with the story, even though there was little progress in finding out what had happened to her.

The *Daily Express* newspaper had the name MADELEINE in capitals and a long article on the case across its front page on the following dates in 2007: 31 July, 3 August, 6 August, 8–11 August, 14 August, 16 August, 17 August, 20 August, 22–24 August. Subsequent editions in September and October 2007 continued to feature Madeleine in front-page headlines on most days, and the 1 November 2007 headline was 'Is Madeleine a child slave in Morocco?'

There was, in fact, no real news to report on Madeleine's whereabouts during this whole period. Frustrated by having no news to report, sections of the press turned their attention on the parents, with accusations of complicity in the child's disappearance, and attacks on their demeanour and behaviour. It is fair to say that the case dominated news coverage in the UK for 6 months in 2007.

How would you explain this type of newspaper coverage? Whose interests does it serve?

Regional newspapers and their ownership

The following are some examples of regional newspapers:

- London area: *Evening Standard* (Associated Newspapers)
- Birmingham area: *Birmingham Post, Birmingham Mail* (Trinity Mirror)
- Manchester area: *Manchester Evening News* (Guardian Media Group)
- Yorkshire and northeast: *Yorkshire Post* (Johnston Press)
- Northeast: *Newcastle Evening Chronicle* (Trinity Mirror)
- Scotland: *The Scotsman* (Johnston Press)
- Southwest: *Bristol Evening Post* (Associated Newspapers)

Application of key concepts to the study of regional newspapers

Look through some regional newspapers. What is their news agenda? What methods are used to attract readers? How do they differ from the national press? How does their advertising content differ from national papers?

Genre

Local newspapers usually use a tabloid format with large, attention-grabbing headlines and a large proportion of pictures.

Representation

These papers focus on local people, places and events, with articles also on local government issues and the provision of local services such as the NHS and police. Their values are mainstream and 'community' based.

Audience

The audience is regionally defined and family-focused. Local knowledge and interest are assumed and the socioeconomic base is broad, with little of the distinction found in the national press.

Values and ideology

Values are 'mainstream' and community-based, with local political/social issues such as the closure of local hospitals and post offices being central. The local MP and councillors feature prominently. Issues include: road safety, education, local crime and policing, policies, social services, the environment, court reports and local celebrities. There are also 'local' angles on national issues, e.g. soldiers from Afghanistan/Iraq returning home.

Institution

Many local titles are owned by one company, with Associated Newspapers, Trinity Mirror, Johnston Press etc. being major players across the country. The Manchester Evening News is part of the Guardian Media Group, and the London Evening Standard is owned by Associated Newspapers. There are often free delivery versions of the paper in local target areas, and also links with local radio.

Language and content

The language tends to be 'tabloid' rather than 'quality' in style. The contents are often subject to press releases from interested groups, e.g. police and local schools. Another feature is local pressure group campaigning, e.g. 'Save our train station', 'Save our playing fields from development'. Other contents include local weather, local advertising and local sport, together with travel/gossip/television/entertainment — all locally focused. Newspapers act as a noticeboard for local jobs and services, with 'find a friend' and 'buy and sell' columns. Local events are publicised and the papers seek to integrate themselves into the day-to-day life of the community.

Advertising

Advertising often has a local 'spin' on national campaigns with, for example, regional openings of national stores. Local restaurants and entertainment are featured and fliers for local businesses are common (e.g. takeaway restaurants). Local property and car and vehicle advertisements are also very important. There is a high advertorial content, which is often difficult to distinguish from real journalism.

Ideas for discussion and development

The Voice (published by Voice Communications Group and founded in 1982) is targeted at young black Britons, with the aim of providing a positive representation of black interests and fighting for 'fairness and equality'. Its circulation is modest at fewer than 50,000 copies and there is now strong competition from ethnically focused local radio stations.

- **In a multicultural environment, will ethnically or culturally targeted newspapers become increasingly important?**

Regulating the press

Controlling the press has always been a sensitive issue in a society where 'freedom of the press' is seen emotively as a measure of democratic freedom in general. Gagging the press is associated with repressive regimes and a loss of liberty.

In fact, issues of press freedom are more complex. The quality press can reasonably demand the freedom to expose politicians and the corruption of those in power, to question performance and judgement, and generally argue for or against current policies and issues. The tabloid press can use the words 'freedom' and 'public interest' to justify publishing material that is damaging to individuals. However, both are constrained by some of the strongest libel laws in the world.

A rich person with good lawyers can still go to court to seek an injunction against a newspaper to prevent it publishing articles he or she considers to be damaging — regardless of whether or not they might be true. In the 1980s, Robert Maxwell, the disgraced former tycoon and owner of the *Mirror* newspaper, successfully used court injunctions to prevent the magazine *Private Eye* from printing articles suggesting that his business empire was corrupt and insolvent. This did in fact turn out to be the case, as was exposed on Maxwell's death in 1991.

Ironically, the Mirror's front page obituary for its deceased former owner featured a large photograph of Maxwell headlined: 'The Man who saved the Mirror'. However, in the days that followed it was revealed that he had robbed the employees' pension fund of £100 million.

On the other hand, Maxwell's *Mirror* had printed articles claiming that miners' union leaders, including Arthur Scargill, were corruptly using union money for their own benefit. This was not the case. Although the newspaper was forced to retract its statements, it published only a tiny article as compared to full front-page coverage of the allegations. These allegations permanently damaged the reputations of those concerned.

The tabloid press frequently abuse 'freedom' to publish unsubstantiated or simply false allegations about the behaviour of individuals, even to the extent of making up quotations and events. Unless the individual concerned has sufficient funds available, there is little that can be done to prevent this practice.

Another case was brought to court in 2001 by model Naomi Campbell, who was photographed leaving a drug rehabilitation clinic in a depressed state. The court ruled that the *Mirror* was right to publish the photographs in the 'public interest' because of Campbell's celebrity status and that her claim of invasion of privacy was invalid. However, the judgement was overturned by the House of Lords in 2004, suggesting continuing controversy about what constitutes the 'public interest'.

The Press Complaints Commission

Concerns about the ineffective nature of newspaper regulation by the Press Council (a self-regulating body set up by the newspapers themselves) led to the establishment of the **Press Complaints Commission** (PCC) in 1991.

The PCC is the newspaper complaints body or 'watchdog'. It was established to monitor newspaper content in response to complaints made by members of the public. Its structure was revised in 1993 following complaints about invasions of privacy. The PCC is intended to provide recourse for those who feel that newspaper content has either offended or

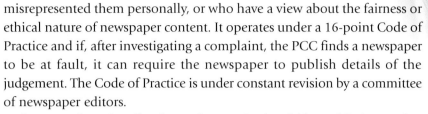

misrepresented them personally, or who have a view about the fairness or ethical nature of newspaper content. It operates under a 16-point Code of Practice and if, after investigating a complaint, the PCC finds a newspaper to be at fault, it can require the newspaper to publish details of the judgement. The Code of Practice is under constant revision by a committee of newspaper editors.

The PCC often cites 'freedom of expression' and 'the public interest' as a justification for publishing controversial stories, and it is still regarded by many as ineffective in defending the rights of individuals against press intrusion. However, it was instrumental in securing the agreement by newspapers to limit the intrusion into the lives of Princes William and Harry.

Magazines

Lifestyle magazines

Lifestyle magazines are a broad category of magazines that define audiences in terms of their way of life and consumption of specific products. Examples include *Gardeners' World, More, Maxim, Marie Claire, Woman's Own, Bizarre* and *GQ*.

Lifestyle magazines seek to reinforce patterns of consumption and behaviour, and they provide readers with a sense of security and identity. Readers' aspirations are stimulated in relation to possessions, appearance, relationships and careers. It is important to remember that all lifestyle magazines are primarily vehicles for advertisers, which are provided with clear readership profiles for targeting their advertisements.

Lifestyle magazines have attractive covers, and they use teasers and photographs of celebrities to draw readers in. Inside the magazine, idealised versions of life are shown, in which representations of the target audience are surrounded by the desirable consumer products. They also adopt a mode of address and include articles that engage with the readers' attitudes, beliefs, values, interests and concerns.

The representations that dominate lifestyle magazines include glamorous and perfected people, models, celebrities, famous and successful individuals, and exotic places. The poor, the unattractive, the sick, the old and the unsuccessful do not tend to feature in these magazines, and there are often limited representations of ethnic minorities.

The target audience of the magazine should be obvious from the images used on the cover, the language register and mode of address, and the nature of advertisements and articles. For example, for a title like *FHM*, a photograph of an attractive, semi-naked female on the cover, advertisements for aftershave and trainers, and articles on a boys' night out, all suggest a lad's magazine aimed at 16–30-year-olds. The related advertisements will be focused on the products the target audience could be expected to purchase, e.g. a magazine for teenage girls will include advertisements for cosmetics, shampoos, clothes and accessories, and perfume. Many of the articles are often little more than recommendations of particular products. Indeed, the percentage of lifestyle magazines taken up by advertisements is substantial. In recent editions of *Marie Claire*, approximately 70% of the pages were advertisements or advertising features.

Content of lifestyle magazines

The content of lifestyle magazines is fairly predictable and does not vary much over time. Here is an illustration of what you can expect to find in any issue.

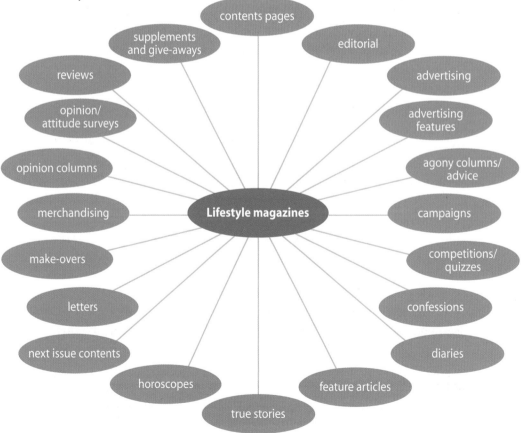

Cover of lifestyle magazines

The cover of a typical lifestyle magazine usually has the following elements:

Issue number

Puffs — self-boosting claims for the magazine

Main cover line

Cover price

Straplines

Feature article photograph

Bar code

Women's magazines

In the 1950s, women's magazines focused on traditional women's roles and family interests. The emphasis was on home and family care, household skills (knitting, cookery, housework etc.) and personal appearance — all of which were intended to please a working husband. With the growth of feminism in the 1960s and 1970s, the magazines adapted to meet the career aspirations and changed values of a new generation of readers. However, many traditional elements are still to be found in the pages of women's magazines today.

Ideas for discussion and development

- **What do the following 1950s titles — some still being published today — tell you about the way women were seen in the 1950s?**

Women's Own

Woman

Woman's Realm

Woman's Weekly

Woman and Home

Case study

Cosmopolitan **magazine**

Cosmopolitan was launched in 1972. It was the first of a new generation of women's magazines to recognise the dramatic changes that had taken place in women's lives during the 1960s. Under its original editor, Helen Gurley Brown, it broke new ground in advocating sexual and economic freedom for women, and in recognising that its readers were interested not only in men but also in appearance, mind, body and career.

The magazine was taken seriously by academics and supporters of the women's movement as an important contributor to the advancement of women's self-confidence, self-esteem and independence. It became a symbol of the changing times by discussing all aspects of sexuality openly for the first time, and it was the first mainstream women's magazine to publish naked male pin-ups.

In spite of its high profile on social and women's issues, *Cosmopolitan* is essentially a consumer lifestyle magazine. Its high-spending readership makes it a magnet for advertisers — its readers spend £1 billion a year on fashion goods and £1.4 billion on new cars.

Cosmopolitan is published in 28 countries and is owned by National Magazines, itself part of the giant Hearst Corporation which also publishes *Esquire, Good Housekeeping, She, Cosmo Girl* and the US edition of *Marie Claire* (under licence from the French title owner Hachette).

Task

Using a copy of a contemporary women's magazine, explore some of the ways in which the front cover communicates with its readership.

Girls' magazines

Girls' magazines have developed from the classic *Girl* newspaper in the 1950s to reflect changing social attitudes towards girlhood and sexuality. Modern magazines such as *Bliss* deal frankly with all aspects of sexuality and sexual behaviour.

Jackie

In the 1970s, the magazine *Jackie* dominated the market, with its combination of agony column advice, readers' letters, photo-strip romance stories and pop star pin-ups.

Jackie reflected the relative innocence of the 1970s 'teenybopper' culture. It concentrated on romance, fashion and beauty, and saw itself as a big sister figure for its readers. Pin-ups were wholesome not raunchy, and pop stars Donnie Osmond and David Cassidy were favourites.

Angela McRobbie's study of the magazine (1978) found that it offered girls narrow horizons and low status, reinforcing stereotypes in relationships, where girls were subservient and passive in relation to boys. Careers advice was limited to traditional areas like beauty therapy, nursing or working with animals. Life was shown to revolve around getting a boyfriend, and letters to agony aunts Cathy and Clare were on subjects like how to kiss and the problem of wearing glasses. Sex and sexuality, contraception and abortion were not covered.

Just Seventeen (J17)

Just Seventeen (later *J17*) was launched by Nick Logan in 1983 and published by Emap. It reflected the changes in social attitudes towards women and girls, and was targeted at girls aged 12–16 who aspired to the age of 17, with its connotations of maturity and excitement.

The magazine's contents identified with a readership interested in sex, future careers, celebrities, mobile phones, fashion and appearance. It also provided advice on sexual behaviour and relationships, and in its day broke new ground with its frank and open discussion of sex and sexuality.

It closed in 2004 following declining sales and increased competition from a new generation of girls magazines such as *Bliss* and *Sugar*.

Bliss

Bliss is published in an A5 handbag size called a 'baby glossy'. It focuses on boys, music, beauty, fashion and teen issues. It claims to be Britain's first interactive magazine, with internet and mobile phone links throughout.

Aimed at girls aged between 13 and 18, the magazine is worldly and sophisticated in its attitude to sex, relationships and all issues affecting self-presentation and identity. It connects with celebrity culture but also features articles on crime and world issues like climate change.

Case study

Bliss content analysis

Issue: May 2006

Cover price: £2.30

Total number of pages: 162

Adverts: approximately 65 pages, with many advertisements tied in to beauty, appearance and fashion features.

Cover contents:
- feature article photo of Paris Hilton with caption 'Dumped by Nicole, now Mischa hates her too — Paris' secret heartache'
- advice on self-presentation and relationships — '289 flirty looks'
- puff 'Britain's first interactive magazine! bliss world'
- advice on relationships 'When will you pull *the one*? We know!'
- fashion advice 'Ditch the tights & flash some flesh!'
- confession/true story 'I'm 16 and in jail… for murdering Mum' and 'Attacked in my bed by psycho stranger'
- makeover 'Do you need a body makeover? Find out how your figure measures up'

Articles include:
- behind the scenes at Channel 4 soap (Hanging out with *Hollyoaks*)
- a global-warming alert
- face and body worries
- horoscopes
- body makeover
- problem pages
- confessions from readers
- articles on celebrities
- advice on relationships (fit lads give their opinion on whether sexual experience matters in a girlfriend)

Comment: the magazine's contents combine all the usual concerns of teenage girls with a glossy and contemporary adult feel. It is a lifestyle magazine, where happiness involves relationships and spending money on make-up, clothes, accessories, shoes and mobile phones. The usual insecurities of teenage life concerning personality, appearance and how to behave in relationships (evident in *Jackie* 30 years earlier) are still present beneath the magazine's sophisticated packaging.

Task

By discussing the contents of the front cover, explore the ways in which the magazine communicates with its target audience. For a Unit 2 production, you could be asked to produce two magazine front covers, one for a lad's magazine and one for a girl's magazine.

Lads' magazines

Reasons for the development of lads' magazines

The following are some of the reasons for the development of lads' magazines:

- A gap in the market — young men with money to spend had no style magazines specifically aimed at them.
- To meet advertisers' and product manufacturers' needs — the magazines are an ideal vehicle for targeting the lucrative market of young men, with advertisements for aftershave, watches, gadgets, cars, bikes, clothes, music, DVDs, computer games and alcohol.
- The 'top shelf' problem — sexually explicit 'top shelf' soft porn magazines aimed at young men were not wholesome enough to attract mainstream advertisers.
- The new male consumer — market research showed young men were spending more on clothes, their appearance and lifestyle products, all of which could be built into the magazines' contents.
- More relaxed views on homosexuality — this made it easier for young men to buy magazines with a focus on lifestyle and appearance without appearing less masculine.
- Male identity and the 'new lad' as a marketing tool — this follows a perceived crisis in male identity in the face of an increased cultural focus on the achievements and advancement of women.

Gentleman's Quarterly (GQ)

The launch of men's style magazine, was held back for many years because of fears about gender identity problems and homophobia. In 1987, *GQ* magazine was launched by Condé Nast, with the first issue having a picture of Conservative politician and businessman Michael Heseltine on the cover. Early editions of the magazine continued to use male role model figures on the covers — for example, movie stars Gary Oldman, Jeff Bridges, Michael Douglas and television comedian Paul Whitehouse — to assert their masculinity and seriousness.

The magazine contains serious articles on topics of interest to its readership. From the mid-1990s, the magazine began to feature attractive semi-naked young women on the front cover, partly as a result of competition from *Loaded* and *FHM*.

FHM, Maxim and Loaded

These are glossy magazines with a content of raunchy, irreverent articles, fashion spreads, partly clothed pin-ups, and a variety of features representing the lifestyle and interests of the 'new lad'. Their content is largely entertainment-based, but the magazines also contain some articles and features on issues of cultural and social importance.

These magazines are vehicles for advertisements for cars, bikes, watches and other expensive consumer items. Some of the back pages of the magazines contain small advertisements for sex chatlines and pornographic websites. The magazines always contain sexualised images of semi-naked young women, and these idealised females represent the sexual aspirations of the readers.

The magazines attempt to define masculinity in the age of 'girl power', but have borrowed most of their style from women's magazines.

Zoo Weekly and Nuts

Zoo Weekly is published by Emap. The weekly magazine's website offers 'today's hottest stuff' and combines soft-porn images of girls with advertised videos and images of sporting personalities. Topics include girls, competitions and what to buy. *Nuts* is published by IPC Media and has a similar formula.

Consider the following questions when analysing magazines:

- Are readers being encouraged to identify with celebrities?
- Who are the people being represented in the magazine?
- Does the magazine reinforce negative stereotypes of young people?
- What kind of behaviour/lifestyle is being encouraged or endorsed?
- What kind of activities are not included?
- Who does the lifestyle model benefit?
- Who is excluded from this lifestyle model?
- What percentage of the magazine is devoted to advertisements?
- Are the magazines anything more than advertising and marketing copy, exploiting the insecurities of their readers for commercial gain?

> ### Task
> Consider the representation of women on three magazine front covers.

Why do women buy magazines?

- Magazines offer escapism, and the chance to fantasise about the lives and loves of celebrities.
- Magazines provide self-help advice by suggesting ways in which readers can change themselves and their appearance.
- Magazines stimulate gossip and curiosity in the form of stories about the behaviour of others.
- Magazines offer ideas about how to attract members of the opposite sex.
- Magazines satisfy affiliation needs — reading the magazine makes readers feel part of an exciting world.
- Magazines offer lifestyle choices and personal gratification associated with the purchasing of advertised products.

Why do men buy magazines?

- Magazines offer escapism.
- They contain pictures of half-naked young women, who are presented as idealised girlfriends.
- Magazines contain jokes and stories about sex and outrageous behaviour, which appeals to young men.
- Music and entertainment reviews, sports coverage and pictures of desirable consumer items tie in with the aspirations of readers.
- Magazines satisfy affiliation needs — there is a desire among readers to be 'one of the lads'.

The UK's leading magazine publishers

The magazine market is highly competitive and dynamic, with over 3,000 established titles. More than 1,000 magazine launches are proposed each year. Of these, approximately 350 make it to publication and only half of these become established titles.

The following is a list of the main publishers with magazines in the UK:

- **Condé Nast Publications:** glossy magazine publisher that is part of a larger US operation (Advance Magazine Group). Titles include *GQ, Vogue, Glamour, Tatler, Easy Living, House and Garden, Brides, World of Interiors* and *Vanity Fair*.
- **Dennis Publishing:** independent, privately owned publisher of *Maxim* (in 21 countries), *Men's Fitness, The Week, PC Pro, Custom PC, Viz, Test Drive* and *Bizarre*.

- **Emap:** the second largest UK magazine publisher, with 150 magazines and 16% of the market. In 2004, Emap closed two well-known but failing titles, *J17* and *The Face*. Remaining titles include *Kerrang!*, *More*, *Heat*, *Red*, *Zoo* and *FHM*.
- **Hachette:** the largest French magazine publishing company, formerly partnered with Emap in the publishing of *Elle* and owner of the *Marie Claire* title.
- **IPC Media:** the UK's largest magazine publisher, with over 100 titles and 22% of the market. It sells 350 million magazines a year. It was taken over by Time Warner in 2001 and its titles include *Loaded*, *Nuts* and *NME*.
- **National Magazine Company** (part of the US Hearst Corporation): Probably the largest magazine company in the world, selling over a quarter of a billion copies a year, with 80 international editions in 100 countries. Its UK titles include *Cosmopolitan*, *Esquire*, *Good Housekeeping*, *She* and *Country Living*.

E-media

The rapid development of this media platform has meant that texts previously available in broadcast and print formats are now available via e-media. As with any medium, the characteristic of the medium determines the shape of the media text. For example, newspapers are printed on sheets of newsprint folded together. The size of the sheet and the physical attributes of the medium determine the shape and content of the media product.

In the same way, e-media have altered the shape if not the content of media texts to suit emerging technologies. The online version of a newspaper, while still consisting of written material accompanied by photographs, has to adapt to the web page format, with links to articles and short videos.

The internet has transformed people's relationship with the media and with each other. Anybody with an internet connection can post whatever they want on the net. An individual website is a business opportunity for some, a means of communicating for others. Either way, website creators are firmly established as media producers, as they construct texts for consumption by a large audience. At the same time, website visitors are consumers of texts.

Online publications

Online versions of newspapers provide an excellent example of the possibilities of new e-media technology. They carry most of the content from the printed papers, and retain their character and distinctive voice with columnists and editorial pages. However, the web versions are highly interactive, with opportunities provided for readers to respond to articles online and to discuss issues among themselves. This makes the relationship between newspaper columnists and readers far more dynamic, with journalists also being more accessible — many through blogs (see page 82). This is also an example of audiences becoming creators of media texts, as readers see their comments on-screen shortly after submitting them. Some contributors produce posts that are as long as the original articles on which they are commenting.

Web versions of newspapers can also be constantly updated as the news priorities alter during the day. In a fast-moving media world, the morning's print headlines can look out of date by the afternoon, particularly as many press releases, especially of political news, are released to coincide with key news broadcasts such as the one o'clock or mid-evening news. Traditional newspapers are left behind, but their online versions can be updated every minute. Web newspapers also blur the distinction between television and print news forms: they provide their own video links, with reporters giving updates on major stories, and also carry links to other sources such as CNN and Sky News.

As with newspapers, e-media versions of magazines are more interactive and many offer links, videos and a whole range of material not available in print.

Task

Using a copy of a national newspaper and the paper's website of the same day, discuss the benefits and disadvantages of each form as a means of communicating with and retaining the interest of the target audience.

Websites

A **website** is a related collection of internet web files located on the same server and accessible via a browser through a unique address, 24 hours a day. Websites include a home page — the first file visitors see — which explains what the site contains and how to navigate through it.

Files usually contain hyperlinks to allow movement within the site or to other sites.

Websites are dynamic, interactive forms of communication, and the use of them involves navigating from one page to another in search of information. The user-friendliness of this process and the ease of access to the information desired are key factors in assessing the success of website design. The principles web designers should consider are: sharing, access, communication, availability and knowing the audience. A site should convey reliability, professionalism and credibility.

Codes and conventions of website production

Questions in your examination may include reference to website design and analysis. Below is a list of website design dos and don'ts, which will be useful when answering such questions:

- Websites should be kept simple. The web is a secondary medium; people often do other things while scanning the web and do not take everything in.
- Up-to-date information and content are more important than gimmicks, fancy graphics and animated logos. Websites should not be overloaded with decoration.
- Relatively unskilled individuals should be able to use the site with ease. Designers should put themselves in the shoes of the site visitor and assume they know very little.
- The home page should make a strong visual impact. Flash movies, for example, have relatively small file sizes and can be embedded in web pages and downloaded easily, without affecting the overall download speed of the page.
- Identifying the target audience is as important as with any media product.
- Access should be straightforward — browser and search engine friendliness avoid complications arising in this area.
- Websites should be easy to update.
- Key words and text should be relevant and easy to understand. Jargon and internally focused text is a turn-off for visitors.
- All pages should have titles, and these should not be too long.
- Irrelevant diverts and useless links should be avoided. Broken links should be fixed quickly.
- Tables should be broken up vertically.
- A website should be easy to read.
- Interactivity engages the user and makes the site more memorable.

- Good organisation should provide visitors with multiple ways of navigation.
- Buttons should be supplied with both text and graphics, and a consistent look and feel should be maintained throughout the site.
- There should be a consistency of design and the clear presentation of the site's identity. Design should conform to established conventions that visitors recognise and should use attractive colour schemes.
- People abandon slow downloads, so download time for the home page should be no more than 15 seconds (remember that graphics pages take longer to download).

In your examination, if a fixed image is supplied as case study material, the real dynamic of a site is difficult to judge. Your commentary should therefore focus on presentation, content and page design, under the headings of representation, audience and institution.

Useful website terminology

You should be familiar with the following terminology:

- **Broadband:** a system of transmission, where a single fibre-optic telecommunications cable, with a wide band of frequencies, carries multiple signals. Broadband allows for a high-speed internet connection, with telephone services on the same line, replacing traditional analogue dial-up services. Large video, audio and three-dimensional files can be downloaded quickly and easily.
- **browser:** a computer software package used to view, download or interact with web pages on the internet. The most popular browsers are Internet Explorer, Netscape and Mosaic.
- **internet service provider (ISP):** a company that provides access to the internet via a telephone link, e.g. Wanadoo, Onetel.
- **server:** a computer that provides an information service to other computers linked to it through a network. On the World Wide Web, the term can also refer to a program that responds to requests for web pages from a browser.
- **uniform resource locator (URL):** an address that specifies the location of a file on the internet, e.g. www.philipallan.co.uk.
- **World Wide Web (www):** the international computer network and information retrieval system that provides global access, via web browsers and through the use of hypertext transfer protocol, to web pages on the internet.

What is a blog?

A **blog** (short for web log) is a type of website journal, usually arranged in reverse chronological order with the most recent entry at the top. It can be on any subject and is often used by journalists as a kind of diary and to provide interaction with readers. Updating a blog is called 'posting' and the articles themselves are called 'posts'. Blog sites are usually conversational in style to encourage interaction, and allow users to leave their own messages to contribute to the ongoing debate.

What is a podcast?

A **podcast** is a digital media file distributed over the internet for playback on portable media players and personal computers. The term means either the content or the method of distribution. Although initially used for audio files, podcasting can be used to download any kind of file, including pictures, videos and even radio shows, which can be listened to directly without having to visit specific radio sites.

The term 'podcast' derives from the Apple iPod, for which the first scripts were developed. The latest iPod combines mobile phone, music player and video player, with users able to access e-mails and the internet as well as storing their private music collection.

Key term

Bluetooth: a technology that allows a connection between phones, laptops, PCs, printers, digital cameras, video games consoles etc. over a short-wave radio frequency. Bluetooth allows for short-range communication — up to 100 metres. The most common use is between a mobile phone and a hands free headset.

Viral images and videos

Viral images and video have gained popularity through the process of internet sharing, through e-mail, blogs and websites like YouTube. Many of these amateur videos are shot on camera phones and distributed virally on the web and by e-mail through **Bluetooth** technology. Viral videos are mainly designed to entertain, but can also be used for promotional purposes, e.g. by bands.

Viral marketing

Viral marketing refers to techniques that use pre-existing social networks to increase brand awareness through self-replicating viral processes. People are encouraged to pass marketing messages on voluntarily. The term comes from 'virus' — something you catch and pass on to many others.

Viral marketing media include word-of-mouth, internet Flash games, adver-games, trailers and advertisements, or text messages. Research has shown that a customer tells three people about a product he or she likes and 11 about a product he or she does not like. Band and music promoters, film producers and cosmetics manufacturers all make good use of viral marketing.

The objective of any media company using viral marketing is to achieve a high social networking potential (SNP), which will be the equivalent of millions of pounds of free advertising. The classic early example is the 1999 film *The Blair Witch Project* (Daniel Myrick and Eduardo Sánchez), which was publicised entirely by viral means.

Cross-media texts

This section deals with two types of cross-media texts: documentary and film fiction.

Documentary

When studying 'documentary and hybrid forms' you are required to investigate how documentaries are presented across different media platforms. This will be primarily in cinema and broadcasting, but you should also consider how documentaries are treated in newspapers and magazines (gossip and reviews) and on the internet (news, updates and audience forums).

You should study the production and reception of documentary texts. Audience 'reception' is arguably becoming ever more important in these days of 'reality TV' and the internet, with the associated growth in interactivity and audience participation. Increasingly, audiences are becoming creators of documentary texts, for example by using mobile phone cameras to film themselves and then posting the results on the internet. Technology is continually breaking down the distinction between audiences and producers of texts.

Origins of documentary

Documentary film-making in the UK was undoubtedly shaped by John Grierson and the GPO Film Unit. It was founded in 1933 with sponsorship from the General Post Office, and it sought to document the lives of ordinary British workers.

The GPO approach to documentary was something of a social and political mission. Grierson and his band of young middle-class film-makers — including Harry Watt, Alberto Cavalcanti and Humphrey Jennings — sought to use documentary to create a more honest and dignified representation of working-class life. Their work is often dismissed by contemporary commentators for being patronising, paternalistic and perhaps a little too sombre. However, the GPO Film Unit has to be understood within the wider social context of the UK in the 1930s, where class division was much more acute than today and where many middle-class people had no idea about the harsh realities of working-class life.

GPO titles included *Coal Face* (Cavalcanti, 1935) and *Night Mail* (Watt/Wright, 1936); these were poetic films designed to expose the working conditions and create a dignified representation of the British industrial worker. The artistic value of these texts was augmented by collaboration with leading contemporary artists, such as the poet W. H. Auden, the composer Benjamin Britten and the writers E. M. Forster and Laurie Lee. After the outbreak of the Second World War, the GPO Film Unit was disbanded and subsumed under the direction of the Ministry for Information as The Crown Film Unit, for the production of propaganda and public information films.

Ideas for discussion and development

- **Is it possible for contemporary television and cinema documentaries to continue the serious, democratic work of the GPO, or are they more directed by commercial constraints and audience ratings towards being more entertaining than informative?**

Characteristics of documentary

It is tempting for us to see documentaries — especially when compared to fictional films — as factual or 'true' accounts. However, in the same way that audiences have come to accept the Hollywood mode of 'realist' editing as 'natural', so too they have become familiar with the codes and conventions of the documentary form. If asked to characterise the documentary genre, most people would probably mention actual settings, live footage, expert and layman opinions, direct interviews, archive footage and voice-over narration. This list of elements represents the development of documentary as it has evolved through its cinematic form, which in recent decades has given way to the less expensive television versions.

Documentary styles

There are a number of different documentary styles currently in use in cinema and television. Contemporary documentary genres mix styles from within documentary and also from broadcast-fiction genres (such as docu-drama and docu-soap). This mixing of styles is a common feature of postmodernism (see page 213).

Expository

The expository form uses a narrator to direct viewers towards a preferred reading. The voice-over is usually paternalistic and authoritative (the so-called 'voice of God'). With this comes the assumption of intellectual and cultural superiority on behalf of the film-maker — a discourse that is often validated through the use of 'experts'. This form may use re-enactment, restaging and 'found' footage.

Observational

This is often associated with the 'direct cinema' and cinéma vérité movements of the 1960s (see page 88). The assumption here is that events captured on film would have occurred with or without the camera being present. There is no overt narration, and the narrative follows the voice and action of the subject, not the director. However, it is highly debatable that such a transparent mode of film-making can ever be achieved.

Interactive

The film-maker/film crew mixes with the subject of the documentary. This is most commonly done in the form of interviews. These interviews may be edited into the text to appear authentic, but they may not have originally been recorded in that manner.

Reflexive

Reflexivity — or self-awareness — is a postmodern trait in documentary film-making. The film-maker casts doubt on the film's claim to 'be real' by drawing attention to his or her presence. The documentary is deliber-ately organised to expose the film-maker's role in the construction of reality. We may, for example, hear the director's voice off-screen or cutting between scenes, drawing attention to the illusions of continuity editing. Subverting the realist techniques normally associated with documentary supposedly invites the reader to query the validity of representation. However, critics say this is more about the publicity-seeking nature of some documentary-makers. Exponents of this approach include Michael Moore (*Bowling for Columbine*, 2002 and *Fahrenheit 9/11*, 2004), Morgan Spurlock (*Supersize Me*, 2004) and Louis Theroux (*When Louis met…*, 2000–02).

Investigative
This takes the form of a journalistic investigation into a current-affairs issue. It is more commonly used in television than cinema, for example *Horizon* (BBC 2), *Dispatches* (Channel 4) or *Panorama* (BBC 1).

When reading any documentary text, consider the following:
- How is the text constructed (e.g. use of mise-en-scène, editing, sound, narrative structure and narrative style) to represent 'reality'?
- What social concerns, issues or values does it raise?
- How effectively does it represent people, places or events in a specific social and cultural setting?
- Who is the target audience and how are their needs, expectations and values addressed?
- How do the attitudes of the documentary-maker affect the representation of 'reality'?
- How is the text affected by the technological equipment available?

Terms associated with documentary
The following terms may be used when referring to aspects of the documentary genre:
- **Mediation:** the means by which, through representation, a media organisation and its employees stand between an event and the public's perception of that event. When we encounter a media text, we are not seeing a definitive account of 'reality' but someone's version of it.
- **Mimesis:** a Greek word meaning 'the imitation of life or nature' in the techniques and subject matter of art, literature or media. Ideally, mimesis should be the driving force behind every documentary, but in reality this is impossible because of mediation.
- **Social realism:** the representation of characters and issues in film and television drama in such a way as to raise serious underlying social and political issues. Social realism involves a drama-documentary treatment in the sense that, while the characters may be fictional, the contexts and circumstances in which they are placed represent existing social realities. Social realism films are usually shot in a naturalistic way, avoiding the use of sophisticated editing and treatments, and with little use made of

non-diegetic sound. Examples include the films of British director Ken Loach, *Kes* (1970) and *Sweet Sixteen* (2003).

- **Subjective shot:** a type of shot in which the camera is positioned as if looking at the world through the subject's eyes. For example, the opening title sequence of *Taxi Driver* (Martin Scorsese, 1976) shows the world through the eyes of driver Travis Bickle (Robert DeNiro) as he views the streets through the rain on his windscreen. The image is blurred and distorted, as is his view of the world.

- **Suspension of disbelief:** the way in which an audience accepts the artificial world of the stage, film or television as real for the duration of a performance. Members of the audience know that what they are watching is only a fictional construction but, in order to feel total engagement and gain maximum enjoyment, they allow their imaginations to take over and accept what is put before them as 'real'.

- **Verisimilitude:** seeming to be like or connected to the real. The term is important in many media genres because it determines the level of audience engagement and willingness to engage in suspension of disbelief. Contemporary war films need to convey a sense of verisimilitude to be credible. Reconstructions of Second World War battle scenes, with special-effects bullets flying around the heads of the actors, are now seen as more real than newsreel footage of the actual events, e.g. *Saving Private Ryan* (Steven Spielberg, 1998).

Key terms

diegetic sound: sound generated within a film narrative, e.g. the sound of traffic in a scene involving a road.

Non-diegetic sound: sound that is outside the narrative, e.g. an orchestra playing rousing music during a battle scene.

Ideas for discussion and development

When studying a documentary about a particular culture or group, look out for the use of 'representative characters' and consider why they have been specifically selected:

- **Are these characters typical of the group or do they conform to a stereotype with which the audience may be familiar?**
- **Are they chosen for other reasons, such as comic value or dramatic impact?**
- **In terms of the representation of the groups' activities or lifestyle, what is selected and foregrounded and what is left out?**

Cinéma vérité: technology or ideology?

Cinéma vérité is a French term that can be roughly translated as 'truth cinema'. It refers to a documentary technique that began in France and Quebec in the 1960s. At its simplest, it involves the use of real people, hand-held cameras and live sound in undirected situations. The technological innovations that made cinéma vérité possible in the 1960s (i.e. lightweight cameras, portable sound equipment and film stock that could be used in lower light conditions) led to a more informal and spontaneous style of documentary that is now commonly referred to as 'fly-on-the-wall'. Proponents of cinéma vérité believed in the possibility of documentary 'truth' or accurate representations of events as they occurred before the camera. This was notably different from earlier descriptions of documentary as the 'creative treatment of actuality' (Grierson).

It is now generally accepted that documentaries can never offer a 'true', unmediated representation of reality. However, in constructing the 'real', as Brian Winston points out, '…the hand-held camera became a central mark of authenticity[…]seep[ing] into public consciousness…as the essence of documentary' (Winston 2000).

Advanced **Media Studies**

Docu-soap

Docu-soaps combine elements of soap opera with documentary, and focus on the lives of real people. They became prominent in popular television in the late 1990s. Although there has been a tradition of 'factual' television programming going back to the 1950s, this was the first time that the genre had been able to compete with fictional programmes for prime-time scheduling. *Driving School*, for example, achieved audiences of over 12 million, and others such as *Hotel* and *The Cruise* enjoyed similar success.

Like cinéma vérité, the docu-soap was partly made possible by new technology. Docu-soaps require the shooting of a great deal of raw footage, and doing this on old-style 16 mm film would have been too expensive for programme-makers. Video film, by comparison, is inexpensive and easy to handle. This allows programme-makers to shoot hours of raw footage in the hope of turning up — and sometimes manufacturing — dramatic moments. Making a docu-soap costs on average a third of the amount required to produce a light entertainment or sitcom programme — mainly because the actors, props and set are already in place.

In docu-soaps, the main focus is on light entertainment rather than on serious issues. Social commentary and analysis are usually abandoned in favour of drama and catharsis. The very term 'docu-soap' was, as Stella Bruzzi notes in *New Documentary* (2006), coined by journalists keen to dismiss this new sub-genre because it 'contaminated the seriousness of documentary with the frivolity of soap opera'.

The main features of docu-soaps include:
- a focus on characters (often informally referred to by their first names)
- short sequences
- intercut (multiple) narrative strands
- fast editing
- overt structuring devices
- opening and closing 'hooks' to keep viewers watching and make them return for the next episode
- celebrity voice-over narration (with regional accent)
- interviews
- non-diegetic soundtrack (often popular music)

Docu-soaps were a phenomenon in the UK and around the world in the late 1990s. Although a few, such as *Airport* (BBC, 1996–) and *Airline* (ITV, 1998–) have continued, by the early 2000s they had largely disappeared from the schedules in their pure form.

Drama documentary

Drama documentary (or 'docu-drama') is a hybrid genre that combines the style and techniques of documentary with those of drama and broadcast fiction. Docu-dramas are dramatic 'reconstructions' of famous events such as crimes, disasters or controversies, but captured and represented in a documentary style. In this way, they blur the distinction between fiction and reality.

Documentary techniques used in docu-dramas include:

- talking heads — witness/survivor/expert accounts delivered straight to the camera
- use of low-resolution film stock and hand-held cameras
- natural sound and lighting
- archive footage or stills
- location shooting

A good way of understanding the genre is to compare *Titanic* (James Cameron, 1997) — a Hollywood film about the sinking of the famous transatlantic liner — with *Herald of Free Enterprise* (BBC, 2006) — a dramatic reconstruction of the sinking of a cross-channel ferry in 1987. There are many similarities between the two texts, in that both use:

- a real event as the basis for action
- a chronological plot structure
- a scripted/acted narrative with binary coded characterisation
- mise-en-scène — props, costumes, setting and music — to signify specific cultural/historical periods
- filmic techniques such as enigma and action codes, symbolism, iconography and non-diegetic sound
- special effects to create a realistic reconstruction of the sinking of the two ships

However, in spite of these shared features, *Titanic* looks and feels like a *fiction* text while *Herald of Free Enterprise* appears to be *factual*. While docu-drama and feature film are both fictional genres, docu-dramas are 'constructed' to look and feel 'real'. The crucial differences between the two texts are as follows:

- *Titanic* has very high production values, whereas much of *Herald of Free Enterprise* is shot with natural light and sound, and has lower production values (including grainy, hand-held camera footage).
- *Titanic* has an all-star cast, while *Herald of Free Enterprise* uses relatively minor or unknown actors. Audiences tend to associate famous actors

with other characters they have played, but unknown actors have no such intertextual history.

- *Titanic* uses realist continuity editing, while *Herald of Free Enterprise* continually cross-cuts between dramatic re-enactment and 'talking heads' — interviews with survivors, ferry company personnel and members of the rescue services.

Although *Herald of Free Enterprise* uses this cross-cut approach, it is interesting how sound/voice editing is used to create continuity. When the survivor accounts fade into the dramatic re-enactment scenes, the 'authentic voice' is faded out more slowly than the accompanying images, thus creating a connection between the 'real' and the 'fictional'.

Although the dramatic element is obviously employed for entertainment purposes, there is a serious side to docu-drama. Docu-dramas are used to raise awareness of important social events, either in a moralistic, educative manner or as a way of seeking justice for those involved. The sinking of the *Herald of Free Enterprise* was not a tragic accident but a wholly avoidable catastrophe. Part of the rationale behind the programme was to argue that the ferry's sinking had been caused by corporate negligence.

Other famous television docu-dramas include *Bloody Sunday* (about the shooting of 13 unarmed Catholic civilians in Northern Ireland by British paratroopers in 1972) and *Hillsborough* (about the 1989 football stadium disaster, in which 96 Liverpool supporters were crushed to death).

Ideas for discussion and development

- **Does documentary have a duty to raise awareness of social issues?**
- **Why might the documentary element rather than the purely fictional/ dramatic element be more believable/convincing to viewers?**

New observational documentary

Observational documentary has not been rendered obsolete by the advent of more interactive and reflexive modes of non-fiction television and film. Instead, the form has developed so that it remains 'observational', while incorporating many of the tactics and devices of newer documentary forms.

The characteristics of the docu-soap and reality-based sub-genres of observational documentary series (e.g. *Wife Swap* and *Faking It*) are their emphasis on entertainment, the importance of personalities who enjoy performing for the camera, fast editing and inter-cutting between alternate stories or personalities, a prominent voice-over, and a focus on everyday experience. As contributors are involved in a 'performance', there has been a relaxation of the boundaries between documentary and fiction.

Task

Can you find any evidence that Michael Moore sacrifices truth and objectivity for the sake of entertainment in the representation of US gun culture in his film *Bowling for Columbine* (2002)?

New documentary

The heavy and educational reputation of documentaries has been a problem in reaching younger audiences, but recent new cinema documentary texts, such as *Bowling for Columbine* (Michael Moore, 2002) and *Supersize Me* (Morgan Spurlock, 2004), produced in feature-film format with an entertainment style, have enjoyed both critical acclaim and commercial success.

Realism

Realism is about making media representations seem real. 'Real' therefore means 'related to the life experiences of audiences at the time of consumption of the media text'. A realist text attempts to present representations in ways that convince audiences of the authentic nature of what is put before them.

Obviously, realist texts are not 'real'; they are subject to selection and construction principles, and treatment styles that change in accordance with cultural expectations and fashion. For example, British new-wave realist films of the 1950s and 1960s, such as *Saturday Night and Sunday Morning* (Karel Reisz, 1960), *The Loneliness of the Long Distance Runner* (Tony Richardson, 1962) and *A Taste of Honey* (Tony Richardson, 1961) were shot on monochrome (black and white) film stock. This was done for cost reasons, but it also made the films seem more like newsreels and documentaries, which at the time were always live (video tapes did not exist) and in black and white (until 1967).

When filming *Schindler's List* (1993), about the Holocaust, director Steven Spielberg used black and white stock because for him the 1940s had always appeared in black and white newsreel and he wanted to create a realist feel for his film. Even now, colour images of the Second World War seem strangely modern, making the events depicted feel much closer to contemporary experience than the more usual monochrome images.

Realism, then, is not about texts being real, it is about them *seeming* to be real because they reflect and represent the world in ways that persuade audiences of their authenticity.

Film fiction

Reference to film occurs throughout this textbook and film is an important medium for any media course. However, as this is not a film studies course, there is no detailed history of cinema, the star system, the studio system and other aspects of the film industry. We are concerned with film as it appears across a range of media platforms and in the way it is consumed by media audiences. We are also concerned with the institutions that produce films along with other media products, and the ways in which they market these products to media audiences.

Contemporary cinema is dominated by large international companies, which see investment in film as a commercial venture tied in with a larger media operation. On the other hand, a vigorous and dynamic independent world cinema movement exists in both the developed and the developing world, and this continues to develop film as an artistic medium and a powerful tool of cultural identity.

The marketing of film

The following strategies may be adopted by institutions to market films:

- **Teasers** — opening campaigns that drop hints about future film releases and encourage the curiosity of the audience.
- **Selling features** — what are the most appealing aspects of the coming attraction.
- **Pre-release publicity** — building on teasers, this might include interviews with stars and directors, descriptions of technical details and special effects, profiles of directors etc.
- **Sponsorship** — association with major companies, product placement, advertising.
- **Genre** — identification of genre contextualises the film and allows comparison with other similar films to attract the same audience.
- **Manufactured controversies** — manufactured arguments or disputes among performers can be used to get the film talked about.
- **Associated texts/intertextuality** — relationship of the product to the book, for example *Harry Potter* (2001–) or *The Lord of the Rings* (Peter Jackson, 2001–2003), or the historical fact, for example *Alexander* (Oliver Stone, 2004), *Gladiator* (Ridley Scott, 2000) or *Troy* (Wolfgang Petersen, 2004).
- **Synergy** — songs are often released before the film to generate interest, for example 'My Heart Will Go On' by Celine Dion from the film *Titanic* (James Cameron, 1997)

- **Publicity outlets** — magazines, newspapers, billboards, radio, television, cinema, publicity, internet.
- **Target audience** — defined by a combination of genre appeal, star appeal and storyline. Contemporary films often have multiple audiences, with plot elements that appeal to different groups. For example, *Titanic* is a love story, disaster movie, thriller and historical re-enactment all in one.
- **Release strategy** — films can be released in stages to build up expectation. For example, an initial release in capital cities plus planned release at major multiplexers across the country.
- **Local campaigns/commerce** — timed to coincide with local release.
- **Newspapers, magazines, television, internet, word of mouth** — can help spread the word and increase interest in the film.

Ideas for discussion and development

Product placement is the payment made by commercial companies to film and television producers for prominent placement of their product in key scenes, often in association with celebrity actors and personalities. In 2007, celebrity chef Nigella Lawson was accused of featuring Waitrose products in her fridge and was filmed shopping in a Waitrose supermarket during an episode of her BBC 2 show. However, she strongly denied any financial deal with Waitrose. Celebrity chef Jamie Oliver advertises Sainsbury's products in television commercials and although they are not placed in his cooking programmes, the association of Oliver with the supermarket chain is fixed in the audience's mind.

- **How is product placement different from advertising? Is it ethical?**

Where do audiences see films?

Multiplexes are large cinemas that operate several screens showing different films. They were developed in the 1980s as a means of generating large box-office takings, and have now become mainstream family entertainment centres, incorporating fast food restaurants and coffee bars. Multiplexes rarely show independent or art house films.

Major multiplex owner UCI is now merged with Odeon under the ownership of finance company Terra Firma, and owns 40% of all UK cinemas. UGC, the largest European cinema operator, was bought out by the UK cinema chain Cineworld in 2004. Both developments have resulted in cinema ownership being increasingly concentrated. However, small

independent cinemas continue to provide an alternative venue for low-budget 'art-house' productions.

Media institutions in cinema

The following are some of the main institutions involved in cinema:

- **Film Distributors Association** — the trade body for film distributors in the UK. Film distribution is part of a multi-million pound business, worth £800 million in the UK in box office takings (2004). Association members include Icon, Twentieth Century Fox, Pathé, Buena Vista, Eros, Columbia Tri-Star, Warner Brothers and Metrodome.
- **Metro-Goldwyn-Mayer (MGM)** — founded in 1924, MGM was one of the five largest Hollywood studios during the 1930–48 'golden age'. It controlled such stars as Judy Garland and Greta Garbo. It was one of the last major independent studios until it was taken over by the Sony Corporation in 2005.
- **Twentieth Century Fox** — a Hollywood studio created in 1935 during the 'golden age' of Hollywood and now part of Rupert Murdoch's News Corporation empire.
- **Universal** — a film production company founded in 1912, which was always smaller than the giant Hollywood studios. In 1995, it was acquired by Seagram. Its operations expanded in the global market, with its acquisition of PolyGram music in 1998, making the Universal Music Group the world's largest music company. It was bought by the French company Vivendi and Canal Plus in 2000 to create Vivendi Universal, a major global media organisation.
- **Warner Brothers** — a Hollywood film company founded in 1918. It merged with Time Inc. in 1990 to form Time Warner, with Turner Broadcasting in 1996, and with AOL in 2000 to create the conglomerate AOL Time-Warner, one of the largest global media corporations.

Some key films

Social attitudes in the UK have changed considerably over the last 50 years and fictional films have helped both to advance those changes and to reflect them. The following is a list of some key films that have reflected changes in social attitudes:

- *Psycho* (Alfred Hitchcock, 1960) — this is regarded as the first slasher horror film. It is also famous for its iconic shower scene in which Janet Leigh's character is murdered. Several scenes from the film were censored.

- *Bonnie and Clyde* (Arthur Penn, 1967) — this film was the first to be made after the abolition of the American Hayes Code, which prevented graphic violence from being shown. It shows bodies being hit by bullets.
- *A Clockwork Orange* (Stanley Kubrick, 1971) — this film was withdrawn from UK circulation by the director after many complaints that its portrayal of graphic violence and rape encouraged 'copycat' behaviour. The film reflected growing concern about teenage gang violence.
- *The Exorcist* (William Friedkin, 1973) — dealing with the exorcism of a possessed child, this film contains scenes which, although often now ridiculed, were shocking to audiences at the time. Its combination of sexual violence, obscenity and the questioning of religious belief was too much for critics like Mary Whitehouse and the Festival of Light, who picketed the film. It was branded as satanic by US television evangelist Billy Graham. The film was banned on video release in the UK for 25 years.
- *Last Tango in Paris* (Bernardo Bertolucci, 1973) — this film contains explicit sex scenes in the context of a casual and transient relationship. Although nowhere near as explicit as some contemporary films such as *Nine Songs* (Michael Winterbottom, 2005), it was subject to a prosecution for obscenity brought by Mary Whitehouse (see page 241) and banned from many UK cinemas.
- *Halloween* (John Carpenter, 1978) — this classic suspense and slasher horror movie has been imitated, parodied and pastiched by many, but perhaps not equalled. It firmly established the generic and narrative conventions of the genre: in particular, the 'point of view' camera positioning on behalf of the killer, the narrative moral that sexual promiscuity leads to a violent end, and the fact that the 'final girl' (Jamie Lee Curtis as Lauri Strode) fights back against the killer and is saved. All these elements had, in fact, been present in *Psycho* (1960).
- *Alien* (Ridley Scott, 1979) — this is a space horror film with one of the first female action heroes, Ellen Ripley (played by Sigourney Weaver). She emerges as the sole survivor of the crew battling an alien monster. The film's most famous scene is the alien offspring exploding from crewman Kane's (John Hurt) chest in a grotesque parody of giving birth.
- *Nightmare on Elm Street* (Wes Craven, 1984) — a teen slasher horror classic, this series combined graphic horror scenes with the implication of teenage sexual guilt. The narratives suggested that sexual promiscuity was punishable with horrific murder.

- *Thelma and Louise* (Ridley Scott, 1991) — this is a buddy/road movie where two women take to the road when one of them kills a predatory male after rescuing her buddy from an attempted rape. They find freedom by breaking away from violent, stultifying and conventional relationships, but become fugitives pursued by the male forces of authority. The film reflected the growing challenge to orthodox representations of gender, with the women portrayed as victims of male sexual violence, indifference and duplicity. It ends with a car chase, where the women choose suicide by driving into the Grand Canyon (a famous freeze-frame closing shot) rather than submitting to the pursuing male police officers.

- *Natural Born Killers* (Oliver Stone, 1994) — this is a reworking of a classic *folie à deux* based on the true story of a runaway teenage couple's orgy of violent crime and murder, and the celebrity status awarded to them by media coverage. The film was heavily criticised for glorifying violence and encouraging 'copycat' crime. It raised important issues about media-generated 'celebrity' culture.

- *Trainspotting* (Danny Boyle, 1996) — this graphic black comedy dealt with the realities of heroin addiction. The film reflected a more open discussion of drug addiction and its social consequences, but was heavily criticised for its portrayal of drug use.

Danny Boyle's 1996 film *Trainspotting*

- *Dirty Pretty Things* (Stephen Frears, 2002) — this film is a graphic representation of the exploitation and deprivation suffered by asylum-seekers and economic migrants in modern-day London. The film challenged stereotypical representations of asylum seekers/migrants as a threat, and showed them instead as vulnerable victims of unscrupulous individuals.

- *Nine Songs* (Michael Winterbottom, 2004) — this is the story of a love affair between a young American woman and her English boyfriend, narrated by the boyfriend against a background of rock music concerts. What makes it so startling is the explicit representation of their sexual relationship in a way not seen before in British mainstream cinema. The film pushes the boundary of what is acceptable in the multiplex

pornography: the representation in print, audiovisual or electronic media of sexual acts regarded as indecent. Softpornography involves portrayal of the naked human body, often in simulated sexual acts. Hard pornography involves images of human genitals and penetrative sex.

cinema and challenges the distinction between **pornography** and the mainstream cinema.

- *Brokeback Mountain* (Ang Lee, 2005) — this is a sympathetic and positive representation of homosexual cowboys in a Western genre setting. It demonstrates the change in social attitudes towards representations of sexuality, particularly in this most macho of film genres.

Task

By referring to any new film release that you have viewed recently, discuss how it represents people, places and social concerns.

Ideas for discussion and development

- **Can film change the way we feel about social issues, people and events?**

Media audiences and institutions

Media audiences

We are all part of different audiences for a whole range of media texts. From the moment we wake in the morning — when we switch on a radio or television, look at a cereal packet, read a newspaper headline or see an advertising billboard on the way to school or work — we are consuming and making sense of media texts.

Media producers have many ways of attracting target audiences towards their products. The Marxist French sociologist Louis Althuser (1918–90) coined the term **interpellation** to describe the process whereby individual responses to media texts can be cued by the repetition of familiar forms. For example, the signature tune and opening titles of soap operas attract an audience's attention, create a receptive state of mind and prepare the audience for what is to follow. The same applies to news programmes, which often have dramatic opening music using trumpets and loud chords to draw attention to their importance. The medieval town crier's bell had the same effect. We are, in effect, being told to sit up and take notice.

What do audiences derive from media texts?

Media texts meet the needs of audiences in various ways:
- by providing information
- by contributing towards personal growth and development
- by providing entertainment and escapism
- by providing a sense of social and cultural involvement and belonging
- by giving pleasure
- by giving a sense of control and empowerment

Ideas for discussion and development

- **Choose six media products from three different media platforms and show how they meet audience needs, values and desires.**

Maslow's hierarchy of human needs

Psychologist Abraham Maslow's hierarchy of human needs (1954) suggests that the fulfilment of needs works like a pyramid, where satisfaction (at the most basic or lowest level) is necessary before the next stage can be reached. According to this hierarchy, consumption of media texts fulfils needs at all levels above the lowest two — the satisfaction of basic survival and safety needs — and can help to explain what satisfaction or pleasure audiences derive from different media texts.

Maslow's hierarchy of human needs (1954)

Self-actualisation needs: to find self-fulfilment and release one's potential

Aesthetic needs: symmetry, order and beauty

Cognitive needs: to know, understand and explore

Esteem needs: to achieve, be competent and gain approval, esteem and recognition

Becomingness and love needs: to affiliate with others, be accepted and belong

Safety needs: to feel secure, safe and out of danger

Physiological needs: to satisfy hunger, thirst etc.

Ideas for discussion and development

- **How could Maslow's hierarchy be used to explain the appeal of *Big Brother* to audiences?**

Note that the system does not allow for the escapist function of media texts — in which audiences escape to a world of fantasy and make-believe where their lives are often transformed or improved. Even those at the lowest levels of Maslow's pyramid may seek psychological wellbeing as relief or distraction from physical discomfort and fear in this way.

Mulvey and the 'male gaze'

The feminist academic and media and film critic Laura Mulvey (1941–) produced a groundbreaking essay entitled 'Visual Pleasure and Narrative Cinema' (1975), describing what she saw as the male point of view being adopted by the camera for an assumed male audience.

Mulvey viewed the practice of the camera lingering on women's bodies as evidence that women were being viewed as sex objects for the gratification of men. She argued that the central active characters in films are male and that the male audience identifies with them in their viewing of the passive females. Women in the audience are also positioned by the narrative to identify with the **male gaze** and see the world through male eyes. Her essay was hugely influential in the development of feminist film studies.

Mulvey's approach owes much to Freudian psychology. Her arguments can be challenged by pointing out that not all central heroic characters in films are male. Also, Mulvey denies the existence of a 'female gaze', which has enjoyed physically attractive men in films from the earliest days of cinema, with stars ranging from Rudolph Valentino to Brad Pitt. Lastly,

Daniel Craig in *Casino Royale* (2006)

Ursula Andress in *Dr. No* (1962)

Everett Collection/Rex Features

Media audiences and institutions

Uma Thurman in *Kill Bill: Vol 1* (2003)

Content: Mine International/Alamy

Ideas for discussion and development

- **Is Mulvey's theory still relevant to modern cinema audiences?**

changes in the representation of women have resulted in fundamental challenges to stereotypical gender roles since Mulvey's essay was written, e.g. *Kill Bill: Vol 1* (Quentin Tarantino, 2003). (For further discussion of Mulvey see page 219.)

The construction and targeting of audiences

Since media products are all produced within a commercial environment, the nature of the audience is extremely important. It is the audience that determines whether or not the media text is successful in commercial terms. This can be simply a matter of numbers or overall viewing figures, particularly in the case of television where ratings wars between stations are common, e.g. *EastEnders* (BBC) versus *Coronation Street* (ITV).

However, in terms of attracting advertising revenue or sponsorship, it is not just audience numbers that are important. There is no point attracting a large number of people to view an advertisement for a product they do not want or cannot afford. Media audiences, therefore, are 'constructed'. That is to say, media texts are designed in such a way as to attract a particular, desirable audience grouping.

Currently, the most desirable target audience group is young and active women aged 25–44, who are seen as ideal targets for commercials and advertising. These people tend to be multi-taskers, are willing to try new experiences, act as decision-makers on family purchases, are loyal readers of magazines and have money to spend.

Case study

Example 1

BSkyB has launched a new television channel, Sky Real Lives, aimed at older women, based on human interest and reality shows. It replaced Sky Travel. Sky's Barbara Gibbon said: 'There is a huge appetite for real-life stories that engage the full range of emotions for our viewers.' BSkyB entertainment boss Sophie Turner Laing said: 'This initiative is driven by consumer demand and fits our ambition to offer the best content in every genre.'

The new channel's target audience is women aged 35–54. Shows will include *Vain Men*, a documentary about young males trying to achieve the perfect body, and *Baby Race*, a programme tracking single women in their late 30s as they try to conceive.

In July 2007, BSkyB said it had added 90,000 customers in 3 months (up by 17% on the previous year) and now has a total 8.6 million customers.

Example 2

In 2005, book publisher HarperCollins employed OMD UK, a media agency, to research and establish the most effective medium for targeting their 18–40-year-old female audience for a new book.

The agency argued for a television slot for the campaign, and established that *Big Brother* was the most popular programme for the target group. The book, *Where Rainbows End* by Cecilia Ahern, was given a 30-second commercial over 10 weeks, running on E4's live stream of the *Big Brother* series. 1.3 million women saw the campaign and over 200,000 copies of the book were sold over 12 weeks, which was well above its forecast sales. This made it HarperCollins' most successful women's fiction launch ever and led the company to reappraise the importance of television in book advertising.

Ideas for discussion and development

- **What evidence can you find that television advertising and programme content are increasingly targeted at women?**

Theories of audience behaviour

There is general agreement that being exposed to media texts affects people in some way. Exactly how and to what extent people are affected has been the main debate in audience theory for the last 50 years.

Theories of how audiences react to media texts have been developed steadily and illustrate a change of focus. Originally, the audience was seen as a passive, manipulated mass — consider the impact of 1930s Nazi Party rallies and propaganda films, as explored by the Frankfurt School of media sociologists working in postwar America. Today, we see the audience as being made up of differentiated consumers, who are actively engaged in selecting from media products to meet lifestyle expectations, while negotiating the meaning of media texts in line with their own background, experiences and needs.

This current, rather flattering, view of audience behaviour is still challenged by some neo-Marxist analysis, which sees 'one-dimensional man' as being totally manipulated by media representations and incapable of mounting a genuinely effective individualist challenge to capitalist constructions of the world. Audience theories are explored further on pages 233–41, which should be read with A2 work in mind. For the present, it is important to recognise the difference between a **passive** view of the audience — where people are seen as being affected directly by what they see (as with 'copycat' violence, where a person imitates violence seen on television and in film), and an **active** view of the audience — where audience members engage in a kind of dialogue with media content to 'negotiate' and make sense of it on their own terms.

There can be no doubt that the interactive nature of much contemporary media content, and the explosion of dialogue via e-media, have made the contemporary audience more active consumers of media texts than ever before.

Media institutions

Nearly all media products are created to make money for the producers, and media institutions are the industrial working groups and organisations designed to research, produce and distribute media texts for profit.

Institutions have their own objectives, ethos and values, which are generally shared by those working for them. Individuals working within institutions are organised into hierarchies. They are responsible to senior managers, have targets and goals for personal advancement and development, and achieve job satisfaction from meeting the expectations of their performance. This job satisfaction and the status conferred by working within an organisation forms an important part of an individual's identity and lifestyle.

The values and goals of institutions can therefore become as important to individuals as wider social or cultural frameworks. Corporate needs can affect an individual's judgement and behaviour, with the economic and commercial needs of the organisation often being prioritised over wider social or cultural concerns. Institutions are driven by commercial values

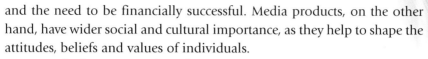
and the need to be financially successful. Media products, on the other hand, have wider social and cultural importance, as they help to shape the attitudes, beliefs and values of individuals.

As a result, there is a conflict of interest between institutions — with their goal of financial success — and the wider social implications of the products they produce. Independent film-makers constantly struggle to produce and distribute their products to a wide audience because, although their products are often culturally valuable, they are usually non-commercial and therefore of little interest to large media organisations.

Media institutions are powerful organisations with enormous influence in our society. They tend to be dominated by mainstream, hegemonic values, supported by consumer advertising. Politically, they seek a climate that allows them the maximum freedom to exploit markets and generate commercial profit.

What do media institutions do?

In short, media institutions produce media texts. Like any other industrial producer, they operate within a system of 'supply and demand' — they produce goods (media texts) to satisfy the needs of the consumer market (media audiences). However, there are a number of shortfalls in viewing media institutions in this simplistic commercial context:

- All media institutions are involved, to greater or lesser degree, in the competitive market of audience ratings. However, not all media institutions are strictly commercial concerns. The BBC, for example, is a public service broadcaster, and is paid for by the licence fee rather than subscription or advertising revenue.
- Some media institutions are public bodies, some are small independent concerns, and others belong to large multinational corporations that are composed of a number of different media and cultural organisations.
- Media institutions do not just operate at the 'micro' level — producing texts — they also work at the 'macro' level — producing meaning and influencing our social world.

'Institution' is an important key concept and is usefully defined in the following two ways:

1 An organisation that has influence in the local or wider community. The BBC, for example, is said to be the 'voice of Britain' and has the role of representing national culture and identity. Hollywood cinema is often said to promote key US values and ideals.

2 An established custom or practice. Every institution has its own identity and style. For example, the look and feel of a BBC 1 text is quite different from a Channel 4 text.

Institutions are, moreover, indistinguishable from media audiences. The influence and customs/practices outlined above only make sense if we look at institutions within the context of consumption. Textual production involves the complex and ever-shifting interplay between institution and audience. Institutions operate within a competitive context — each trying to win a share of the audience market for themselves. They must then produce texts that satisfy the needs (tastes and values) of the audience. As we all know, it is difficult to please everyone, so institutions must think carefully about identifying their target audience.

Advice on defining audiences

Be careful not to generalise about target audiences. You should avoid bold statements like 'the text is aimed at older people', or 'the target audience for this institution is adults'. Be more precise about age ranges (e.g. teenagers or twenty-somethings) and consider other factors like profession, occupation, class, race, gender, sexuality or ethnicity.

Always remember that although texts may be produced with a target audience in mind, this does not prevent the text from being consumed by people outside that specific audience demographic.

Types of institution

Media institutions generally fall into three main categories, although crossovers do occur:

- independent institutions
- public service broadcasters
- commercial corporate institutions

Independent institutions

Independent (or 'indie') institutions are commercial media companies, but operate on a smaller scale than corporate institutions. They are often managed and run by the same creative staff who produce the actual media texts. The hardest job for independent companies is breaking into existing media markets, where distribution and exhibition are owned and controlled by corporate institutions. As a result, independents generally target their products at niche markets, e.g. 'indie' music fans or 'art house' cinema-goers.

However, there are independents who are commercially successful because they produce texts for larger corporate institutions. Tiger Aspect or Kudos are both examples of independent television producers who are 'commissioned' by larger mainstream institutions to make programmes on their behalf.

Case study

Tiger Aspect is a UK-based independent television producer which makes programmes in a range of genres, including comedy, drama, entertainment, factual, animation and wildlife, for all of the UK's main terrestrial and non-terrestrial broadcasters. For example, they have created shows like *Murphy's Law* and *The Vicar of Dibley* (BBC 1), *Charlie and Lola* (CBeebies), *Mr Bean* (ITV) and *Teachers* (Channel 4).

Like many successful independent production companies, Tiger Aspect has been bought up and is now controlled by the multinational marketing/ entertainment group IMG (International Management Group). This prompts the question of just how 'independent' it is.

Digital technologies — particularly the internet, which has no overt distribution/exhibition control — have encouraged a huge growth in the number of independent production companies. The interesting thing for these independent companies (like the independent record labels before them) is that any measure of popularity/commercial success is met by 'takeover' bids from larger corporate institutions. For example, YouTube is now owned by Google, and MySpace is in the hands of Rupert Murdoch's News Corporation empire.

Ideas for discussion and development

Outsourcing production is a common practice in contemporary television.

- **How many of the television programmes that you watch are made by 'independent' producers?**
- **How many of the 'interactive' networking websites, such as MySpace and Bebo, are still owned by independent producers?**
- **Are larger corporations (and the corporate advertisers they bring with them) an inevitable consequence of popular success?**

Public service broadcasters

In the UK there are two institutions with public service remits: the BBC and Channel 4. Channel 4, however, is an anomaly in that it has a public service remit but is funded, like other terrestrial/commercial broadcasters, by advertising revenue rather than the licence fee.

Public service broadcasting is centred on eight basic principles:

- It aspires to universal accessibility — it should reach everyone in the UK.
- It aspires to universal appeal — it should, at some point in the schedules and across the whole network, have something for everyone.
- It works from the premise of public responsibility rather than consumer sovereignty — so it should have a concern for 'national' community and identity.
- It should cater for minority as well as majority tastes and interests.
- It should encourage competition in good programming rather than in audience ratings and viewing figures.
- It should remain free from political and commercial influence and interest.
- It should strive to educate, inform and entertain — the entertainment part being no more important than the need to educate and inform.
- Programme makers should be given free creative rein rather than being inhibited by corporate policy.

In essence, public service broadcasting should provide an important service to the public.

Example institution: the BBC

The BBC, originally formed as the British Broadcasting Company in 1922, was established, under Royal Charter, as the British Broadcasting Corporation in 1927. See page 6 for a summary of its organisational

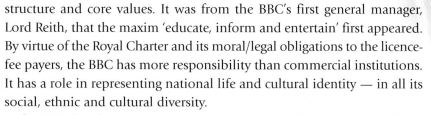
structure and core values. It was from the BBC's first general manager, Lord Reith, that the maxim 'educate, inform and entertain' first appeared. By virtue of the Royal Charter and its moral/legal obligations to the licence-fee payers, the BBC has more responsibility than commercial institutions. It has a role in representing national life and cultural identity — in all its social, ethnic and cultural diversity.

The BBC does have commercial interests. It buys in programming from independent producers and it sells successful programmes — like *The Office* — to foreign markets. It does not, however, derive any income from advertising revenue or make a profit. All money generated by the BBC's commercial arm — BBC Worldwide, established in 1979 — is reinvested in new programme-making initiatives. Similarly, the licence fee is not set by the BBC itself but by the government, which likewise elects the BBC's governing body. So while the BBC is supposedly free of governmental interference, the relationship between the two is complex.

The BBC, originally a radio broadcaster, had a monopoly on British television between 1936 and 1955, until Independent Television (ITV) was created following the Television Act 1954. The duopoly of BBC and ITV — comprising a number of regional broadcasters such as Granada and Thames — remained generally amicable for most of the postwar period. From the late 1980s onwards, a series of technological, political, social and cultural developments began to destabilise what many now see as the outmoded ideals and practices of public service broadcasting. The main developments were:

- **Globalisation** — media institutions are now more multi-national than national concerns.
- **1990 Broadcasting Act** — the Independent Broadcasting Authority was replaced by the Independent Television Commission with the aim of 'restructuring' British broad-casting. The Act allowed **deregulation**, which led to the emergence of Channel 5 and the growth of multi-channel, 'pay-per-view', and subscription cable and satellite channels. It also stipulated that the BBC, normally an 'in-house' producer, had to outsource 25% of its output to inde-pendent production companies. Although the Act expanded consumer choice in the number of institutions and channels available, many critics claim that it has led to 'dumbing down' as institutions, governed by ever-increasing competi-tion, fall back on repeating inexpensive/successful formulas.

- **Market liberalism** — focus has shifted from programming to advertising. As more money for production funding comes from commercial sponsorship, there is more of a need to maximise audiences. Thus programming is less risky/less experimental.
- **Hutton Report 2004** — this was a report into the death of Dr David Kelly, a Ministry of Defence employee who apparently committed suicide after being named by the BBC as the source of 'leaked' quotes, claiming the government had 'sexed up' documents that led to the military invasion of Iraq in 2003. The report cleared the government but the BBC was so heavily criticised that its chairman and director general were forced to resign. Many now question just how 'free' the BBC is to follow its public service broadcasting remit.
- **Licence fee shortfall** — successive governments (obviously not wishing to upset voters) have set licence fee increases below the rate of inflation, leading to a shortfall in the BBC's production budget.
- **Digital broadcasting and new media** — the growth of digital technology, the internet and mobile telephones have transformed media consumption, leading to audiences who are less tied to television schedules and who expect more interaction with media products. Younger audiences, for example, spend as much time, and in some instances more, consuming media products online than they do watching television or listening to the radio.

Ideas for discussion and development

- **Does the licence fee still represent an appropriate way of funding the BBC?**
- **Is an 'impartial' broadcasting institution — free from political and commercial influence — a vital part of national democracy?**
- **How much of your own media consumption is taken up by the BBC? Do you think it represents the tastes, values and interests of your own particular social group?**

In this context, it is easy to see the how the BBC's public service status is under threat. In the current era of globalisation, the BBC is well equipped to deal with change. BBC World Service radio (and now television and internet coverage) is a well-established global network. However, in the de-regulated context of corporate capitalism — driven by profit, competition and appealing to the largest number of consumers — it is perhaps less well equipped. Many also argue that the BBC is being increasingly subjected to more political pressure from the government.

Such debates are prompting changes. In a recent broadcast, Mark Thompson, current director general of the BBC, announced a plan of restructuring and staffing cuts, explaining that change was precipitated by:

'digital technology, which is shifting audience expectations and their relationship with the BBC through on demand, interactivity and person-alisation.'

(BBC website, 20 October 2007)

The BBC could go down the route of public–private partnership — popu-larised by the New Labour government since the late 1990s — but such a move may prompt licence payers to reconsider why they are paying the fee in the first place.

The BBC already commissions programmes from independent production companies — such as Kudos, which produced both *Spooks* and *Life on Mars* — and makes money from BBC Worldwide, but it still has to keep a tight hold over its public service broadcasting status and meet the conditions laid down in the Royal Charter.

Ideas for discussion and development

- How do we account for the BBC's decision to cut the budgets for serious news/current affairs programmes, like *Newsnight* and the *Today* programme, while maintaining spending on popular entertain-ment programmes, such as *Tonight with Jonathan Ross*?
- Is the decision to increase funding for BBC 3 — a minor channel with a small, but young audience — a worthwhile investment in the future?

Interestingly, the very language of BBC media has changed. Traditional, generic terms like 'radio' and 'television' have been rebranded as 'audio and music' and 'BBC Vision' in an attempt to reflect the way that people receive images and sound, not just on television screens or radio, but increasingly on their computers and mobile phones. Similarly, the term 'new media' has been replaced with 'present media' to reflect the 'now-ness' of its contemporary dominance.

The BBC has always been seen as a paternalistic institution, dictating output in terms of decency and taste. Many pop songs, like Frankie Goes to Hollywood's 'Relax' and the Sex Pistols' 'God Save The Queen', have been banned from the airwaves for their supposedly indecent lyrics. However, even the BBC itself now admits that when it comes to questions of power, the balance has swung in favour of the audience. As a recent posting on the BBC's news website put it, viewers and listeners are not watching or listening when the 'scheduler dictates', but are downloading material to their BBC iPlayer whenever and wherever they like.

Commercial corporate institutions

Commercial media institutions are, like any other capitalist business enterprise, driven by the logic of competition and profit. Unlike the BBC with its licence-fee revenue, commercial broadcasting institutions have fewer guaranteed or fixed sources of income. There are four main ways in which commercial media institutions can generate revenue:

- **Subscription** — viewers pay a monthly/annual fee for a specialist service, such as Sky Sports or Setanta Sports. These services are confined to digital or satellite broadcasting services.
- **Pay-per-view** — viewers make a one-off payment for a single, special-event broadcast, such as a high-profile sporting event.
- **Sponsorship** — many genre programmes, such as one-off dramas, sitcoms and soap operas, are partly financed by commercial sponsors, e.g. Cadbury sponsors *Coronation Street*.
- **Advertising revenue** — commercial companies pay to have their products/brands advertised during commercial breaks in the schedules. Breaks in primetime slots/popular programmes command more revenue than quieter/less popular times, because the advertisement will be seen by a greater number of potential consumers. Commercial media institutions thus need to maximise viewing figures in order to maximise advertising revenues.

The income generated by the above methods must be greater than the amount spent on production and distribution costs. While advertising revenue is a lucrative source of income, it is also difficult to command. Advertisers are only willing to pay premium advertising rates if they know they can reach a mass audience at a specific time.

For example, when BARB — the organisation responsible for recording British broadcast viewing figures — revamped their service in January 2002, audience ratings figures were temporarily unavailable. According to a report in the *Guardian* (Owen Gibson, 7 January 2002) media buyers (i.e. the people responsible for placing advertisements on behalf of advertisers) had to work 'blind'. The buyers had no sound justification for where and when to place crucial advertisements for the January sales. Understandably, advertising revenues fell dramatically in the blind period.

There are certain premium slots (e.g. live international football matches) that are definite crowd-pullers. However, not all broadcasting output is that easily guaranteed, so programme makers must do what they can to ensure that their output achieves high audience ratings. This has inevitably led to charges of 'dumbing down', as commercial broadcasters focus on repeating successful formulas like reality television and soap operas. These generate larger audiences, which in turn generate higher advertising revenues. This has led to the current bewildering situation where we have a great deal more choice in terms of channels, but arguably less choice in terms of textual diversity. Financial security is more important to commercial institutions than experimentation or creativity.

Expansion

Another way in which commercial institutions survive is through expansion. In a highly competitive market, one way of staying ahead is to out-grow your competitors (or, better still, buy them up). When we looked at independent institutions on page 107 we touched upon the idea of commercial success leading to outside investment. Corporate growth is no longer measured in terms of **vertical integration**. This was the business model of choice for the Hollywood Studio System (in its classic period between the 1930s and 1960), where studios like Warner Bros or MGM would own not only the production facilities but also the distribution networks and the exhibition cinemas. The studios therefore ensured a smooth passage for their films, from production straight through to reception.

Modern media institutions are likely to be sub-companies within a much larger parent company, multinational **conglomerates** (international companies with a wide and varied range of commercial interests) such as Time Warner, News Corporation or Viacom. The idea behind conglomerates is that all the companies within the organisation protect and reinforce each other by concentrating profits rather than spreading them out unevenly. Like the Hollywood studios — which have all evolved into multinational institutions themselves — conglomerates operate beyond merely creating media texts. Unlike the vertical integration model, conglomerates have developed in terms of **horizontal integration** — into what is known now in the jargon of media-corporate-speak as **synergies.**

Synergy, by definition, is when two bodies or organisations combine 'energies' to create something greater than the sum of their individual parts. For example, Time Warner has integrated both vertically — in film and television production, distribution and exhibition — and horizontally — into magazines, book publishing, internet services and theme parks.

Synergy does not in itself guarantee commercial success, but it does provide strength in numbers. Having interests in film, television, digital communications and publishing means that the media corporation can neatly producing, distribute, market and exhibit the product, as well as producing accompanying material, such as books, interactive websites and video games.

Cross-media ownership

One of the most sensitive issues to come out of corporate media expansion is the area of **cross-media ownership**. This is where a media institution in one sector of the industry — e.g. newspapers or film — branches out and buys into another sector of the media industry — e.g. broadcast television or an internet P2P site. In the UK, where a diverse newspaper industry and public service broadcasting have traditionally dominated national media culture, cross-media ownership continues to been a highly political issue. Since the deregulation legislation of the 1990s, both Conservative and Labour governments have been unsure of where to go next. The biggest fear is that a single media corporation such as Rupert Murdoch's News Corporation may end up controlling too much of the overall market and thus be in a position of extreme power.

This is good news for larger media institutions because they are able to control almost every aspect of the production–consumption process in-house, therefore ensuring that profits are not leaked out to middle-men in other institutions. For audiences, and some would argue for democracy, this may not be such a good thing. In the marketplace of corporate capitalism, there is little room for alternative or independent production.

Ideas for discussion and development

- **Why do you think many people in the UK media industry are wary of cross-media ownership?**

Is there a solution to the contradictions of the deregulated free market? On the one hand, de-regulation has opened up a whole spectrum of consumer choice — the number of different channels now available is enormous. On the other hand, deregulation has led to concentration in ownership, with only a handful of large multi-national corporations controlling everything.

Does ownership influence production?

The main thing that you will need to be able to respond to in the AS examination paper is **institutional context** — the ways in which the 'construction' of media texts are affected/constrained by the institution that produced it.

As we saw earlier, media texts produced by the BBC are constrained to a large degree by the public service imperatives of 'educate, inform and entertain', with a strong emphasis on meeting cultural diversity and minority needs. Commercial broadcasters, on the other hand, need to generate advertising revenue and will strive to produce media texts that have a broad audience appeal.

However, one of the ways that media institutions can avoid going directly head-to-head with their rivals, both in terms of scheduling and content, is to target their products at niche markets or specific target audiences. Thus, for example, a soap opera on Channel 4 (*Hollyoaks*) will have a very different production style and narrative content to one produced by BBC 1 (*EastEnders*) or for ITV 1 (*Coronation Street*). Channel 4, as befits its status as the relative newcomer, targets a younger audience; BBC 1 and ITV 1 are more typical of mainstream, family-orientated broadcasting institutions.

Example of a media conglomerate: Time Warner

Time Warner is one of the top global media corporations, alongside Disney, Viacom and News Corporation. It has 87,000 employees worldwide, had a revenue of $44.7 billion in 2006 and has assets in film, telecommunications, internet, television and publishing.

Originally, Time Warner was the result of a merger in 1990 between Warner Communications Inc. and Time Inc. Warner Inc. had grown out of a number of large media institutions including Warner Brothers Pictures, Warner Music Group and D. C. Comics. Time Inc., which produces *Time Magazine*, is the world's largest producer and distributor of magazines.

In 2001, Time Warner was bought up by the internet service provider AOL (America On-Line) to become AOL Time Warner. That one of the USA's largest media institutions was taken over by an internet company was a real sign of changing times. However, in 2002, following the dotcom crash, AOL's market value decreased considerably and AOL, now a subsidiary company, was dropped from the company's title.

Case study

Time Warner's key values, taken from their website, are:

- **Creativity.** We thrive on innovation and originality, encouraging risk-taking and divergent voices.
- **Customer focus.** We value our customers, putting their needs and interests at the centre of everything we do.
- **Integrity.** We rigorously uphold editorial independence and artistic expression, earning the trust of our readers, viewers, listeners, members and subscribers.
- **Diversity.** We attract and develop the world's best talent, seeking to include the broadest range of people and perspectives.

(Source: adapted from Time Warner official website)

When the AOL Time Warner merger (the largest business merger in world history) was announced in January 2000, the combined market capitalisation was $280 billion. However, by 2004, Time Warner's market value was reduced to $84 billion. Despite heavy losses, Time Warner remains a global leader and the diversification into internet communications is thought by many business commentators to be a shrewd move.

In terms of synergy, there are mutual benefits for both the old and new media institutions involved. For Time Warner, AOL provided the logistical facilities for a mass-scale move onto the internet. AOL was already a successful internet service provider and was one of the few organisations with the network facilities to deal with a major operation like Time Warner. For AOL, this allowed it to move on to the next technological stage of internet development. AOL had been a market leader in getting people online but needed the investment strategy and technology to get them onto the next level — Broadband access. Time Warner had previously acquired a telecommunications service, Road Runner, which had the technology and network capacity that allowed for Broadband access at fast and efficient levels. Broadband access is much faster than dial-up, allowing for more complicated tasks, like video streaming, consequently transforming the communications aspect of the internet to incorporate media communications: watching live news, and downloading music, videos and television. From a strategic perspective, the merger was beneficial to all involved, creating a globally powerful institution that combines both old media power and content with new media speed and access.

Time Warner divisions

Time Warner is split into several key divisions, with the company owning a diverse range of media, telecommunications and entertainments brand names:

- **New Line cinema** — film and television distribution, exhibition and merchandising.
- **Warner Bros.** — includes film, television, production and distribution, animation, cinemas, video and DVD production, interactive entertainment and D. C. Comics.
- **Time Inc.** — magazine publishing and distribution, with over 150 titles available worldwide.
- **Time Warner Cable** — telecommunications research, manufacturing and installation (Road Runner).

- **AOL** — a range of internet service provisions, including instant messaging, games, phone, Broadband and brands like CompuServe and Netscape.
- **Home Box Office (HBO)** — subscription television cable network, television production and distribution, and multiplex cinema network.
- **Turner Broadcasting System** — a range of television, radio and Broadband production and broadcasting services, which include CNN, Cartoon Network and Boomerang.

Time Warner also invests in what it calls 'early to mid stage' companies — fledgling institutions, many in the digital/internet communications industries. In this way, it is always looking to expand into new media markets, and thus into new consumer markets. Despite this, Time Warner is run on a fairly conservative basis with a board of directors composed of only 13 people.

Time Warner's global presence

While Time Warner is essentially a US-based company, it has a presence around the globe. CNN has certainly taken on Sky and the BBC as a global news service. The AOL-affiliated internet services have a major influence on current online media developments. Hollywood cinema continues to dominate the global film market.

One area of interest, particularly in the UK, where Time Warner does not have a direct ownership/control foothold, is terrestrial television. However, its influence, in the shape of HBO, is felt in terms of content. Some of the most popular television shows in the UK, like *The Wire*, *The Sopranos* and *Sex and the City*, are imported HBO productions.

There are a number of possible explanations as to why these shows are on our screens, particularly on Channel 4 and Five. First, they are well made and have high production values. In the case of *The Sopranos*, they use known film actors such as James Gandolfini, Steve Buscemi and Edie Falco, and quality directors like Mike Figgis and Peter Bogdanovich. Second, high-budget production and proven commercial success in the USA make these shows attractive to UK institutions and to advertisers. Quite simply, it is less expensive to buy such shows in than to make them from scratch. In addition, exposure on the internet allows these shows to generate a fan base before hitting the small screen, thus ensuring a more reliable advertising revenue.

Interestingly, when successful British shows — like the BBC's *The Office* — are exported to the USA, they are re-shot and re-formatted for the US market. HBO's success on UK television is relatively small in terms of overall viewing figures across all channels, but is quite considerable on the actual channels where they are shown. This has encouraged HBO's plans to launch its HBO SVOD (video on demand) service in the UK, marking the first time the cable channel has launched its own channel in the UK market. The new on-demand service will be available on BT Vision, Tiscali TV and Virgin Media, featuring original mini-series, television series, comedy specials and documentaries.

Network viewing share (%; January 2002 to September 2007)

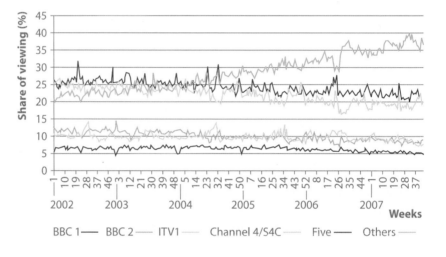

It could be argued that terrestrial television channels like Channel 4 and Five are now caught up in a global economy of **cultural imperialism** — where Western, particularly US, cultural values and ideology dominate the world. Economic constraints, such as low production budgets and the need for advertising revenue, force companies to buy US imports. Channel 4, however, would argue that the increased revenue from popular foreign imports is reinvested in new programming.

Ideas for discussion and development

• Are HBO texts, like *Sex and the City* or *The Sopranos*, taken up by Channel 4 because of content/audience appeal or because they are cheaper to buy than produce 'in-house'?
• Would you consider HBO texts to be 'content-led' or 'advertiser-led'? Do they represent innovative and original programming?

Television statistics

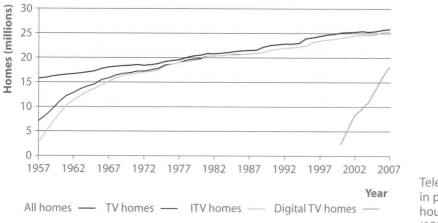

Television ownership in private domestic households (1957–2007)

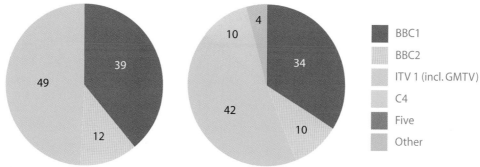

1981

1991

- BBC1
- BBC2
- ITV 1 (incl. GMTV)
- C4
- Five
- Other

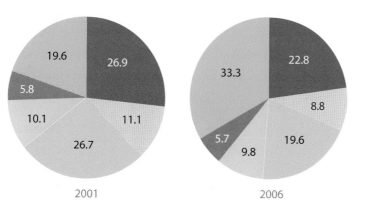

2001

2006

Television viewing — annual % shares of viewing (individuals), 1981–2006

NB. Shares for 1981 and 1991 have been rounded to nearest whole number.

119

Media audiences and institutions

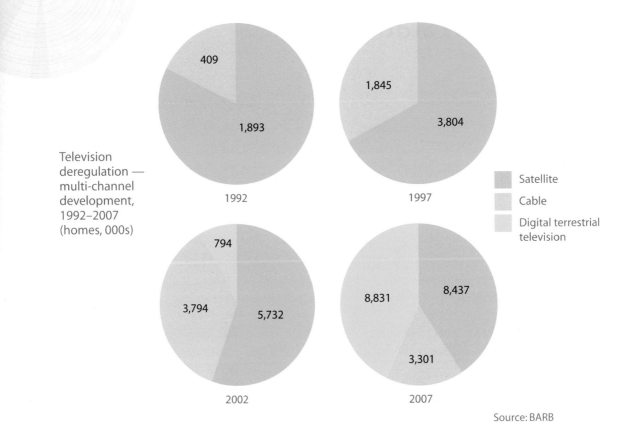

Television deregulation — multi-channel development, 1992–2007 (homes, 000s)

1992
- 409
- 1,893

1997
- 1,845
- 3,804

2002
- 794
- 3,794
- 5,732

2007
- 8,831
- 8,437
- 3,301

Legend:
- Satellite
- Cable
- Digital terrestrial television

Source: BARB

Representation in the media

Representation is perhaps the single most important media concept because it addresses the very essence of what the media do. Everything we receive from media output involves representation of aspects of the world we inhabit, and we are dependent on these representations to make sense of this world.

News

The production and manufacture of news

We live in a culture obsessed with news. Twenty-four hour coverage by BBC News 24 and CNN provides a constant stream of material, with an on-screen 'crawler' continually providing updates. Maintaining this constant stream of information puts huge demands on news organisations.

News is a cross-platform product — available on dedicated television news channels, mobile phones, on the internet, in traditional newspaper form, on radio, satellite and free-to-air television stations. For newspapers, websites are becoming as important as the daily paper as they provide the constant updates required in the modern news environment.

News provides the background representational context to our whole world. As consumers of news, we often tend to accept what is presented to us without question. The news is seen as a fixed, factual body of information. In reality, the news is a selective, constructed representation of some of the millions of events that take place in the world. Key questions must be asked as to what constitutes news and how it comes to be presented the way it is. Increasingly, news is seen as an extension of the entertainment industry, with the term **infotainment** being used to describe the modern mix of hard and soft news items.

What is news?

What is the news and where does it come from? Is the news the same throughout the world? Why are some events and issues considered to be news and others not? Is the news biased? Can any event, place or person be presented as news?

Attempts have been made at explaining the nature of news and how it is constructed, most notably by Johan Galtung and Marie Ruge in the 1960s. These Norwegian researchers devised a set of news values, which describe the circumstances and conditions required for events to become news. This approach has been adapted by other researchers, resulting in a comprehensive list of news values:

- **Frequency** — news needs to happen on a daily and frequent basis to meet broadcasting schedules.
- **Cultural proximity** — news needs to be close to home or related to home issues.
- **Threshold** — news needs to be of sufficient importance to attract attention; big events get noticed more than small ones.
- **Negativity** — bad news has priority over good news.
- **Predictability** — news tends to anticipate and justify expected outcomes.
- **Unexpectedness** — news has to seem unexpected, even though most of it takes place within predictable patterns.
- **Continuity** — follow-up elements of a big story are frequently seen as newsworthy.
- **Unambiguity** — events with a clear meaning are more likely to be reported than complex issues.
- **Composition** — news is subject to editorial construction and reflects individual editorial choices, the constraints of the medium and organisational values.
- **Personalisation** — events that can be made personal in any way are prioritised.
- **Reference to elite nations** — powerful, mostly Western, nations have priority coverage.
- **Reference to elite persons** — celebrities get more coverage than unknown persons.
- **Narrativisation** — news is constructed as a story and all elements of narrative theory apply.
- **Visual imperative** — television news and tabloid journalism tend to be driven by pictures and what is available.

News as entertainment

Television and radio news

Television news traditionally operates through flagship fixed programme slots, e.g. the *Six O'Clock News* and *Ten O'Clock News* (BBC 1), *News at Ten* (ITV), *Newsnight* (BBC 2) and *Channel 4 News* (Channel 4). BBC radio news still operates in a similar way on Radio 4, providing reports on the hour and full news review programmes in the early morning up to 9 a.m. (*Today*), at 1 p.m. (*The World at One*) and at 5 p.m. (*PM*), followed by the evening six o'clock news and the ten o'clock news (*The World Tonight*).

24-hour news

Multiple channel television has led to the launching of 24-hour news channels: BBC News 24, CNN and Sky News, for example. These channels, plus the availability of news 24 hours a day on the internet (and so via mobile phones), has changed the public's means of accessing the news. There is no longer the need to wait patiently for fixed television news slots.

The advantage for consumers is that the news is always available; the disadvantage is that the 24-hour channels have difficulty maintaining their news coverage without constant repetition. The end result is a mixture of news and entertainment, with headlines being repeated and very little depth to much of the coverage.

'Dumbing down'

The movement away from hard news and factual content in media products, and the increasing use of entertainment and trivial material to maintain audience interest, is called **dumbing down**. The disparaging nature of the term underlines the disapproval felt among some media professionals about turning news into entertainment at the expense of serious content. However, despite this criticism, the tendency to dumb down has spread to all news programmes, and indeed to all media platforms.

The need to attract and hold the attention of an increasingly channel-hopping and fickle audience can be seen in the tendency for television news programmes to run exclusives and scoops which themselves can then become the news. In this way, for example, BBC news can claim to have broken a story, or Channel 4 news can announce the exposure of a scandal. The programme thus makes its own breaking of the news part of the story.

News management and agenda setting

The order in which media producers, particularly of news, present reported events is called the **agenda**. Events placed high on an agenda are perceived by audiences to be of great importance. Items low on the agenda are of less importance, and items not on the agenda or not reported remain unknown to an audience.

Determining the agenda, or **agenda-setting**, is seen as a means of exercising power over public opinion and responses to events. This may be done by editors of newspapers or producers of television news programmes for personal, political or commercial reasons, or as a result of the perceived level of interest in a topic. It can also lead to matters of public concern receiving very little media coverage. For example, owing to agenda-setting in the UK tabloid press, the relationship between celebrities Victoria and David Beckham receives more prominent coverage than scientific reports on the progress of global warming.

The Jo Moore scandal (see case study) became symbolic of New Labour's obsession with 'spin' and news management. Moore had tried to manage the release of news items to the best advantage of the government, bearing in mind the other news dominating on a particular day. She was trying to ensure that items she did not want to receive wide coverage would be pushed down the agenda by other more important events. On a day when there was little of importance taking place, a news item such as one relating to councillors' expenses might receive a great deal of attention in the media. This would then create difficulties and embarrassment for the government. On a day when there were far more important items to consider, it would probably go unnoticed.

The perceived significance of any news item on a particular day will affect the amount of coverage it receives, and the coverage it receives will depend on what other news there is. It is in the nature of news that more important items push lesser items off the agenda. In the absence of important items, relatively insignificant items are given more coverage and therefore come to be seen as more important by the audience.

Task

Find examples of 'bad news' buried in the inside pages of newspapers, where seemingly less important but more appealing stories are given front-page coverage.

Case study

Spin: 'a good day to bury bad news'

In February 2002, Jo Moore — a government 'special adviser' on media issues (a 'spin doctor') — resigned from her job as a result of the controversial comments she made about hiding the release of bad news behind the terrorist attacks of 11 September 2001, when all attention was focused on the tragedy.

Her actual words were: 'It's now a very good day to get out anything we want to bury. Councillors' expenses?'

Advanced **Media Studies**

CNN: the world as seen from the USA

CNN claims to cover world news. On a superficial level, it certainly has news from around the world, with world weather reports, world financial reports and feature items such as one on militancy in the world religions of Islam, Judaism and Christianity.

If you watch more critically, you might notice the preference given to US stories over other news, along with the shallow, repetitive nature of the reporting and the empty, conversational tone of the journalists as they fill time by making comments and jokes to each other. You will notice the heavy intrusion of advertising and sponsorship, and the constant trailers for items coming up on the show.

You may see cameras pointed at empty presidential podiums waiting for a spokesperson to appear while the commentator makes small talk and continually repeats the same details, to fill time before the next advertisements (which are for CNN). You will find a very limited number of stories, all of which feature a US agenda of news priorities and a US commercial television style throughout. The attention span of the average viewer is seemingly assumed to be in the region of 2 minutes — after this, news items are repeated.

Task

Record half an hour's worth of CNN news and analyse it with fellow students. Do you agree with the above analysis? What were the top stories?

Remember that producing the opening sequence of a news broadcast could be part of a production task for Unit 2.

News representations

News representations, like all representations, are based on a selection of elements. Characteristics of people, places and events are combined in an entertaining fashion to an audience via a media text. The presentation of that media text suggests that the representation is a realistic portrayal of these people, places and events. Representations are selective and metonymic in nature — i.e. a part of something is used to represent a whole. For example, a photograph of a demonstrator hitting a policeman can be used by a newspaper to suggest that the whole demonstration was violent, even though this may not have been the case.

Task

You are a news editor of a UK tabloid newspaper. You have two photographs to choose from to represent a large demonstration against the potential environmental damage caused by the planned expansion of Heathrow airport.

Photograph 1: a smiling couple in their twenties talking to a smiling police officer, who stands in front of them with his arms folded.

Photograph 2: a teenage girl is being frogmarched by two police officers, one male and one female, away from a barrier. She is clearly in a state of distress and the shirt she is wearing is torn at the shoulder.

Which photograph would you use on the front page of your newspaper? What impression would your choice give of the demonstration?

Remember that choosing front-page photographs for two tabloid newspapers could be part of a production task for Unit 2.

Political correctness

'The weight of this sad time we must obey
Speak what we feel, not what we ought to say'

(*King Lear*, William Shakespeare)

How often do you hear people say that they can no longer 'speak what they feel' because of **political correctness**? What is political correctness, where does it come from and how is it reflected in media content?

Language and political correctness

The idea of political correctness originated in the USA in the 1970s, when 'liberation' movements for African Americans, women and homosexuals were fighting for equality and trying to change people's perceptions. Linguists Edward Sapir and Benjamin Whorf argued that people's use of language determined the way they saw the world, and that if you wanted to change attitudes you had to make people change their use of language.

Language, after all, is a primary means of representing the world and the people in it. For feminists working for women's equality, this meant changing words that defined women in terms of male activities or where the masculine version of the word dominated, such as actor (actress), waiter (waitress), policeman (policewoman).

Feminists argued that because the English language favours the masculine (mankind, man-made, manager), using the feminine form somehow diminished women. For example, an actor is a serious figure but an 'actress' can be a figure of fun or even, on occasion, a prostitute. Even the word 'girl' can be used negatively to describe someone as weak and light-headed, such as in the phrase 'a big girl's blouse'. Similarly, a 'manageress' seems a less important figure than a 'manager'.

The substitute of the word 'person' for the gender identity where possible, like 'chairperson', or the use of a gender-neutral word, like 'police officer', was thought to further gender equality. Gender neutrality means that no negative or stereotyped connotations can be attached to the female in the role; in fact, her gender cannot be identified in the title. This approach then became a requirement in education ('head teacher' replaced 'headmistress'/'headmaster'), public life and the media, and resistance or criticism of the process was seen as negative, reactionary and, by feminists, sexist. In fact, these changes have now become totally integrated into current practice and expectation.

Attitudes, beliefs and values

This approach was also transferred into attitudes, beliefs and values, whereby certain views were deemed unacceptable and the expression of them was constantly challenged and suppressed. These views might relate to gender (sexism), sexuality (homophobia), and to matters involving race and religion (racism).

The movement coincided with equal opportunities legislation in most Western countries, whereby discrimination on the grounds of race, gender, disability or sexuality, and even the expression of certain views on these topics, was made a criminal offence. This process even went as far as advocating **positive discrimination** — the practice of employing or advancing people because of their ethnicity, gender or sexual orientation, rather than because they were the ideal candidate for a job. This practice was designed to redress the imbalance in the numbers of people from these groups present in certain kinds of employment. For example, homosexuals had been excluded or oppressed in areas like the police or the armed forces, and women were (and still are) under-represented at senior management level. Ethnic minorities tend to dominate at lower, unskilled levels of employment rather than in the professions, and disabled people are still under-represented in all levels of employment. Political correctness became synonymous with positive representation and the advancement of minority groups. It also advocated **multiculturalism**, whereby all cultural and religious groups were encouraged to flourish and develop their own religious and community values within the host community.

Being seen as politically correct became important to politicians seeking office, as it meant that they could not be challenged by so-called progressive forces in favour of these changes. Not to change was seen as reactionary, and men in particular who resisted were called 'dinosaurs', doomed to extinction. To accept the changes was 'modern' and 'going with the flow'. It formed part of a tick-list of desirable attributes that became a new orthodoxy. All these changes were reflected in media language and representations, where checks for language use and political correctness became standard procedure.

In media institutions, this has even led to repeats of 1960s/1970s comedy series, like *Porridge* and *Steptoe and Son* (BBC), being checked against current standards and cut where offence was thought likely. The fact that this is seen as necessary shows how much society has changed. However, from originally being a positive force for change, political correctness has come to be a force suppressing opinion. Having successfully challenged an existing order and forced people to reconsider their negative attitudes and behaviour, the practice encourages a standard response to all matters involving gender, race, religion, multiculturalism and sexuality. In spite of the best intentions behind the practice, some now see politcal correctness as a reactionary force in its own right, replacing the reactionary views it sought to challenge.

Nor has political correctness been able to deal with changing social and cultural circumstances. For example, a new form of oppressive reactionary religious thought — principally in radical Islam but also in evangelical Christianity and creationism (which denies centuries of scientific progress) — has required a rethink of some politically correct dogmas. This is particularly true of radical Islam's attitude to gender equality issues, homosexuality and the application of *sharia* law, including the death penalty, which appear incompatible with the sharing of secular values in a tolerant, multicultural environment.

The need to challenge undemocratic and illiberal views in relation to gender and sexuality is set against the desire to show tolerance and a lack of prejudice towards different ethnicities, cultures and religions. For example, the overt racism directed against white people by Robert Mugabe's oppressive regime in Zimbabwe was not 'racism' according to politically correct terminology because 'racism' is usually only defined in terms of white attitudes towards black and Asian people.

Political correctness drew attention to embedded prejudice in Western societies against ethnic and sexual minorities and against women.

The correction of language and thought helped to advance the liberation movements and change social attitudes. The question is whether the approach now needs adjusting to meet the challenges of a changing world.

Media representations and stereotyping

Stereotyping is the social classification of individuals, groups of people and places by identifying some common characteristics and universally applying them in an oversimplified and generalised way, such that the classification represents value judgements and assumptions about the individual, group or place concerned.

Stereotypes are resistant to change because, once established in people's minds, they tend to stay there. Research generally shows that individuals will seek out information that confirms their existing viewpoints and opinions, and reject information that challenges them. This is partly explained by the theory of **cognitive dissonance** developed by Festinger. Put simply, having formed a judgement, people like to be proved right and resist evidence that puts them in the wrong.

Do stereotypes change over time?

Stereotypes can eventually change over time, particularly if media representations are used to challenge them. This, for example, is why it is so important to represent ethnic minorities in a positive light, as integrated, socially equal and financially successful members of society, present in all levels of society. The more people are exposed to positive representations of this kind the more they will come to accept them as the norm.

Stereotypes are, by their nature, crude generalisations used as a form of mental categorisation. They become the first point of reference in perceiving and assessing individuals, groups and places.

The term carries with it negative connotations and the implicit understanding that a closer and more detailed evaluation of the individual, group or place will result in more accurate assessment.

The fact is that nobody really believes that all French people are good cooks, all Italians make good lovers, all Yorkshiremen are mean and all blondes are dumb, but everybody is probably guilty of using stereotypes to make instant judgements about new people and places. We need to remember to be open-minded, to judge by our actual experience and set these stereotypes aside. Relying on stereotypes can be harmful, as it leads to negative and prejudiced reactions to others, their origins, race and culture.

Example of changes in stereotyping: nurses

The traditional representation of nurses is exemplified in the classic ITV series *Emergency Ward 10* (1957–67), which in 1959 had an audience of over 12 million. The series tended to romanticise the nursing profession by showing nurses (all females) as professional, dedicated carers, saving lives while seeking romance with higher status male doctors.

Angels (1975–83) was an unglamorous depiction of the nursing profession, showing student nurses facing up to problems of sexual promiscuity, alcoholism and other hard-hitting social issues in a pressurised NHS. With a multiethnic cast, this BBC series aimed at authenticity, with actresses being required to spend time on a hospital ward to add to the realism of the programme. This treatment was carried through into the BBC's *Casualty* (1986–) and spin-off *Holby City* (1999–).

The cast of
Emergency Ward 10

ITV/Rex Features

By contrast, *No Angels* (Channel 4, 2004–06) used comedy drama to show four women balancing a difficult job in today's NHS. The three series showed these women navigating complicated personal lives involving sexual promiscuity, single parenthood and personal aspirations.

The move from *Angels* (a traditional, admiring term for nurses) to *No Angels* suggests a change in attitude to the health service as a whole.

The cast of
No Angels

Representations of ethnic minorities

Stuart Hall (1932–), a leading academic figure in the development of media and cultural studies theory, wrote a study on the representation of race on British television in the 1970s. This began a debate about media representations of black people. Hall has since (1995) investigated representations of black people in period films, identifying three types: faithful, happy slaves; primitive and cunning natives; clowns or entertainers. Hall sees such negative stereotypes as reinforcing dominant ideology, by making slavery and colonialism appear acceptable and inviting black people themselves to accept the hegemonic position.

Key term

racism: practices and behaviour involving social and economic discrimination, based on the false assumption that one particular ethnic group or race is culturally and biologically inferior to another. Racist behaviour is based on centuries of economic exploitation and has been deeply embedded in European culture. Concerns have been expressed about the role played by the media in sustaining and reinforcing race stereotypes.

In 1971, Hall criticised British television's negative representation of black people. He analysed programming in terms of positive and negative representation:

- **Positive representation** — when a group is repeatedly represented in a positive light and in ways that enhance the group's self-esteem, social position and value, and furthers their interests.
- **Negative representation** — when a group is repeatedly represented using negative stereotypes and negative or damaging aspects of their behaviour and social status. Negative representation can lead to scapegoating, discrimination and exclusion, and has negative social and economic consequences for the groups concerned.

The most serious example of the consequences of negative representation and stereotyping is provided by the Nazis' treatment of the Jews in the 1930s and 1940s. **Racist** propaganda encouraged the worst kind of prejudice and the resultant persecution culminated in the Holocaust. This took place against a background of general indifference from the rest of the population, who were persuaded by Nazi propaganda that the Jews were unwelcome, undesirable aliens.

Ideas for discussion and development

Blue eyes and brown eyes

A US teacher Jane Elliot devised a game in 1968 to demonstrate the effects of stereotyping and labelling. She divided her class into two groups: the blue eyes and the brown eyes. The brown eyes were given special privileges and were expected to perform well. They were not allowed to mix with the blue eyes, who were looked down upon and treated as failures. She was shocked to find how quickly the students adopted their roles, with the blue eyes behaving like failures and the brown eyes treating them badly and actually performing better because they were expected to.

- **Have you ever thought how photographs of suspected criminals, chosen and published by the press, always seem to make the individual look menacing or threatening? Why is it that once someone has been accused of being a criminal, he or she suddenly looks like one?**

Current issues involving representation of ethnic groups

Immigrants: convenient scapegoats for social ills?

Recent news stories concerning the number of asylum seekers and illegal immigrants entering the UK have led to concerns about negative representations of this minority group.

Asylum seekers are those who seek refuge (asylum) or a place of safety from oppressive political conditions in their own countries, where their lives may be at risk. The UK has a long tradition of welcoming those suffering from such oppression, including Jews in the 1930s escaping from Nazi persecution in Germany. However, the large numbers of people claiming this status, and concerns about the legitimacy of their claims, have led the tabloid press and the media in general to coin phrases such as 'bogus asylum seeker', which effectively neutralises the sympathy attached to the original term. High-profile cases of asylum seekers committing crimes and even being associated with terrorist activities have further reduced public sympathy for claimants.

The term 'economic migrant' has also been developed to describe those who travel to the UK in search of work, either legitimately (in the case of EU nationals, such as Poles) or illegitimately (in the case of, for example, Africans seeking to enter the EU illegally via boats setting out from the north African coast).

Public opinion seems increasingly hostile to large-scale clandestine and even legal immigration, regardless of migrants' race or origin. The public's views are further manipulated by tabloid headlines, which frequently cite abuses of the system and evidence of official incompetence in managing the situation. In particular, cases where social housing has allegedly been allocated to new immigrants ahead of existing residents have stirred up strong reactions. This, and the continual use of emotive terminology by the press and others engaged in the debate, means that the genuine hardship of many would-be immigrants and the important economic contribution made by many legitimate migrant workers is easily overlooked. It could be argued that this has become a case of 'moral panic' (see pages 63–65).

Muslims: Islamophobia or legitimate fears?

Increasing evidence of clashes between Islamic and Western values in the media have made reporting of Islamic affairs in the West a sensitive area.

Salman Rushdie

Salman Rushdie, a British citizen of Muslim Indian origin, was condemned by Muslim clerics for his novel, *The Satanic Verses* (1988), which satirises aspects of Islam. A *fatwa* (order of death) was levelled upon him in 1989 by the then spiritual leader of Iran, the Ayatollah Khomeini, and Rushdie was forced into hiding under the protection of the British secret service for many years. His knighthood in 2007 revived Islamist calls for his death — including a call from the Pakistani minister for religious affairs that Muslims would be justified in taking violent action.

Once again, issues relating to freedom of expression and the use of death threats by Muslim extremists to coerce Western governments and media became a top story. Very few Muslims will have read Rushdie's original offending book, as devout Muslims are not allowed to read it and would rely on information passed on from spiritual leaders.

Bad news is good news

Increasing concerns about terrorism have resulted in widespread coverage of the activities of minority Muslim extremist groups, e.g. holding demonstrations attacking the British way of life. Small vociferous groups can easily dominate news coverage by the sensational nature of their behaviour. This ensures maximum coverage and then metonymically comes to be seen as representative of the whole Muslim community.

Positive behaviour, such as abiding by the law and working quietly at a career and home life, does not attract media coverage. It is therefore in the nature of news that only negative representations are shown. This provides a serious problem for community workers seeking to improve the positive representations of the Muslim community. Pressure groups such as the Muslim Council of Britain, which claims to represent Muslim interests but which has no democratic legitimacy in the Muslim community, can often exacerbate the situation by expressing strong controversial opinions and making claims about irrational Islamophobia in UK society.

Community relations are sensitive in this area, even after years of attempting multicultural solutions to race relations, and there are calls to develop more integrationist and anti-extremist responses from within the Muslim community to counter the growing perception of an extremist threat within the UK.

(See also the 'Ideas for discussion and development' box on page 11, which deals with the protests surrounding publication of cartoon images depicting the Prophet Mohammed.)

> ## Task
>
> Examine a range of national daily newspapers, looking for stories involving the police, race and community relations. How balanced are the stories in reporting controversial issues?

Case study

Police, race, community relations and the media

Undercover Mosque was a Channel 4 documentary produced for *Dispatches* by independent producer Hardcash and broadcast on 15 January 2007. It reported on the extremist views being expressed at the Green Lane Mosque in Birmingham and at other mosques in the UK. Muslim clerics were shown making defamatory and threatening statements about women, homosexuals and non-Muslims in general.

The Crown Prosecution Service (CPS) and the West Midlands Police (WMP) investigated the documentary to see if there were grounds to prosecute the Muslim clerics concerned. They decided that there were not. However, in August 2007, the WMP decided to investigate the programme itself under the Public Order Act 1986, and chose to refer the contents to the CPS, which said there was insufficient evidence to bring charges against the programme. WMP themselves then referred the documentary to Ofcom, the television watchdog, on the grounds that the footage used had been edited in such a way as to represent the clerics 'out of context' and therefore encouraged 'race hatred' against Muslims.

The referral caused some surprise because the WMP were originally investigating extremist views as expressed in the documentary to see if any prosecution could be made against the clerics responsible, and they now seemed to be taking on the role of television critics, involving themselves in criticism of the broadcaster rather than the disturbing contents of the broadcast. Critics suggested that this was another example of politically correct policing, avoiding a sensitive issue in the interest of community relations — the West Midlands has a large Muslim population.

Channel 4 vigorously defended the accuracy of the programme and asked for the police to provide evidence of any lack of context in the quotations used. This was not forthcoming, and Ofcom dismissed the police complaint in November 2007.

The case highlights the sensitive and difficult balance involved in guaranteeing free speech, respecting the rights of minority groups and maintaining good community relations, while also allowing legitimate investigation and exposure of those spreading dangerous and antisocial opinions.

(For further information on the representation of the police force in the media, see pages 14–15.)

Representations of young people

Origins of youth culture

Teenagers as a social group were first defined in the early 1950s, when marketing agencies and record companies identified a target group for their products. The growth of a youth culture based on music and recreation became part of the growing affluence found in the USA and Europe in the 1950s. Teenagers had money to spend on records and clothes, and so became appealing to advertisers.

Media attention on teenage behaviour became an early moral panic. Rock and roll music was seen as encouraging sexual promiscuity and therefore threatening mainstream society. Protecting and controlling the young has always been an obsession of adult society, and the media found easy targets and plenty of material for sensational journalism concerning the growth of the 'sex, drugs and rock and roll' culture and the many stars and celebrities it produced.

Moral panic representations tend to focus on conflict and fighting between different youth groups (e.g. mods and rockers in the 1960s, skinheads against ethnic minorities in the 1970s and 1980s), degenerate behaviour, antisocial practices such drug taking and sexual promiscuity, and even fashion. Hippies, punks, goths and New Romantics have all been called degenerate and criticised by the media in this way. In this kind of representation, the young are seen as illustrating the moral decline of society as a whole.

Case study

'Minister labelled racist after attack on rap "idiots"' (*Guardian* headline, 6 January 2003)

Government minister Kim Howells blamed the killing of two black Birmingham teenagers in crossfire between rival gangs in Birmingham on rap music.

'For years I have been very worried about the hateful lyrics that these boasting, macho idiot rappers come out with… It's a big cultural problem. Lyrics don't kill people but they don't half enhance the fare we get from videos and films. It has created a culture where killing is almost a fashion accessory… Idiots like the So Solid Crew are glorifying gun culture and violence.'

Critics of Howells answered that gun culture was a function of urban deprivation and that music reflects the experience of young people and doesn't create it. He was accused of racism for identifying what at the time (2003) was seen as a specifically black problem. More recent cases of teenage gun crime and knife crime provide clear evidence that the problems are no longer restricted to the black community.

Ideas for discussion and development

- **Should music lyrics that seem to encourage violence and negative attitudes towards women be banned, or are the concerns expressed just another moral panic?**

Contemporary youth culture

How can modern youth culture be summed up? Bearing in mind the impossibility of describing youth culture to the young, and in particular the clued-up readers of this textbook, here is an attempt to assess the current scene:

- Emos dye their hair black or dark brown with red coloured streaks. The Emo 'sweep', usually seen in males, is where the fringe is swept to one side. 'Emo' is short for 'emotions', which are willingly displayed, particularly at rock concerts when listening to Criminal Damage or Panic At The Disco. They usually wear baseball boots, and have their jeans at hip height or lower.
- Grebos and moshers (depending on where you live) are nu-metal fans who follow bands like Slipknot and Linkin Park, and watch MTV2 and Kerrang! channels. They wear band-named T-shirts with hoodies and baggy jeans, and skating trainers as footwear. Long and greasy hair is common for both lads and girls.
- Chavs are working-class. They listen to rap music and use racist and slang language, are anti-culture, wear sports clothes with caps sideways — often, of course, with Burberry check. They hang out in large groups and follow fashion.

These are broad generalisations that will no doubt offend many readers, as youth culture is constantly changing. What the variety indicates is a search for genuine identity through the sharing of cultural values and tastes with others in the face of the imposed conformity of mainstream media culture. Bricolage in the creation of youth culture style is alive and well.

Ideas for discussion and development

- **How far would you agree with the above descriptions of youth groups? What are the characteristics of other groups not mentioned?**

Some critics would argue that because all youth cultures are constructed around patterns of consumption, including music, its proponents are in fact just manufactured and manipulated audiences and, like any other media audience, delivered to advertisers. However, media representations of contemporary youth cultures are usually content with broad generalisation and stereotyping rather than acknowledging the subtle differences between groups. It is a feature of group identity that recognition of subtle signs of similarity and difference creates a restricted code where only those closely engaged can recognise the meanings.

Television stereotypes

Television stereotypes of the teenager have included figures like 'Kevin the Teenager', played by Harry Enfield in *Harry Enfield and Chums* (BBC, 1990–97) and reprised in a 2000 film, and Vicky Pollard, played by Matt Lucas in *Little Britain* (BBC, 2003–06). Members of youth culture groups would probably see both of these examples as hopelessly stereotyped and inaccurate, but this does not matter, as the audience for both is essentially not teenagers.

Youth soap: *Hollyoaks*

Hollyoaks is a Channel 4 soap opera based largely on the lives of young people and students living in the Chester area. Always stylish and with high production values, the soap has recently become more violent and edgy in subject matter and treatment, but is still mainly concerned with boy–girl relationships. The soap has been used to air controversial issues of public interest over the last few years, including:

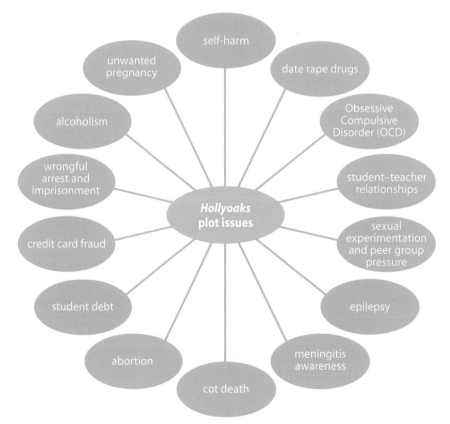

Some of the reasons for *Hollyoaks'* success might be the following:

- It has a cast of glamorous young people — including 'babes', who attract a male audience and thus generate spin-off coverage in lads' magazines, and who produce workout videos for the female audience.
- The transience of university life — this forms the background of many of the characters, allowing for a steady introduction and removal of characters before they go stale.
- It has a good mixture of age ranges in its characters.
- It has developed high production values, with film treatment software giving a glossy and polished feel to the production. It has a high standard of camera work and editing.
- It balances light-hearted, comic plot elements with serious and controversial issues. Plot lines are relevant, somewhat edgy and usually well developed.
- The treatment fits perfectly with teen lifestyle magazines and mainstream youth culture.
- Acting standards are generally high.
- The early evening prime-time slot catches the audience before it goes out.
- It attracts advertising, as it is an excellent way to reach a teenage target audience.

Classic film representations of youth and youth culture

- *The Wild One* (Lázló Benedek, 1953) — Marlon Brando's classic outlaw biker film was blamed for the destruction of cinemas and teenage violence. It was frequently banned in its day.
- *Rebel without a Cause* (Nicholas Ray, 1955) — James Dean's famous film about a rebellious teenager. This film, together with *East of Eden* (Elia Kazan, 1956) and his early death in a road crash, led to Dean becoming a mythic figure for youth.
- *Easy Rider* (Dennis Hopper, 1969) — featured the strapline 'A man went looking for America and couldn't find it anywhere…', probably because most of this classic hippy road movie is seen through a cannabis-induced fog.
- *A Clockwork Orange* (Stanley Kubrick, 1971) — a futuristic urban dystopia featuring violence, violent sex and cult gangs dominating the streets. It was withdrawn in the UK by Kubrick himself, who was shocked by so-called 'copycat violence' involving scenes from the film.

- *Tommy* (Ken Russell, 1975) — a musical film based on The Who's 1969 concept album *Tommy*, about a boy who becomes a pinball wizard.
- *Romper Stomper* (Geoffrey Wright, 1992) — a classic skinhead film.
- *Donnie Darko* (Richard Kelly, 2001) — a strange and moody film, principally about the alienation of youth in a world of moral contradictions.
- *Sweet Sixteen* (Ken Loach, 2002) — the title of this film is ironic, as it follows the tragic life of a Scottish boy who, in spite his best efforts to improve his life, is drawn into crime and ultimately murder just as he reaches the age of 16.
- *This is England* (Shane Meadows, 2006) — a representation of 1980s skinhead gang culture. Set in 1983 in a world of New Romantics, mods and skinheads, the film centres on 12-year-old Shaun (based on the director himself). It deals with masculinity, race and violence, with a background of working-class life, mass unemployment and xenophobia.

Representations of gender/ sexuality

Gay culture

Homosexuality was illegal in Britain until 1967 and consequently was represented as part of a hidden, twilight world of crime, blackmail and corruption, e.g. in Joseph Losey's *The Servant* (1963).

The representation of gay men and lesbians has changed dramatically over the last 30 years, from the camp and stereotypical character of Mr Humphries, played by John Inman in *Are You Being Served?* (BBC, 1972–85) to *Queer as Folk* (Channel 4, 1999–2000). The latter was a ground-breaking series that focused on the lives of young gay men in Manchester, and was criticised for openly representing promiscuous gay relationships. *Tipping the Velvet* (BBC, 2002) was based on lesbian life in England in the 1890s.

Ideas for discussion and development

- Can you find examples of gay representations that do not rely on some elements of the old stereotypes?

It is now possible to laugh at gay characters without being accused of homophobia. For example, the 'only gay in the village' character Daffyd, played by Matt Lucas in *Little Britain* (BBC), shows how far representation of gay people has come, although in this case the distinguishing uniqueness of the character is more important than the stereotypical representations of his sexuality.

Women

The changing status and role of women is one of the most striking aspects of social change in the last 40 years. Women, as half the population, hardly rank as just a social group, but the massive shift of power and the transformation of gender relations make the representation of women a key area of concern to students of the media.

Feminists would see any media representation of women which confirmed a stereotype as **sexist**, in particular the display of women's bodies as sex objects — for example in lads' magazines — for the entertainment of men.

Key term

sexism: representations that discriminate on the basis of sex, especially against women, which is seen to derive from and sustain patriarchy (a male-dominated society). In general terms, feminists have argued that representations of women that present them as objects of sexual desire for the entertainment of men are sexist. Women are defined in terms of the sexual desirability of their bodies to men, rather than as individuals (see Mulvey's theory of 'male gaze' in on page 101).

Sexism in advertising

Television advertisements from the 1950s and 1960s are a useful reference point to establish just how women were perceived. Women are shown as supporting dominant males, looking attractive to keep their attention, looking after the house and cooking exciting meals:

- **Washing up and washing powder.** In the classic series of Persil washing-powder advertisements, the conscientious and house-proud mother compares her glowing white washing with her jealous neighbour's grey-white washing. The male voice-over confirms the choice: 'Persil washes whiter — and it shows.'
- **Floor cleaners.** The user of the product (the clever woman) demonstrates to her neighbour (the stupid woman) the benefits of using 'Flash' floor cleaner. The male voice-over confirms the choice.
- **Margarine.** Women in the street are asked by a suited male to compare Stork margarine with butter. They cannot tell the difference. The male voice-over confirms the excellence of the product (or the stupidity of the women).
- **Persuading husband to buy car/washing machine.** A 1950s newspaper advertisement shows a woman leaning on the arm of a seated man (who is smoking a pipe and reading a paper), having persuaded him to buy her a washing machine.
- **Oxo stock cubes.** Katie, the housewife star of Oxo gravy advertisements, thinks up enticing ways to please the men in her family (husband and

son) by using Oxo cubes in the dinner. Slogan: Oxo 'gives a meal man appeal'.

In most adverts of these decades, the male voice-over provided the 'expert' view. Women were shown as being concerned solely with washing, cleaning, cooking and pleasing the men in their lives.

Scene from an Oxo commercial featuring the 'Oxo family', 1983

Advertisements in the 1960s and 1970s for alcohol and tobacco often featured women as sex objects, for example:

- **Manikin cigar advertisement.** The central image shows a woman emerging from the sea in a revealing wet T-shirt. A very small inset photograph shows a Manikin cigar packet. The caption reads: 'Sheer enjoyment'.
- **Bacardi rum advertisement.** The photograph shows the lower half of a woman's body dressed in shorts. The woman is holding a glass of Bacardi. The caption reads: 'Get into Bacardi shorts'.
- **Smirnoff vodka advertisement.** The central image shows a young, apparently innocent woman in her late teens or early twenties, partly dressed, looking at herself in her bedroom mirror and obviously getting ready to go out. The caption reads: 'I wonder if I dare discover Smirnov? Smirnov — the effect is shattering.'

These advertisements would no longer be permitted under the current regulations for alcohol advertising and the total ban on tobacco advertising.

Feminism

The feminist movement emerged from the liberation culture of the 1960s, although arguments for women's rights had been put forward centuries earlier. Feminism has provided an important perspective for the critique of media products, especially from the standpoint of representation, and has sought to challenge dominant ideologies that reinforce patriarchal values. **Feminism** is explored in greater depth on pages 217–24.

> **Key term**
>
> **feminism:** political movement to advance the status of women by challenging values, social constructions and socioeconomic practices that disadvantage women and favour men

Contemporary representations of women in film and television

The following are some more recent representations of women that show them as being equal to men:

- science-fiction hero — Ellen Ripley, played by Sigourny Weaver in *Alien* (Ridley Scott, 1979), *Aliens* (Ridley Scott, 1986), *Alien Resurrection* (Jean-Pierre Jeunet, 1997)
- police superintendent — Jane Tennison, played by Helen Mirren in *Prime Suspect* (Granada Television, 1991–2006)
- police commander — Claire Blake, played by Amanda Burton in *The Commander* (ITV, 2003–07)
- superhero — Lara Croft, played by Angelina Jolie in *Lara Croft: Tomb Raider* (Simon West, 2001)
- action hero — Trinity, played by Carrie-Anne Moss in *The Matrix* series (Wachowski Brothers, 1999–2003)
- warrior — Guinevere, played by Keira Knightley in *King Arthur* (Antoine Fuqua, 2004)
- avenger — The Bride, played by Uma Thurman in *Kill Bill: Vols 1 and 2* (Quentin Tarantino, 2003/2004)

Representing celebrity culture

A **celebrity** is any individual who has become the focus of media attention and is therefore widely known and recognised by the public.

Tabloid newspapers exploit celebrity recognition and popularity to increase sales. Coverage tends to focus on the ups and downs of relationships, broken marriages, affairs, and scandals involving drink, drugs and violent or disorderly behaviour. Celebrities are therefore represented as either objects of admiration or of condemnation (often in rapid succession), depending on the aspect of their lives attracting media attention. This narrativisation of celebrities' lives emphasises a 'rise and fall' morality, whereby individuals are elevated by the media and public interest, receive all the benefits of a luxury lifestyle and are then brought down by their own behaviour. It acts as a form of moral retribution and *schadenfreude* (a German word meaning to take pleasure in the misfortune of others).

Key term

publicist: an individual who manages the profile and public relations of an individual in the public eye. A publicist usually operates by manipulating press stories to create a more positive image and by suppressing negative storylines. The high-profile publicist Max Clifford is quoted as saying: 'The biggest part of my job is stopping stories'.

Celebrities often welcome publicity if it raises their profile and improves their career prospects. However, such publicity is resented when it draws attention to their excesses, marital disputes and failures. Celebrities often use **publicists** to manage the relationship with the media to their advantage.

For the audience, celebrities represent idealised individuals. They are often wealthy, with all the freedom of life choices that wealth brings. People who are obsessed with celebrities often see them as role models with whom they can identify. The intrusive nature of media attention can make people feel that celebrities are personally known to them, and this creates a false sense of intimacy. People can also enjoy seeing celebrities brought down to earth as a form of moral retribution for their failures and excesses.

Jade Goody

Jade Goody was transformed from non-entity to 'celebrity' following a notorious appearance on *Big Brother* in 2002, where her rudeness to other contestants and ignorance of basic general knowledge (she thought Cambridge was a part of London and Saddam Hussein was a boxer) made her a talking point in the tabloid press. Despite being called 'Miss Piggy' by the *Sun* newspaper, she managed to take advantage of the limelight she received on the show, with advertising and business contracts, a fitness programme, and other lucrative deals with magazines.

Goody appeared on *Celebrity Driving School* and *Celebrity Weakest Link*. She also developed her own perfume, and in 2005 opened a beauty salon called *Uglys* in Hertford, which later closed. In 2006, when Goody was just 25 years old, HarperCollins published her autobiography, *Jade: My Autobiography*. The book was 'ghost written' by *Heat* features editor, Lucie Cave.

In 2007 Goody was invited back on *Celebrity Big Brother* and achieved further notoriety after being accused of racism towards fellow housemate Shilpa Shetty. She was evicted from the show in the midst of a highly publicised row, which drew comments even from the prime minister.

Goody has no particular talents or skills. She is a creation of *Big Brother* and the media coverage she has received, and has subsequently turned into a rich, notorious celebrity. She is a classic example of how modern media and marketing industries can manufacture and exploit the concept of celebrity and apply it to anyone simply because of the publicity they provide. The quantity of coverage dedicated to Goody is also a reminder of the task facing media reporters, columnists and producers — which is to fill an ever-increasing amount of space in their programme schedules and print columns.

Kate Moss

Tabloid newspaper headlines in March 2006 drew attention to statistics indicating a dramatic increase in cocaine use among schoolchildren. A photograph of model Kate Moss was used to illustrate the front-page article, as she had been previously identified as a cocaine user and therefore a negative role model for the young. The implication of the association is that Moss, increasingly criticised by the tabloids, is partly responsible for making cocaine use seem more acceptable to the young.

However, notoriety can be an attractive commodity for celebrities. In 2005, Moss was photographed taking cocaine and associating with partner and 'rock and roll bad boy' Pete Doherty, and these photographs appeared in tabloid newspapers. After universal condemnation, she was interviewed by the police and forced to make a public apology. For a short period her contracts with some major perfume and couture producers were suspended. However, within 2 months she was back on the cover of *Vogue* magazine. Moss is currently the highest paid model in the world and has doubled her earnings to £9 million a year. She signed a new contract with Calvin Klein worth £500,000 in 2006.

Ideas for discussion and development

Fame and the tabloid press

'They are either at your feet or at your throat — never in between.'

· **Discuss this view.**

Representations of the regions of Britain

British regions, particularly the north of England and Scotland, have traditionally suffered from negative stereotyping when compared to London and the southeast of England. This 'north–south divide' has its origins in the industrial past, as the north was the centre of the heavy industries of coal mining, shipbuilding and steel and textile manufacturing. The Birmingham Black Country was the so-called 'workshop of the nation', with its wide range of manufacturing industries including, in the mid-twentieth century, the car industry. These were working-class areas, with large industrial cities dominated by smoking chimneys and the back-to-back houses of the industrial workforce. There were, of course, vast areas of countryside in these areas, with agricultural land, country estates and elegant houses, but the essential image was that of heavy industry and its associated labour force.

London, the centre of the crown, government, the financial markets and the cosmopolitan playground of the rich and middle class, was surrounded by wealthy suburbs and looked towards continental Europe.

Today, there is still a significant divide between London and the rest of the UK, reflected in income levels, house prices, work opportunities and entertainment options. London has become a multicultural world city, welcoming tourists and immigrant workers from all over the world.

The northwest of England

Coronation Street (Granada/ITV, 1960–)

Coronation Street was seen as a breakthrough in television soap drama when it first appeared. Its realism and regional accents made it comparable to the British 'new wave' cinema of the time, such as *Saturday Night and Sunday Morning* (Karel Reisz, 1960), with its hard-edged portrayal of working-class life in Nottingham.

Set originally in the working-class area of 'Weatherfield', based on Salford in Manchester, it is now ITV's longest running soap opera. *Coronation Street* has become a national institution and now inhabits a world of its own that increasingly seems out of touch with the reality of life in cosmopolitan, contemporary Manchester. The street itself, a set in the central Manchester

studio, looks dated in a city dominated by a dramatic new skyline of shops, offices and loft apartments.

Shameless (Channel 4, 2004–)

Shameless fictionalises modern Manchester as it would prefer not to be represented. Unemployed drunks and dysfunctional families live in no-go areas on a sink estate — all producing a negative comic stereotype of northern underclass life.

Emmerdale (ITV, 1972–)

Emmerdale is set in a west Yorkshire village and much of its action revolves around The Woolpack pub (see page 42 for more on pubs in soap operas). The area has seen more than its share of disasters — with barn fires, gas explosions, burning churches, devastating storms, plane and car crashes, blown-up buildings and even murder accounting for the demise of many of the characters. It is certainly not a lucky village, but the drama involved means that ratings remain high, with up to 8 million viewers tuning in to an episode where a truck crashed into a lake.

Ideas for discussion and development

The phrase 'it's grim up north' used to represent the southern view of the north of England as a decaying, industrial wasteland.

- **Do current representations of the north still confirm this stereotypical view?**

Scotland

Scotland has suffered from a so-called 'tartan' representation for many decades. This emphasises the Highland culture of traditional dress (involving kilt and sporran), bagpipes, stag hunting, lochs, glens, trout streams, large estates and gothic castles. The reality is that most Scots live in the lowlands, not the under-populated Highlands, and their urban existence has been characterised by high levels of unemployment and deindustrialisation since the closure of steel, coal and shipbuilding industries in the last quarter of the twentieth century. In recent years, increased political independence (with the formation of the Scottish Parliament) and a greater sense of national identity have helped the move away from traditional stereotypes.

Monarch of the Glen (BBC, 2000–05)

Set in the fictional Glenbogle estate in the Highlands and based loosely on the writings of Compton Mackenzie, the series reinforced stereotypes about Scottish rural life. It centred on the characters of a feudal (English) landlord and his (Scottish) tenants.

Trainspotting (Danny Boyle, 1996)

In this classic film, a group of young Scottish men take heroin to avoid the realities of unemployment and Scottish life in general. The film involves some negative stereotypes of Scots as lazy, dysfunctional or violent. The film ends with a note of hope as the leading character, played by Ewan McGregor, accepts the need to join the rat race and get a proper job. The film was praised and criticised in equal measure for its open portrayal of drug taking.

Rab C. Nesbitt (BBC, 1988–99)

Created by Ian Pattison and starring Gregor Fisher, this sitcom centred on an unemployed, drunk, overweight Glaswegian who spent his time dressed in a pinstripe suit and string vest. The show featured all the negative stereotypes about Glaswegians but also dealt with some darker themes, almost always in a blackly comedic way.

Braveheart (Mel Gibson, 1995)

This film is Mel Gibson's rousing story of medieval Scottish cultural and physical resistance to the invading English (even to the extent of subverting the English crown when Gibson's William Wallace fathers a child with the French-born English Queen, Isabelle). Under horrible torture before his execution, Wallace's last word yelled at the crowd watching his grisly end is 'Freedom' — a clarion call to nationalists delivered more in a Glaswegian than a Highland accent, but securing the film's status among patriotic Scots. In spite of its rewriting of history, the film actually confirms many negative stereotypes of quarrelling Scottish tribal leaders in kilts being outwitted by the all-powerful English and their own treachery — Wallace is in fact betrayed to the English by Scottish leader Robert the Bruce.

Rob Roy (Michael Caton-Jones, 1995)

In this film, Liam Neeson plays the kilted hero fighting oppressive landlords and the English during the Jacobite Scottish rebellion of 1715. Having suffered much personal abuse and even the rape of his wife,

Rob Roy ultimately triumphs over Tim Roth's evil English upstart, Archibald Cunningham, in the final duel scene. As with *Braveheart*, the underlying nationalist theme is the betrayal of the 'true' Highland spirit by traitor Scottish nobles in league with the hated English invaders.

(See also *Sweet Sixteen*, summarised on page 140.)

Case study

Scottish Tourist Board advertisements: Visit Scotland

This series of television advertisements provides an interesting insight into how Scotland is marketed to England and the rest of the world. They combine many of the traditional elements that are associated with Scotland, but also attempt to develop the clichés in a more contemporary context.

Winter advertisement

Description: A blonde woman is lying on a hillside covered in heather. There are lovely views of woods, mountains and a lake, with traditional, gently mournful Scottish pipe music playing.

Her voice speaks words that invoke the sense being represented: 'hear it' to the sound of water and reeds, then 'smell it', 'touch it', 'taste it' to the sight of fresh mussels, then 'see it', 'live it'.

The advert is sensual and gently erotic, focusing on the woman's sensual experiences. It ends with a meal in an exotic restaurant and a romantic encounter seen through the woman's eyes.

The final caption is: 'Live it. Visit Scotland'.

Scotland

Description: A traditionally dressed piper and pipe band are shown playing *Scotland the Brave*. There are helicopter shots of a loch and sunset. Two words are superimposed on the images: 'music', 'relaxation'. The final caption again is 'Visit Scotland'.

Scenes from the 'Visit Scotland' campaign

Task

1 Which of these two ways of representing Scotland seems to you to be the most effective in encouraging tourists, and why?

2 As part of your Unit 2 production work, you have been asked to create a television advertisement encouraging people to live and work in Scotland. Briefly describe the theme, content and sequence of your advertisement (as a storyboard if you wish) and provide a final caption.

The south of England

Americans looking for representations of 'merrie England' are comforted by such films as *Four Weddings and Funeral* (Richard Curtis, 1994) and the endless cycle of 'whodunnit' crime series set in a thatched-cottage England that never existed. Usual features of this stereotypical landscape include beautiful old churches, the village post office and the pub. Stock characters include publicans, gardeners, spinsters, doctors, vicars and rich families with guilty secrets.

Midsomer Murders (ITV, 1997–)

This series is set in the imaginary county of Midsomer, where a considerable number of murders take place. Everybody in the series lives in beautiful thatched cottages, idyllic farm houses or stunning country mansions. The series is supposedly contemporary but relies heavily on escapist rural nostalgia, reinforcing all the stereotypes of British rural life from 50 years ago.

Miss Marple (BBC, 1984–92 and ITV, 2004–)

These series feature Agatha Christie's busybody and attentive heroine, who continues to outwit the professionals in the nostalgic settings of an English country scene that no longer exists.

London

EastEnders (BBC, 1985–)

This soap opera shows the East End of London as it never was. Barbara Windsor, popular star of the *Carry On* films of the 1960s and 1970s, currently resides as the idealised landlady of The Queen Vic pub, with 'wide boys', barrow boys and wheeler-dealers confirming many traditional stereotypes of London working-class life.

Ideas for discussion and development

* **Why do so many representations of the south of England focus on nostalgia?**

A combination of sexual antics, unfaithfulness, unwanted pregnancies and disputes between neighbours keeps the show's plots going round, but a trip to the East End of London will confirm that *EastEnders* has a totally inadequate representation of the ethnic groups which now form a large percentage of the area's population.

Representations of sport

Sports coverage is one of the most important areas of media representation. More people watch sport on television than play it, and its packaging for television consumption has involved transforming the way the contests are perceived.

Sport on television

Televised sport involves the narrativisation of a contest; it is turned into a story with a beginning, a middle and an end. There are heroes and villains, disappointments and triumphs, winners and losers, victory and defeat. Contests are seen as battles between individuals already well known to audiences, who are encouraged to share their emotions and identify with them at a personal level. Celebrity culture means that there is often more than just the game at stake. The reputations of the celebrities are often on the line, as audiences follow their every action and reaction, constantly assessing and criticising their performances.

The need to generate excitement and a sense of drama involves a long run-up period to any particular contest or match and an emphasis on the individual personalities involved. It is important that audiences be taken into the heart of a contest, and pre-match discussions with coaches, players and experts are part of the process that raises tensions and expectations. Teams are portrayed as favourites or underdogs, players are heroes or villains, and their private hopes and fears are paraded for all to see.

Camera positioning in matches often gives a far better view of the whole game than any live spectator has, and close-ups take the viewer right into the centre of the action. Controversy and conflict are an important part of the dramatic narrative constructed around a game, as are the expectations and failings of individual team members. Action replay allows controversial decisions or actions to be immediately reviewed and debated. Exaggerated language from excited commentators is designed to raise the temperature of the game, and controversial referee decisions and foul play add to the drama.

The after-match post-mortem — how the victors won and what went wrong for the losers — is an important part of the ritual. Interviews with the losers straight after the game are designed to catch and exploit the immediate emotional trauma of defeat, while the triumph of the victors is their reward. Audiences can identify with the often hyped emotions of the individuals concerned and share the experience as it happens. At a strategic level, experts discuss tactics and failings like historians discussing a battle, offering judgements and opinions on what went right or wrong. The press has its day in the post-match analysis and written post-mortems.

Regardless of the sport involved, transforming this process into a media experience is similar in all cases. All sport has sponsors and advertisers, who are reflected in the teams' strips or team colours in the same way that medieval soldiers wore their lord's coat of arms and colours. Advertising and sponsorship embed sporting events in the daily lives of ordinary people, with the products and services they use firmly identified with the sport and players.

Fortunately for sponsors, defeat does not appear to reflect badly on their product, although they generally do not continue to back teams/players that always lose. The more successful a team, the more media exposure it will receive and therefore the more exposure the product advertised will receive — so it pays to sponsor winning teams.

Media representation has changed the experience of watching sport, as anyone who attends a local football match between school teams will realise. Watching the real thing is arguably not as exciting as viewing the reported, represented event on television.

Cross-media sport

Sport, as a modern media genre, makes an ideal model for cross-media study. Media sports coverage, from broadcasting, the press, and increasingly the internet and mobile downloads, has significant popular appeal for institutions, advertisers and audiences alike. This section attempts to cover sport as a generic form, but it is inevitable that football — as the ubiquitous media sport in the UK — will occupy the default position.

There are endless games, pastimes and activities that come under the broad banner of sport. Only a few, however, are given any significant media coverage. For example, football — in its professional men's variant — commands cross-media representation on a daily basis. Croquet, on the other hand, does not. When looking at the cross-media relationship between sport and the media we need to concentrate on the following ideas:
- the 'type' of sports given major media coverage and the nature of that coverage
- the triangular relationship between sport, media and advertising/sponsorship

- the social and cultural role of (media) sports
- changing patterns of production and consumption

Media institutions and sports coverage

Media coverage of sport on television and radio, in the press and in new media technologies represents a significant area of media production and consumption. As discussed earlier, modern mass media institutions are defined by the market logic of competition and profit, underpinned ultimately by audience ratings. The competition to secure sports audiences is one of the fiercest media battlegrounds.

Sports that are given regular media coverage are, on the whole, 'masculine': team sports like football, rugby or cricket, or pub/club pastimes like darts or snooker. The key audience group for these sports is males aged 16–30, for whom other media forms — like reading a newspaper or watching a soap opera — do not traditionally appeal. In terms of audience appeal, sport represents a viable way of delivering this otherwise uninterested audience group to the paper/screen — and thus the advertisers.

As Gary Whannel shows (1992), British media institutions have always regarded sport as a genre — particularly in broadcasting and the press. Here are some of the generic conventions of media sport:

- Newspapers are organised in reverse order — back-page sports news is the top story of football, rugby or cricket, with lesser stories/sports working their way towards the centre of the paper. For many newspaper readers, the back page acts as an alternative to the front page, with the same conventions of lead story, picture values and headlines.

- All radio and television news programmes have a sports bulletin towards the end of the programme, with emphasis given to major sports (football, rugby and cricket) and to national/larger clubs. Regional news programmes provide the same service for local teams.

- Major sporting events are given a lot of pre-match 'hype' and are deemed important enough to change the normal broadcasting schedules.

- Multiple camera positions, including overhead and pitch-side **steadycam**, create an action/movement point of view.

> ## Key term
>
> **steadycam:** a portable camera strapped to a cameraman with a harness to produce a smooth floating image of the subject.
>
> Steadycams provide an alternative to the hand-held camera's crude wobbling effect and can make the viewer feel that he or she is floating through the action and around the characters. Steadycams are often used for point-of-view shots and are also used extensively in sports coverage.

- Major incidents (goals/tries etc.) and controversial issues (offsides, sendings off and penalties) are always subject to 'action' replays.
- Television and radio coverage of games operates a 'buddy system'. Studio half-time/full-time analysis consists of a host and two or three ex-professional pundits, such as the dour Alan Hansen and the more gregarious Ian Wright. They are often chosen to create 'blokeish' banter.
- Post-match interviews feature star players and managers. On television these take place just inside the tunnel in front of the sponsors' board.
- Sport holds dedicated slots in the broadcasting schedules. For example, the BBC's *Match of the Day* is synonymous with late Saturday evenings, while terrestrial coverage of UEFA Champions League matches takes place during prime-time slots on Tuesday and Wednesday evenings.

All sports coverage has traditionally had a twin attraction for media institutions. First, as a live event that exists outside the media, it is cheap to record or report on. Second, its status in popular culture ensures that it will attract sizeable audiences.

Sport, media and advertising/sponsorship

In terms of contemporary media sports coverage, it is best to consider the audience as being the subject of a triangular relationship between sport, media and advertising/sponsorship. Media sports are highly popular in terms of audience figures and consequently are economically lucrative. Intense bidding wars are a regular feature whenever the FA Premiership tenders out the rights for live and highlighted football coverage. Satellite broadcaster Sky Sports, for example, recently paid £1.3 billion for a 3-year deal to show 92 live Premiership matches per season. Setanta, a rival institution, paid £392 million to show 46 matches per season. Sky Sports is widely held to have instigated the formation of the English Football Premiership in 1992 — encouraging the bigger teams to break away from the Football League and its more conservative policies on commercialisation.

Even the BBC, which under the terms of its public service broadcasting remit is supposed to be free from commercial interest or interference, is a site for branding and advertising. Team shirts are emblazoned with logos, and leagues and cups are sponsored by major brands (to which commentators inevitably allude). The BBC initially banned shirt advertising, which had begun in 1977, causing teams to have a television strip and a non-

television strip, but it backed down in 1983 and, in line with all other sporting and media institutions, has submitted to market forces.

The BBC's relationship with sport is crucial in terms of its public service broadcasting remit. The responsibility to reflect the cultural life of the UK is met in coverage of domestic fixtures and 'national' participation in international events (such as the Olympics and Commonwealth Games) and by focusing on events where there is a 'British' interest. Curling, for example, gained previously unheard of coverage when the British women's team won the gold medal at the 2002 Winter Olympics.

The commercialisation of sport has altered consumption in many different ways. There is far more choice for audiences in terms of availability — though perhaps not in terms of diversity. Channel 4, however, as part of its public service broadcasting agreement, provides coverage of 'extreme' sports such as surfing, skateboarding and BMX biking. Unsurprisingly, these are popular with the 16–25 age group that make up a large section of Channel 4's target audience. It is in this construction of audiences and audience positions that media sports are most interesting.

David Beckham and Juan Sebastián Verón at the launch of a new Pepsi advertment

Media coverage of sports has led to the creation of new audience groups. Football, for example, is traditionally the preserve of working-class male audiences. (It is one of the few rural pastimes that made the transformation into industrialised urban culture.) However, increased money from media coverage rights and commercial sponsorships have generated a higher level of sophistication and brought an element of glamour into the game. Increased media coverage, plus the introduction of expensive foreign players and huge increases in player wages, have helped to produce the concept of football stars and celebrities.

This 'civilising' process has extended football's reach to new consumer groups, including middle-class and female audiences. Again, wider audience shares equate to increased advertising and sponsorship revenue. The representation of football has gone far beyond events on the pitch. It now includes the type of sensational and exclusive representations that had previously been reserved for film and television stars.

Ideas for discussion and development

- **Why do media institutions invest so heavily in securing the rights to cover major sporting leagues and tournaments?**
- **Is extensive media commercial involvement good for the development of sport?**

Cultural issues in sports representation

Gender identities

Sports audiences are, as noted earlier, mostly male. It has been argued by many social commentators that spectator sports perform a social function by allowing men to act out or reproduce masculine notions of loyalty and courage, not on a real battlefield but within the more rationalised confines of a sports arena (and by extension, in media representations). In terms of media representation, sport is often located within discourses of masculinity and nationalism.

Feminist critics argue that media representation of masculine sports serves to reinforce and reproduce ideologies of patriarchal superiority. Coverage of women's sports seems to be representative of female sub-ordination, focusing on the sexualised/objectified or maternal aspects of femininity. Women's sports tend to include tennis, gymnastics and swimming and be undermined by the demeaning 'ladies' prefix.

Tennis, in particular, is arguably subject to sexist representation, whereby players can be referred to as 'babes' in the tabloid press and judged by their physical attributes rather than their sporting skills. While there was a great deal of press/broadcast coverage when the British women's curling team won the gold medal at the 2002 Winter Olympics, much of it was fore-grounded on the team's 'skipper', Rhona Martin, and the idea that she was a mother and an 'ordinary housewife'. Although the BBC covered many of the football matches in the 2007 Women's World Cup, they were relegated mainly to BBC 2 (or the digital channels) and were limited to games in which the England team was involved. Most of the coverage was dedicated to reminding us that we were watching women's football as opposed to 'proper' men's football.

Look out for the ways in which male sports are 'normalised'. A male football match, for example, is

Ideas for discussion and development

- **Is there still a tangible gender imbalance in media sports coverage?**
- **In what ways do media representations of male and female sports differ?**

never prefixed with 'male', but a system of 'otherness' is used for women's representation. In match/event commentary or reports, look at how often the players/athletes are referred to as women. Are male players/athletes subjected to the same referencing?

National identities

The historian Benedict Anderson (1983) makes a compelling case for seeing the media's role as central to the formation of modern 'national communities'. Modern nations are too vast for every citizen to know each other personally. Yet fundamental to the notion of national identity is a shared sense of interests, values and concerns. Media sports coverage is clearly an arena for 'national' interest and concern.

According to Neil Blane and Raymond Boyle (1998), media representations of sport are 'deeply incorporated into people's sense of who they are and what other people are like'. Blane and Boyle are referring to the ways in which media representations of sport employ stereotyping and binary oppositions as narrative strategies. Indeed, the coverage of a sports fixture is equally as reliant on narrative structures as a broadcast fiction or film text.

England football and rugby union internationals often invoke the historical and political struggles between the home nation and their opponents. For example, after England defeated France in the 2007 rugby World Cup semi-final, the *Daily Telegraph* ran the following 'intertextual' headline (15 October 2007):

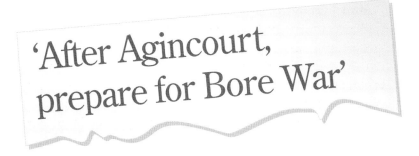

'After Agincourt, prepare for Bore War'

The headline evokes England's defeat of France at the Battle of Agincourt (1415), and the 'English' characteristics of strength, bravery and dogged tenacity that played a part at that battle, being reignited on the rugby pitch. Similar references are made to the Boer War with South Africa, albeit with the deliberate spelling error punning on England's lack of open play. Sport, then, is employed as a metaphor for the nation and its sense of identity and self-hood.

We can also see this narrative strategy being employed to represent the 'other' opposing nations. For example, the German national football team is routinely represented in the press in terms of its (military) machine-like organisation, energy and clinical strategy. Tabloid headlines often use the indexical semiotic signifiers of military strength and ruthlessness. For example, 'The German blitzkrieg trampled through Croatia and now their stormtroopers aim to blast Terry Venables' men out of the tournament' (*Daily Star* front page story, 24 June 1996). Football is used here to connote the historical antagonism between the English and German nations.

Examine the press or television build-up to an England football or rugby international. Look at how the language (linguistic and symbolic) of 'nation' and 'English-ness' are invoked and the way audiences are positioned within those 'nationalistic-patriotic' discourses.

The tabloid press — especially the *Sun* and the *Daily Mirror* — are arguably more extreme in their nationalistic rhetoric than most, but sport does make headline news across the media. For example, when England beat France in the aforementioned rugby match, it was the lead story on the BBC's late night television news bulletin — ahead of coverage of the political situation in Iraq.

Ideas for discussion and development

- **Is the media representation of sport still a key site for playing out ideas and images of national identity?**

Changing patterns of production and consumption

Developments in policy, technology and economics have resulted in significant changes in the ways in which media sports coverage is produced and consumed. It could, moreover, be argued that sport itself has been transformed, economically and culturally, and is now inseparable from the media. The following list of changes is neither comprehensive nor exhaustive, but it highlights the fact that sport is a prime site for observing the effects of cross-media production and consumption.

- The 1990 Broadcasting Act (see page 109) led to the formation of digital and cable subscription and pay-per-view channels, allowing for wider channel choice.

- Under the guidance of Sky Sports, the top-flight English football clubs broke away in 1992 to form their own league — the Premiership.
- Digital technologies have increased and transformed the consumption of media sports: news, information and features are available on terrestrial and digital television as well as online and as mobile phone downloads.
- The internet is a major site for audience consumption and interaction. All sports clubs have their own websites, as do supporters' groups. Blogging is a common practice for contemporary sports audiences.
- Social networking sites with video streaming facilities have led to more broadcast exposure for minority sports, as participants/fans post their own videos on the internet.
- Increased money from advertising, sponsorship and media revenues has led to increased player wages/expensive foreign imports, thus creating the culture of multi-millionaire footballers.
- The image of the sports star has entered the popular cultural phenomenon of 'celebrity'. Players are as much reported on for their off-pitch antics and lifestyles as for their particular sporting skills.
- Out of the celebrity status of sports stars has emerged the culture of WAGs — wives and girlfriends — who are given endless press/ broadcasting attention and are held up as style icons or as representatives of success. (See the *OK!* magazine cover, right, for an example of coverage of the Beckhams.)
- Sports stars are increasingly used in advertising to promote both sports and non-sports related brands. Advertisers feeding on/promoting the iconic status of sports stars like David Beckham or Cristiano Ronaldo create ideologies of success and style that consumers may aspire to.
- Sports stars and WAGs regularly feature on celebrity versions of reality shows, as guests on talk shows or, as in the case of former Arsenal player Ian Wright, as the host of his own radio and television chat shows *Friends Like These* (BBC 1) and *Wright and Bright* (BBC Radio Five Live).

- Speculation about the financial aspects of sport — sponsorship, transfer markets and club ownerships — makes headline news in both press and broadcast media.

It is important to remember that the media are not simply a means for reporting or broadcasting sporting events. The media have an institutional influence on modern sport, helping to redefine the ways in which sports are organised, structured and consumed. Modern sports simply do not exist outside the institutional power structures of the media.

Television, in particular, has dynamically changed many popular sports. The concept of one-day cricket was conceived purely for this medium. Likewise, the scheduling of many international sports fixtures, such as football or rugby world cups, are not arranged for the benefit of players or local supporters but to fit in with the needs of media producers and consumers. A *Guardian* newspaper headline posed the question 'Is too much football on TV killing off the game?' (3 October 2007) in response to the news that only one of the forthcoming weekend's Premiership matches would kick off at the 'traditional' Saturday afternoon time of 3 p.m. — the time that best fitted in with the industrial working patterns of the working-class football supporters. One of the ironies of media intervention in match scheduling is that it makes it logistically difficult for many people, particularly away supporters, to attend matches, but half-empty stadiums do not fulfil the narrative conventions of televised football matches.

Ideas for discussion and development

- **Why are new media technologies, such as satellite broadcasting, the internet and mobile phones, of interest and value to producers and consumers alike?**
- **Could sport exist independently from the media, or is it so tightly bound up in the economics of sponsorship, advertising and media revenues that it is no longer able to support itself financially?**

Unit Focus 1
Investigating the media

This unit is split into two sections:
- **Section A** (AO1) = 48 marks or 60% of the total.
- **Section B** (AO2) = 32 marks or 40% of the total.

Section A

Section A comprises four short-answer questions worth **12 marks each**. The assessment objective (AO1) requires you to demonstrate knowledge and understanding of media concepts, contexts and critical debates.

Question 1 Media forms

Discuss the use of codes and conventions in the construction of this website. (12 marks)

This question tests:
- knowledge and understanding of the generic conventions of websites and web pages
- knowledge and understanding of semiotic analysis

Suggested content relating to codes and conventions is:
- title and strapline
- banner advertisement
- column with web-page contents
- column with advertisements and links

Courtesy of the multicultural Time Out, www.livelistingsmag.com

- headings, headlines and thumbnails (images plus copy) with click-throughs to more
- advertisements for the institution's products with links, e-mail and telephone contact details

Student answer A

As this is from a website it uses typical conventions to achieve its purpose. The layout resembles the rules of recognition used in any website due to its conventions. Located down the left-hand side are the hyperlinks and the subheadings of what is available for the reader to view. Therefore, we know by the subtle, sophisticated blue colour that the codes are used to signify the main aims of the website — to address a multicultural society.

The site makes use of a standard layout and includes links. As it is a table format, the pictures are minimised to thumbnails so that when uploading it does not hinder the reader's time or attention span. The thumbnails are also signifiers of what you can find if you click on any of the links.

Although this is a website page, there seems to be a considerable amount of information loaded into a small space. As well as the subheadings down the side of the page, there are many small sections which, if found on a traditional print media text, would be off-putting. The awards are located at the bottom and can be useful to show the reader that this is a reputable website, that it can be trusted and that the company actually cares about what it is trying to achieve.

Overall, there are many typical codes and conventions that you would normally find on a website page, from layout to iconic features such as thumbnails and text bars.

Grade and examiner's comment

Level 3 — 7 marks

Although there is some good knowledge of generic conventions and some appropriate use of media terminology, the referencing of details is more descriptive than technically accurate.

To gain a secure level 3 or higher, the candidate needs to formulate a more fluently linked response. There is a random selection of points that do not necessarily run together. Use of appropriate media terminology needs to be more consistent and knowledge of website conventions needs some revision. For example, at no point does the candidate note that we are looking at a 'home page' and thus he or she does not consider the generic codes/conventions or purpose of home pages.

Student answer B

The 'Live Listings' web-page text employs the recognisable codes and conventions of a website home page. It is a portal through which consumers can quickly 'click-through' to a range of different pages — in this case, pages detailing a variety of different cultural events and publications centred around metropolitan/cosmopolitan London life.

The page appears to be very crowded and unlike a print magazine has a low image-to-text ratio; the pictures are small thumbnails but are printed in full colour to attract attention. However, the page is not as text-heavy as it appears and it follows the generic convention of headline/strapline on each click-through to more detailed pages. The headline and thumbnail picture — like a conventional print text — interpolate the reader and the strapline summarises the main thrust of the page. Some of the click-throughs, however, return us to the traditional print media world (this is, of course, the online version of an existing print magazine). Thus, 'International Women's Month' and the 'Black Heritage' journal are given banner advertising prominence across the top of the page — functioning as a promotional opportunity to attract potential subscribers and readers.

Advertising is a key convention of web home pages, as they are free to access and need to generate revenue from somewhere. Indeed, all of the click-throughs, whether for dance, cinema or visual arts, will have been commissioned by advertising subscription. The more important advertisements have assumed banner prominence at the top of the page and others roll down the page in columns. A column for less prominent links is found in smaller font on the left-hand side of the page and further information is found in the conventional 'small print' section at the foot of the page.

Semiotically, the page is generically quite uncomplicated, despite the range of information to be found on it. Variations on blue dominate the colour scheme, giving the home page a 'house' colour — possibly signifying sophistication, neutrality or 'cool'. Copy fonts are normally black sans-serif on white, signifying a factual/business-like feel.

Stylistically, the page is organised into clear geometrically organised blocks, which make the pages easy to locate and navigate around. Only the logos for 'Live Listings' and 'Barb Wire' betray the generic sense of angularity and uniformity by breaking with the 'blue' coding and having funkier serif fonts. This is perhaps connoting something about the institutional persona of the parent magazine itself.

Grade and examiner's comment

Level 4 — 12 marks

The candidate shows a complete knowledge and understanding of all the generic design features of web-page construction. Most of the points are backed up with textual evidence, and examples and specialist media terminology and technical language are used with consistency and confidence.

The analysis is widened to consider institutional context and to make meaningful comparisons with traditional media forms (print magazines).

Question 2 Media representations

Consider the representation of people and places on this website.

(12 marks)

This question tests knowledge and understanding of how representations — of both people and places — are constructed and conveyed within media products.

Suggested content relating to representations of people is:
- women
- men
- race
- multiculturalism

Representations of place should refer to London as multicultural/inclusive, diverse and cosmopolitan:
- diversity of the arts scene
- wide range of music
- film and theatre choice (choice of two black 'political' figures)
- international visual arts and dance
- events and issues (marriage, dating)

Student answer A

Due to the layout and conventions of this website, it has a significant intended audience by using a range of contrasting codes. The website makes use of subtle blue, a sophisticated back colour that connotes a 'trendy' London image. This level of sophistication is also signified by the use of complementary pastel colours. The page is crammed with information to connote a busy city and busy lifestyles. This connotes a sense of London as a 'buzzing' metropolitan place, where lots of different cultures live and there are lots of events and entertainments going on.

We also get the impression that the representation of people is one of a multi-cultural society, due to the pictures of black icons like Martin Luther King. These pictures are anchored by 'black heritage' and 'black heroes' to signify pride and importance. The people are also represented as an eclectic society, whereby in the city of London with lots of different people and cultures there will be lots of different ideas, lifestyles and preferences. This also relates to the idea about London being a multicultural society. We can see this in the wide range of subheadings used to signify the different cultural practices and events.

Therefore, the representation of people and places on this website is one of a very multicultural London. It is a diverse and busy urban environment, which is connoted in the range of topics covered and also the sheer amount of content included on the page. For example, the way in which many different events and ideas — from black heritage to women's history, and from rap to opera — are situated next to each other resembles our busy contemporary multicultural lives.

Grade and examiner's comment

Level 3 — 8 marks

This is an 'emerging' media studies response with a good understanding of how representations are conveyed. There is some relevant use of media terminology but no real specific reference to the text itself to illustrate ideas.

To gain a secure level 4 mark, the candidate needs to back up every point with specific textual references and detailed analysis of purpose and effect. The response could be more fluent, with links made between paragraphs, and the use of appropriate media terminology could be more consistent.

Student answer B

In terms of style and content, the 'Live Listings' website represents an urbane sense of London and Londoners, which is cosmopolitan, metropolitan, socially and historically aware, politically correct and (multi)culturally eclectic.

In terms of content, the text appears to be interpolating an educated, middle-class readership that may be from a wide range of ethnic backgrounds. There are references to gender and racial politics and to a wide range of cultural activities. Indeed, the text seems to fall into Frederic Jameson's postmodern formulation concerning the collapse of the distinction between high and low art, by managing to situate the popular cultural genres of rap, pop and clubbing alongside the traditionally high arts of visual art, dance and theatre. A 'knowing' metropolitan audience would appreciate the ironies. Moreover, London is being represented as a 'happening' place at the forefront of the nation's cultural and artistic development.

For instance, if we look more closely at the pop-culture aspects of clubbing and rap we see that the website is interested more in the radical/marginal fringes of the form: 'Exer parties with a Serbian/Balkan theme'. This signifies a representation of an inclusive and multiethnic immigrant city, where there are a wide range of activities and ideas not excluded by the boundaries of race or gender.

The site then represents the values and ideologies of fairly prosperous and hedonistic people who are simultaneously socially and politically aware. For example, the thumbnails have images of cultural/political icons as diverse as Kylie Minogue and Martin Luther King. The artistic side of things is likewise in the vanguard of things, with an avant-garde and international flavour. For instance, there are references to Japanese rap and to South African art. Moreover, the copy is written for a knowing audience and is peppered throughout with references to a wide range of cultural texts and sociopolitical ideas.

In the 'Special Events' section we see the audience being referred to directly as 'the average urbanite', connoting a sense of metropolitan culture and sophistication. The audience is further represented as young and possibly single, with references to dating, marriage and generally events out and about on the town. However, the audience may also be in relationships and with young children as there are references to 'stuff for the kids'. There is a lot of content directly addressed to a female audience — perhaps trying to redress the imbalanced representation of the public sphere as a predominantly male environment.

Stylistically, the web page connotes, through its subtle pastel shades of blue and pink, a sense of sophisticated cool. There are no harsh primary or block colours and everything is organised in a minimalist fashion. There is also a sense of playful fun with the 'Barb Wire' logo, which is self-consciously in a retro 1970s design.

Grade and examiner's comment

Level 4 — 12 marks

The candidate shows a full knowledge and understanding of the concept of representation and the ways in which media representations are constructed and conveyed. The response is written with confidence and technical accuracy, and all points are backed up with detailed textual analysis and evidence. The response has been widened to show that different representations can co-exist within a single text and there are many possible readings available.

Question 3 Media institutions

What does this website tell us about the media institutions involved?

(12 marks)

This question tests knowledge and understanding of how the institution's brand image and brand values/style are created and conveyed by visual, narrative and technical codes.

Suggested content relating to visual narrative and technical codes is:
- logo/title (colour, style, position)
- emphasis on women and black heritage (size, position)
- business — advertising and subscription
- design — non-showy, understated, 'real'
- award winner

Student answer A

Media institutions are the companies that are involved in producing and distributing media products. All institutions have their own particular house style or image and they will usually target themselves at a section of the audience markets.

This website is no exception and is produced by an institution that is not well known but is trying to establish itself and be original while going for a very 'with it' segment of the multicultural London public.

Institutions use particular colours or codes/styles to attract their own target audiences and this 'Live Listings' site does this as well. The soft blue colour signifies 'cool' sophisticatedness, and the range of topics suggests that it is quite trendy and not mainstream commercial, e.g. things about women's history and black heritage. There is a lot of multicultural interest with art from South Africa and clubbing from the Balkans. The site does not use any bright, 'in your face' colours, and the pictures are all quite small and subtle. So too are the headlines.

The website is a commercial website but not a big commercial institution because, although it does have advertising sponsors, it does not feature big capitalist companies like Coca-Cola or Pepsi. It is more about advertising the arts and entertainments of London.

The site also uses a lot of awards at the bottom to show that it cares about what it is doing for London, and maybe the people who read it are also people who would be interested in that kind of thing — i.e. caring about what goes on in society. For example, the two headings about 'International Women's Month' and 'Black Heritage' are at the top of the page and bigger than the rest to signify that this institution makes them the most important things.

To conclude, the website tells us a lot of things about the institution that was involved in making it.

Grade and examiner's comment

Level 2 — 6 marks

The candidate shows a basic knowledge of how institutions convey their brand image/identity and values through design. Some short — and sometimes descriptive — references are made to the text. This is definitely an 'emerging' media studies response.

To gain a secure level 3 mark, the candidate needs to make more detailed/concrete references to the text and to follow up points with more developed discussion (many good points are not elaborated on). Use of media terminology needs to be more thorough, and direct reference to the ideas of 'brand image' and 'brand values' would give a more conceptual response.

Student answer B

Live Listings as a brand is lively, of the moment, non-sensational and ideologically sound. It embraces multicultural interests and manages to be both cutting-edge and traditional.

Looking again at the content and design of the website page, we can deduce a number of factors about Live Listings as a media institution.

It is not an enormous global player, nor does it seem to be integrated under the umbrella of a multinational corporation. It appears to be an ethical, independent institution that has won awards — e.g. 'Global Women of Invention & Innovation' and European design prizes — for its treatment of social and cultural issues. It is, however, an independent commercial institution and relies on advertising subscription and revenue to maintain its operational costs and perhaps generate enough profit to fund expansion.

In terms of values, Live Listings is an ideologically sound, socially and culturally aware institution that embraces multicultural issues and the politics of race, ethnicity, identity and gender. Indeed, the banner advertising at the top of the page champions both 'International Women's Month' and 'Black Heritage', and a lot of emphasis is placed on listing cultural events that probably lie outside the mainstream of commercial popular culture. For example, where we have rap or clubbing there is a distinctively gendered or international flavour that is 'cutting edge'.

In terms of style and brand identity, the institution has gone for a minimalist look. To connote that it is in touch with what is happening on London's streets, it has gone for a non-showy colour and design scheme, which is subtle and simple. Pastel shades of a neutral blue dominate and signify understated cool. The logo is a more metrosexual pink and flowing to signify a sense of liveliness.

The use of thumbnail images is quite interesting — mixing the modern with the traditional. For example, the pop star Kylie Minogue is held as an 'icon' of women's achievement and is indeed given more prominence on the page than Martin Luther King — icon of the black US civil rights movement. Such icons and 'knowing' cultural references are used throughout to connote a brand image of social and cultural awareness, and an explicit and unapologetic adherence to political correctness.

All in all, Live Listings represents itself as a happening and 'with it' barometer of metropolitan London life. It is in the cultural zeitgeist.

Grade and examiner's comment

Level 4 — 12 marks

The candidate shows a full knowledge and understanding of the concept of institution, and is able to demonstrate through textual analysis how the institution's brand and values are represented in the content and style of the text.

A good wider discussion is used to make a distinction between this institution and other types of media institutions. Specialist media terminology is used with a high degree of consistency and confidence.

Question 4 Media audiences

Explore some of the ways in which this website communicates with its target audiences. (12 marks)

This question tests knowledge and understanding of the concept of audience, identifying target audiences and how they are hailed and addressed by the home page and its contents.

Suggested content relating to possible target audiences is:

- Londoners (urbanites)
- ethnic groups, including recent immigrants
- people with a multicultural outlook
- single people and parents
- consumers of arts and cultural events ('culture vultures')

The audience could be said to be hailed and addressed as follows:

- welcomed
- intertextual references
- rhetorical questions
- clear, brief information with click-through choices for more
- informal — direct, second-person address ('you've missed it!')
- unsensational, neutral mode of address

Student answer A

The website communicates with its target audience in many different ways.

As mentioned earlier, the sophisticated soft-blue colour scheme signifies a cosmopolitan middle-class society that is wealthy and educated. The website could also be aimed at students due its significant layout. There is a range of activities for lots of different age ranges and backgrounds.

The content is controversial and therefore identifies with the 'buzzing' atmosphere of London, whereby everyone is interested in a wide range of topics and events. By including an ordered and formal range of events, the page communicates with its target audiences, as it has made use of a liberal range of topics that are entertaining or up-to-date. For example, the heading 'clubbing' is juxtaposed alongside that of 'theatre', instantly highlighting the range of people the website is trying to connect with.

The layout and conventions of the page are well structured, and a wide range of topic headings (such as male and female topics and things for different ethnicities) are listed. The page communicates well with its audiences because it addresses a range of things for a diverse and multicultural society.

Grade and examiner's comment

Level 2 — 6 marks
The candidate shows some knowledge of the concept of audience and some of the ways in which the text is constructed to communicate with specific target audiences. There is some use of media terminology.

To gain a level 3 mark, the candidate needs to identify a clearer sense of target audience(s) and back up *all* points with detailed and specific references to the text. Use of media terminology needs to be more thorough, and some mention should be made of audience theories, debates and ideas.

In terms of media audiences, the use of interpolative strategies in this website home page denies notions of media 'effects'. The audience is treated as far from dumb, and is being hailed through intertextual references to wider social, political and cultural narratives that only a high degree of what Bourdieu refers to as cultural capital/competence could facilitate.

Student answer B

Although one should always avoid generalising when it comes to locating 'target audiences', this site appears to be hailing an educated and middle-class readership. Moreover, there is a definite sense of multiculturalism and an explicit move away from the ethnocentric certainties of more mainstream publications. This text has been produced for a metropolitan audience with an awareness that London is very much a multiethnic immigrant city where lots of different communities co-exist.

By reference to politics of race, identity and gender, the site is making it clear that this co-existence has not always been harmonious, but the site aligns itself with the readership in the drive for social equality and inclusion. For example, a broad range of cultural interests and tastes are catered for — from low art to high art. Clubbing and rap sit alongside dance or visual arts. However, each of these is cutting edge or fairly avant-garde, signifying that the audience has a more engaged sense of 'culture' than mainstream media audiences.

The site also operates an informal second-person mode of address and directly welcomes the reader as 'urbanites'. There are references to dating and marriage, which may signify a younger singles crowd (as would clubbing), but the site, by referencing more traditional cultural forms and by listing 'stuff for kids', also seems to be addressing young families. This is very much in the realms of the young(ish) urbane capital-city dweller.

The mode of address is also fairly understated and neutral, and no garish colours or sensational headlines or images are used to draw the reader in. Alongside the multitude of intertextual references, rhetorical questions are used which, to work, need to be within the cultural and ideological grasp of the audience. While recent ethnographic audience studies have started to veer away from the thorny issue of ideology, there is an overt sense of politicisation in this text. We are not looking at a text that is ostensibly for entertainment, but Marxist or feminist (etc.) readings may reveal underlying meanings in a text that is clear in its ideological stance.

In short, the audience being targeted is drawn from a multicultural, politically and socially aware demographic, with a high degree of cultural capital and competence.

Grade and examiner's comment

Level 4 — 12 marks

The candidate shows a full knowledge and understanding of the concept of media audiences, with a broad analytical discussion of how audience theories may be useful in decoding the audience–text–institution relationship.

Media terminology is used consistently and with confidence, and all ideas are backed up with references to the text. The concept of hailing and addressing is covered extensively.

Section B

Section B comprises two either/or questions — of which you answer only one. The assessment objective (AO2) requires you to apply knowledge and understanding when analysing media products and processes to show how meanings and responses are created.

In this section, you will have undertaken a cross-media study in class. The questions are designed to assess your ability to apply knowledge and understanding of the products and processes in your chosen topic area. This should be done across the range of media platforms (broadcasting, print and e-media), and by exploring how meanings and responses are created.

Remember that quality of written communication will be on the examiners' tick-list of requirements. So plan your answer and check it through afterwards.

Question 5

Explore the ways that audiences consume and respond to media products across different media platforms. Support your answer with reference to examples from your case study.

(32 marks)

Advanced **Media Studies**

Responses to this question will be dependent on the nature of texts/ platforms studied in your specific case study.

Question 6

Write a talk to present to media producers, making a case for using a range of media platforms to reach consumers. Support your answer with reference to examples from your case study.

(32 marks)

A response to question 6 requires you to focus on 'advantages'. AQA stresses that you should be able to take an 'advantages for the institution' or 'advantages for the audience' approach to this task. To get top marks, however, you should adopt an approach that considers both institution and audience.

Simplified mark schemes

Question 1 Media forms

Level 4	10–12 marks	<ul><li>Show full knowledge and understanding of all the generic design features that go into web-page construction.</li><li>Back up every point with textual evidence and examples.</li><li>Use specialist media terminology throughout.</li><li>Widen your analysis to make comparisons with other media — e.g. print magazines.</li></ul>
Level 3	7–9 marks	<ul><li>Show satisfactory knowledge and understanding of some of the generic design features that go into web-page construction.</li><li>Back up your points with some textual evidence and examples.</li><li>Use some media terminology.</li></ul>
Level 2	4–6 marks	<ul><li>Show basic knowledge and understanding of the generic design features that go into web-page construction.</li><li>Refer generally to the text, rather than giving clear and definite examples.</li><li>Use descriptive language rather than specialist media terms.</li></ul>

Level 1   1–3 marks
- Simple knowledge and understanding of generic features of web-page design.
- Undeveloped, common-sense explanation written in everyday language.
- Little or no textual evidence used.

Level 0   0 marks
- Nothing written.
- Nothing relevant written.
- Nothing suitable written.

Question 2 Media representations

Level 4   10–12 marks
- Show full knowledge and understanding of how representations are constructed and conveyed.
- Back up every point with carefully selected textual evidence and examples, then analyse their use and effects in detail.
- Use specialist media terminology throughout.
- Widen your analysis to show that you understand representation conceptually, i.e. that a diverse range of representations is available.

Level 3   7–9 marks
- Show satisfactory knowledge and understanding of how media representations are constructed and conveyed.
- Back up your points with some textual evidence and some analysis of use and effects.
- Use some media terminology.

Level 2   4–6 marks
- Show basic knowledge and understanding of how media representations are constructed and conveyed.
- Refer generally to the text, rather than giving clear and definite examples.
- Use descriptive language rather than specialist media terms.

Level 1   1–3 marks
- Simple knowledge and understanding of the media representations available in media texts.
- Undeveloped, common-sense explanation written in everyday language.
- Little or no textual evidence used.

Level 0   0 marks
- Nothing written.
- Nothing relevant written.
- Nothing suitable written.

Question 3 Media institutions

Level 4	10–12 marks	• Show full knowledge and conceptual understanding of institution.
		• Show how the contents/style/design of the web page represent the institution's values.
		• Back up every point with detailed textual evidence and analysis.
		• Use specialist media terminology throughout.
		• Extend your analysis beyond the present text to show a wider understanding of the concept of institution — such as questions of power and influence, and the importance of brand identity.
Level 3	7–9 marks	• Show satisfactory knowledge and understanding of how the institution and its values/image are represented in the web page.
		• Back up your points with some textual evidence and analysis.
		• Use some media terminology.
Level 2	4–6 marks	• Show basic knowledge and understanding of how the institution uses the website to show its values and ideas.
		• Refer generally to the text, rather than giving clear and definite examples.
		• Use descriptive language rather than specialist media terms.
Level 1	1–3 marks	• Simple knowledge and understanding of how the institution is shown in the text.
		• Undeveloped, common-sense explanation written in everyday language.
		• Little or no textual evidence used.
Level 0	0 marks	• Nothing written.
		• Nothing relevant written.
		• Nothing suitable written.

Question 4 Media audiences

Level 4	10–12 marks	• Show full knowledge and understanding of the concept of media audiences.
		• Be able to identify target audience(s) and explain how the text hails/addresses them.
		• Back up every point with textual evidence and detailed analysis.

- Use specialist media terminology throughout.
- Extend your analysis to show how audience theories — such as effects, uses and gratifications or encoding/decoding — may be useful in aiding our understanding of the text–audience relationship.

Level 3	7–9 marks	• Show satisfactory knowledge and understanding of how the text addresses its target audience(s). • Back up your points with some textual evidence and analysis. • Use some media terminology.
Level 2	4–6 marks	• Show basic knowledge and understanding of how the text gets its message and ideas across to its audience. • Refer generally to the text, rather than giving clear and definite examples. • Use descriptive language rather than specialist media terms.
Level 1	1–3 marks	• Simple knowledge and understanding of the ideas behind media audiences. • Undeveloped, common-sense explanation written in everyday language. • Little or no textual evidence used.
Level 0	0 marks	• Nothing written. • Nothing relevant written. • Nothing suitable written.

Question 5

Level 4	26–32 marks	• Show full knowledge and understanding of the ways in which different audiences consume media products across all three media platforms. • Show excellent knowledge and understanding of how meanings are created and conveyed. • Back up every point with evidence and examples from the texts in your case study. • Plan and structure your response with a clear line of argument, fluent links between paragraphs and integrated use of relevant supporting evidence. • Write succinctly, use media terminology throughout and make reference to media theories and ideas. • The examiner is looking for confidence and engagement with the question.

Level 3	17–25 marks	• Show satisfactory knowledge and understanding of the ways in which media audiences consume texts across all three media platforms.
		• Show satisfactory knowledge and understanding of how meanings are created and conveyed.
		• Back up most points with evidence and examples from the texts in your case study.
		• Show personal knowledge of media texts, platforms and institutions.
		• Use media terminology and ideas accurately, and write a consistent response with a clear structure and good use of relevant supporting evidence.
Level 2	9–16 marks	• Show a basic understanding of how media audiences consume media products.
		• Show that you have knowledge and understanding of at least two media platforms.
		• Make some reference to case-study texts and back up some points with details or examples.
		• Use some media terminology/ideas and try to get some ideas across clearly.
Level 1	1–8 marks	• Very simple awareness of how audiences consume media products.
		• Awareness of one or more media platforms.
		• Writing is less consistent and at times confusing.
		• Little or no textual evidence used — limited to naming texts or making reference to vague details.
Level 0	0 marks	• Nothing written.
		• Nothing relevant written.
		• Nothing suitable written.

Question 6

Level 4	26–32 marks	• Show full knowledge and understanding of at least three media platforms and the distinct advantages each has in reaching different consumer groups.
		• Have an informed awareness of the commercial and promotional aspects of media institutions.
		• Show excellent knowledge and understanding of how meanings are created and received.
		• Support your ideas with examples from the texts in your cross-media study.

- Plan and structure your talk with a professional audience in mind, using appropriate media terminology and ensuring that your advantages are clearly outlined.
- The examiner is looking for confident application of media concepts and ideas.

Level 3	17–25 marks	• Show satisfactory knowledge and understanding of three media platforms and the advantages each has for presenting and promoting media products. • Show satisfactory knowledge and understanding of how meanings are created and received. • Demonstrate your ideas with clear examples from your cross-media study. • Write for a professional audience and be able to use some appropriate media terminology. • The examiner is looking for some good use of media concepts and ideas.
Level 2	9–16 marks	• Show a basic knowledge and understanding of at least two different media platforms and some of the advantages each has in reaching different types of audience. • Show basic knowledge and understanding of how meanings are created by media institutions and received by audiences. • Needs to be recognisable as a talk/presentation, and should use some media terminology and be backed up with some examples. • Better responses will show some awareness of media concepts and ideas.
Level 1	1–8 marks	• Very simple awareness of how audiences consume media products. • Awareness of one or more media platforms. • Writing is less consistent and at times confusing. • Little or no textual evidence used — limited to naming texts or making reference to vague details.
Level 0	0 marks	• Nothing written. • Nothing relevant written. • Nothing suitable written.

Unit Focus 2
Creating media

This practical unit involves an externally set brief, which is internally examined and externally moderated. You will be assessed for your ability to demonstrate:

- independent research skills
- technical and creative skills
- knowledge of relevant codes and conventions
- understanding of the relevance of platforms and large audiences
- production skills in broadcast, e-media and conventional print media
- evaluation skills in relation to your own work

You are required to produce two linked production pieces taken from two of the media platforms studied in Unit 1. This should develop out of your work for Unit 1. It allows you to pursue your own interests, structured by the media concepts you have studied.

Process for completing the unit

Research

It is important that you do some research before you start. You must cover theoretical issues as well as primary texts related to the brief, e.g. the viewing of public information advertisements or current affairs programmes.

Intentions

You should make your intentions clear from the start. How are your productions going to work? How is the specified audience going to be targeted by both the chosen content and the platform?

Pre-production

Pre-production work involves researching the two production pieces you are going to create. You will need to assess existing products similar to the ones you intend to produce and research your target audience. Remember that planning is essential throughout, and that mock-ups and storyboards can be evaluated. Evidence of your research, your purpose and all pre-production work should be submitted and considered in your evaluation.

Production

Organise your time efficiently and set yourself deadlines and targets for completion of the different elements. Fully realised productions are expected and each is worth 37.5% of the total marks for the unit. Original images should be used wherever possible, rather than found images. This means that imaginary images of celebrities and politicians should be used rather than real ones. However, if you do use found images and can demonstrate that you have extensively manipulated them, then you can submit the original image along with your work.

Evaluation

The evaluation should be a thorough and honest assessment of both pieces of practical work and should be 1,500 words long. You should discuss the intentions of both pieces of work in relation to your research, but the main focus of the evaluation should be an analysis of how the productions work in relation to their target audiences, research, media concepts and contexts. You should explore the success and weakness of the productions in relation to your intentions, and assess their overall fitness for purpose.

An evaluation should never make excuses or blame others for failures or errors, but it should explain, for example, why things did not always go to plan and how you sought to overcome any difficulties you encountered. You will be rewarded for explaining your thought processes and demonstrating what you have learned from the experience. If appropriate, this might include how you would change your approach if repeating the exercise.

It is important to remember that in the evaluation you are asked to imagine how your work — involving your two chosen platforms — could be adapted to meet the needs of the third platform. For example, if you have produced a video advertisement for television and a viral image for e-media, you should suggest how images from these productions could be adapted for a print media advertising campaign.

Assessment of the unit

The assessment of this unit is broken down as follows:
Production: 60 marks
Evaluation: 20 marks
Total: 80 marks

Mark scheme

The unit is marked on the principles of 'best fit' by assigning work to the most appropriate band. If the work is totally characteristic of one band descriptor then it is placed in the middle of the band. If it contains elements of a higher or lower band then it is placed at the top or bottom of its band accordingly.

When you read through the following assessment criteria you will notice that they seem quite vague and generic. This is because they have to be applied to a wide range of production pieces. There are, however, important differences in the key words that identify the different levels and what is expected from you. For example, in assessing the production piece, at Level 4 the key words are 'proficiency' and 'sound understanding', at Level 3 'competence' and 'satisfactory understanding', at Level 2 'some competence' and 'basic understanding', and at Level 1 'minimal competence' and 'rudimentary understanding'. These same principles apply throughout the assessment criteria.

Production (total 60 marks)

Level 4   46–60 marks

- The candidate demonstrates technical proficiency in the use of chosen technologies and sound understanding of the needs of the production process, and has demonstrated some creativity.

- Appropriate codes and conventions are used throughout, and the production will be 'fit for purpose' in the light of the candidate's research.

- The candidate's chosen discourse will be employed with fluency.

- At the top of the band there will be considerable attention to detail and a genuine sense of engagement with the chosen media and the subject matter.

- Note: the term 'fit for purpose' is commonly used to describe a situation where a product or service is considered to be suitable for the use for which it is intended. For example, if you produce a short advertisement for use on television, could it actually be used in the way that you intend? Is it realistic and professional enough, and does it follow the appropriate convention of the medium?

Level 3	31–45 marks	• The candidate demonstrates competence in the use of the chosen technologies and has demonstrated satisfactory understanding of the necessities of the production process.
		• The candidate has generally used appropriate codes and conventions, and the production will be largely fit for purpose in the light of the candidate's research.
		• The candidate's chosen discourse will be employed with accuracy for the most part.
Level 2	16–30 marks	• The candidate demonstrates some competence in the use of the chosen technologies and has demonstrated basic understanding of the necessities of the production process.
		• The candidate has used appropriate codes and conventions but in an inconsistent manner, and some of the production will be fit for purpose in the light of the candidate's research.
		• The candidate's chosen discourse will be employed with some inconsistency.
Level 1	0–15 marks	• The candidate demonstrates minimal competence in the use of the chosen technologies, with rudimentary understanding of the necessities of the production process.
		• The candidate may have used some appropriate codes and conventions but in a limited fashion, and little of the production will be fit for purpose in the light of the candidate's reasearch.
		• The candidate's chosen discourse will be employed inconsistently.

Evaluation (total 20 marks)

Level 4	16–20 marks	• The evaluation and pre-production materials contain extended evidence and application of research; they give a clear description of the target audience(s) and how the candidate intended to make the productions appeal to them.
		• There is effective analysis of the strengths and weaknesses of the productions, which demonstrates

sound understanding of the media concepts and contexts relevant to the work undertaken, with clear reference made to the third media platform.

- The candidate uses the language of media studies with confidence.

| Level 3 | 11–15 marks | • The evaluation and pre-production materials contain substantial proof and competent application of research, and offer evidence of the target audience(s) and how the candidate intended to make the productions appeal to them. |

- There is competent analysis of the strengths and weaknesses of the productions, which demonstrates satisfactory understanding of the media concepts and contexts relevant to the work undertaken, with some discussion of the third media platform.

- The candidate makes appropriate use of the language of media studies.

| Level 2 | 6–10 marks | • The evaluation and pre-production materials contain some proof and application of research, and offer some evidence of the target audience(s) and how the candidate intended to make the productions appeal to them. |

- There is some analysis of the strengths and weaknesses of the productions, which demonstrates basic understanding of the media concepts and contexts relevant to the work undertaken, with some mention of the third media platform.

- The candidate makes some use of the language of media studies. There are likely to be some errors in spelling and syntax, and the meaning may be confused at times.

| Level 1 | 0–5 marks | • The evaluation and pre-production materials contain little proof or application of research, and offer limited evidence of the target audience(s) and how the candidate intended to make the productions appeal to them. |

- The candidate tends to describe the productions and/or processes rather than analysing the strengths and weaknesses, demonstrating rudimentary understanding of the media concepts and contexts relevant to the work undertaken.

- The candidate makes minimal use of the language of media studies. There are likely to be extensive errors in spelling and syntax, and the candidate may struggle to communicate effectively.

Production work

You need to produce two linked productions taken from two of the three media platforms specified. Your work should be based on one of three production briefs provided by AQA. You will have three options to choose from for each of the three media platforms. The work you submit should be your own and not more than 20% of the work can rely on 'found' images.

Found images should only be used where it is impractical for you to produce your own material, for example a photograph of a celebrity you wish to include in a magazine production piece.

Production tasks

The following scenarios are AQA's example questions. These tasks will change on a 2-year rolling programme. The brief for each year is published on the AQA website.

Broadcasting

1 Create a 2-minute cinema trailer for a new '15'-rated hybrid genre film and with a budget of roughly £30 million, partly supplied by lottery funding.

2 Create two television advertisements aimed at young women (18–25 years of age), designed to promote sensible drinking.

3 Create the opening sequence for a new current affairs programme to be screened on Channel 4 at 6.30 p.m. and aimed at the 18–21 demographic.

Print

1 Write two features/reviews on the release of a new hybrid genre film rated '15' and with a budget of roughly £30 million, partly supplied by lottery funding. Candidates should aim to produce an A4 page for each piece, including images and text. The pieces should be specific to a named publication such as a newspaper, lifestyle magazine or specialist film magazine, such as *Sight and Sound* or *Empire*.

2 Create three or four advertisements for a pre-Christmas campaign discouraging young women from drink-driving.

3 Create the front pages for two mid-market black-top newspapers, each with a different gender bias.

Web-based digital (e-media)

1 Create three web pages for the official site for a new hybrid genre film rated '15' and with a budget of roughly £30 million, partly supplied by lottery funding.

2 Create a viral moving-image marketing tool to promote sensible drinking. The piece is intended to be disseminated via mobile phones.

3 Create three web pages of an internet site dealing with current affairs, aimed at women under the age of 30.

Formats specified for e-media can include:
- viral videos
- DVD
- video
- print
- website on CD-ROM
- MP3 podcast
- CD-ROM

Preparation for practical work

The following notes cover all the tasks specified in the 'Production tasks' section (pages 184–85).

Broadcasting

1 Create a 2-minute cinema trailer for a new '15'-rated hybrid genre film and with a budget of roughly £30 million, partly supplied by lottery funding.

Before undertaking this task, you should view and make notes on a range of film trailers, and research the costs involved in producing a trailer, to see exactly what you would be able to achieve with the money available. The fact that it is partly lottery-funded means that there is a degree of public accountability involved and the funding source should be acknowledged in the trailer. You should refer to the conventions of a film trailer in preparation for this task.

2 Create two television advertisements aimed at young women (18–25 years of age), designed to promote sensible drinking.

Research

The issue of young women drinking is controversial and has recently attracted a great deal of media attention. You should find out as much as you can about the issues involved: health problems, antisocial behaviour, risks to personal safety etc. You should also research and view public information films on television to see what the tone and style of such a short advertisement might be. Look at conventions like voice-over, captions and slogans, and think about the intended impact on the target audience. Advertisements like the campaigns against Christmas drink-driving or about AIDS often contain a shock element. You might want to look at the 1980s television advertisements about AIDS on the internet.

Intentions

Your intentions are going to be to follow the set brief and create a 'fit for purpose' television advertisement aimed at young women between the ages of 18 and 25, designed to promote sensible drinking. Specify how you intend to communicate with your target audience and influence their behaviour.

Pre-production

You should produce a shooting script and a storyboard, with an assessment of how they will work in practice. (A shooting script is a script listing the scenes to be shot in the order in which they are to be taken.)

The following are two alternative scenarios for this task.

Scenario 1

A young woman in a bar drinks too much, becomes drunk and has difficulty in fending off the unwanted attentions of a male. She cannot find her way home and is sick. She is sitting in the street, where she is rescued from a group of harassing males by a friend who helps her home. Sitting with the friend later, the girl discusses her drinking and promises to 'think before she drinks'.

Having outlined a scenario similar to this one, you should produce a storyboard and shooting script for the production of the video. A storyboard helps you to control the shoot efficiently and ensure that everything is covered.

Pre-production

For the storyboard you should sketch the individual shots in the form of the frames of a strip cartoon and explain them in a brief note beneath each frame. You should also add details about location, lighting, camera moves (long shot, close-up, following shot, tracking shot etc.), music, special effects (SFX) and shot duration. Script and dialogue should be identified in relation to each shot. This is a working document for you to use during the shoot. Here is an outline of the general sequence of the storyboard for this scenario:

1 The woman is laughing and drinking in the company of friends and young men. She is clearly drinking heavily — there are several glasses in front of her.
2 She is drunk in the bar and is being pestered by a man.
3 She staggers into the street, looking lost, and is sick.
4 She is sitting on the pavement and being accosted by several men.
5 Her friend turns up and rescues her.
6 She is escorted home.
7 Later she is sitting with her friend and promises not to drink so much again. Her friend says, 'Just think before you drink'.

Production overview

Slogan: 'Think before you drink'.
Locations: bar, street, woman's home.
Cast: probably around seven — five men and two women.
Equipment: video camera, edit suite facilities.
Dialogue: background noise, exchanges between the woman and the men, possible voice-over comments?

Production

Be realistic in your production objectives. Remember that everyday locations and realistic situations are important for the sense of realism necessary to produce a convincing video.

Camera use

You should have practised using the camera in your school or college before going out on location. However, here are a few basic tips:

- **Framing and mise-en-scène:** everything in the frame (the image you see) should be there because you want it to be there — make sure that distractions like furniture or the family cat are not in the frame. The position you adopt in relation to your subject will affect how the audience sees the subject and reads the story you are telling. Make sure the camera concentrates on the principal subject of the piece and not on unnecessary characters/details which detract from the story you are telling.

- **Location:** choose your locations with care to set the scene for the story you are telling. Shoot all the scenes in a given location at the same time, rather than shooting the story in running-order sequence.
- **Camera work:** long or distance shots can be used as scene-setting establishing shots, to identify the location and contextualise the piece. Close-ups are important for emotion, reaction and creating a sense of involvement with the characters. Do not be afraid to use low- or high-angle shots if appropriate. A 'reaction shot' can be created by shooting one person's behaviour, then filming another person's reaction to it separately. These shots can then be edited together. Avoid creating a 'stage' effect with the camera as a fourth wall — it is old-fashioned and dull. Move the camera to engage the audience and create a sense of real life.

Evaluation

Discuss your intentions and how you communicate with the target audience. Explore how the work relates to the other production piece and assess the strengths and weaknesses of your production. You should also consider how the work could be adapted for the third media platform.

Scenario 2

Production

Bedroom scene — a couple in bed.
The woman wakes up; the man is still asleep.
Flashback to busy pub. The couple are drinking and laughing.
The woman says: 'Where am I?'
She looks around and sees some of her clothes scattered.
Flashback to drunken woman staggering and being escorted by the man to his flat/house.
She looks at the man and says to herself: 'Who are you?'
Flashback to the couple in his house — they are kissing; she is clearly drunk.
He stays asleep throughout. She gets out of bed flustered and panicking and gets dressed. Before she leaves the house/flat, she looks for something in an agitated manner and cannot find it — she says to herself 'Where is it?'

Flashback to the woman dropping her bag/purse in the street and not noticing. Looking very confused and concerned she leaves, running down the street. The final shot shows her sitting outside her house, head in hands — she has lost her front door key.

Production overview

Slogan on screen: 'Think before you drink'.
Locations: man's house/flat, pub, street scenes, outside the woman's house.
Cast: man and woman, pub crowd.
Equipment: video camera and edit suite.

The storyboard and shooting script should always be used to make the most effective use of the time available, for example by filming all interior bedroom scenes together and then all external and bar scenes. Timing is important — the advertisement could be as short as 30 seconds. Time similar television advertisements to find an average length. An advertisement that is too long could lose impact — less is more in this case.

3 Create the opening sequence for a new current affairs programme to be screened on Channel 4 at 6.30 p.m. and aimed at the 18–21 demographic.

To research this, you could watch *Hollyoaks*, which is currently on Channel 4 at 6.30 p.m. — half an hour before the *Channel 4 News*. (You might want to link your programme to this anchor point of Channel 4's evening schedule.) Also look at *Hollyoaks'* graphics, as you might want to borrow some ideas from them to appeal to the target audience specified.

Topics referenced from the opening scene could be drawn from:
- clubbing and venues
- alcohol abuse and related illness/experiences
- drug abuse
- job hunting after university
- 18–30 holidays, gap years, backpacking
- cosmetic surgery disasters
- youth celebrity success
- music stories about up-and-coming bands, biographies, history, break-ups, scandals
- young soldiers in the army (experiences, video diaries)
- video diaries about young people, different experiences, places, entertainment, holidays, jobs etc.

Print

1 Write two features/reviews on the release of a new hybrid genre film rated '15' and with a budget of roughly £30 million, partly supplied by lottery funding. Candidates should aim to produce an A4 page for each piece, including images and text. The pieces should be specific to a named publication such as a newspaper, lifestyle magazine or specialist film magazine, such as *Sight and Sound* or *Empire*.

Your research should begin with *Sight and Sound*, the magazine of the British Film Institute. It is the market leader for quality film reviews, so reading and noting the techniques and structure of its reviews would be useful. Look at more reviews from the internet and other cinema magazines, such as *Empire*. Before writing your features/reviews, consider the language register and the target audience. The two pieces must be 'fit for purpose', i.e. suitable for and credible as journalistic articles in your chosen magazine.

2 Create three or four advertisements for a pre-Christmas campaign discouraging young women from drink-driving.

Using ideas taken from the broadcast scenarios on pages 186–89 you could construct scenes for a series of dramatic photographs — the slogan 'Think before you drink' would still be appropriate. Remember the pre-Christmas context of the campaign.

Research

You should look at similar public information campaigns in print media, particularly the Christmas drink-driving campaigns, which should be available on the internet. Consider which publications are suitable for your campaign, taking into account the target audience of young women. You will be able to access the circulation figures and gender/age breakdown of the readership of both magazines and national newspapers on the internet.

Intentions

You will need to make clear how you intend to reach your particular audience with the campaign and the ways in which you are going to make your work appealing to this audience.

Pre-production

You should experiment with a range of options for the advertisements. Remember that they should be linked both to each other and to your other production piece. This means using the same locations and models, and the same slogan or variations on it. You should collect all the material and evaluate the different versions before deciding on what to do for the final production.

Production

All the production work can be done by scanning images into a computer and manipulating them with software such as Adobe Photoshop. Remember, it is quality rather than quantity that is important. To achieve the highest grade, the advertisements must be 'fit for purpose', i.e. usable in the publication for which they are designed. A colour printing facility is desirable, but do not underestimate the benefits of using monochrome (black and white) images — they can be very dramatic and effective, particularly with this kind of message.

Here are some ideas relating to the composition of the photographs:

1 Young woman sitting in the gutter looking dishevelled, with her head in her hands and a shoe missing. Slogan: 'Think before you drink'. She could be wearing some tinsel around her head or a Santa hat to signify Christmas.

2 Scene in a bar. A young man and woman — obviously not boyfriend and girlfriend — are standing together. He has his arm around her, and is looking down smiling, clearly drunk. She is looking away, with a worried expression — giving the impression that she is thinking about what to do and possibly trying to leave. Both have glasses in their hands. Slogan: 'Think before you drink'. Remember to include Christmas decorations in the bar.

3 A car is positioned as if it has been run off the road, with the impression of damage (broken glass etc.) — a collision with a bollard is suggested. A young female driver is sitting on the pavement with her head in her hands. A police officer is taking the registration of the car. Slogan: 'Think before you drink'. An alternative could involve a shot of the woman blowing into a Breathalyser. Remember, Christmas details are needed.

Evaluation

The evaluation should review the work you have done and provide an insight into why you selected and rejected particular photographs from those you originally took. You should be able to explain the logic of your decisions and how they relate to your chosen audience, publications and overall intentions. The evaluation should discuss the relationship between the productions and how that relationship was intended to work if the productions were to appear in the real world.

3 Create the front pages for two mid-market black-top newspapers, each with a different gender bias.

Research

Before undertaking this task you should ensure that your school or college has the facilities for producing a realistic A3 tabloid front page with appropriate use of colour printing. A cut-and-paste mock-up is not acceptable. The main tabloids you should research are the *Daily Mail* and *Daily Express*, but you could also investigate the *Sun*, the *Star* and the *Mirror*. You should buy copies of the relevant papers on the same day and also look at their websites.

Make notes on the different lead stories and the priorities these suggest for the newspapers, and also identify any political agenda, e.g. whether it is for or against the government. Identify the characteristics of the tabloid you are replicating, paying attention to details such as price, masthead design, font style and spacing policy — this includes use of white space, i.e. blank space around the columns and photographs.

The task involves creating two front pages with a different gender bias. You might find that the *Daily Mail* — the tabloid with the highest percentage of female readers — is the paper to use for the female audience and the *Daily Express* is the most suitable for a male audience.

Intentions

Your intention is to produce front pages for two black-top tabloids, each with a different gender bias, making them as realistic and 'fit for purpose' as possible. Specify how each would communicate with its target audience.

Pre-production

At this stage you can use the cut-and-paste facilities in a word-processing package to put together your front pages. You will need to take digital photographs for the images on the front page — found images are not acceptable. All your preparatory materials and drafts should be kept for submission alongside the final artefacts.

Production

You will need to spend a considerable amount of time on the computer at home and at college/school. Ideally, you need to be able to transfer files between the two so that you can work on either system.

To produce a tabloid-sized front page you need to work with A3 printing facilities. Two A4 sheets can, if necessary, be taped together, but be aware that the finished piece should look as professional as possible.

Microsoft Publisher has all the functionality you need to complete this task, although you may have access to other software. It is essential that you liaise with technicians at your school or college to establish how you should prepare files for A3 printing.

For details of the conventions of a tabloid front page, see page 54.

Evaluation

Remember to cover your intentions and target audience, and to discuss the work in conjunction with your other production piece. You should assess your work's fitness for purpose, and consider any shortcomings or disappointments. You should also consider how your front pages might be adapted for use in the third media platform.

Web-based digital (e-media)

1 **Create three web pages for the official site for a new hybrid genre film rated '15' and with a budget of roughly £30 million, partly supplied by lottery funding.**

Research for this piece should involve viewing a range of film websites and noting their characteristics. For further information on how to proceed with this option, see the section on pages 80–81 on the conventions of website design. Ideally, the three web pages should be linked to simulate the process of moving through a website. Remember to mention the support of lottery funding somewhere on the site's home page.

2 **Create a viral moving-image marketing tool to promote sensible drinking. The piece is intended to be disseminated via mobile phones.**

Research

Viral image marketing is relatively new and you should research definitions and examples from the internet. Download examples and store them in a file for reference if possible. You should then analyse and evaluate these images and establish their main characteristics. You might want to consider a vlog (video blog) approach using a webcam for this task. Social networking sites are an obvious area to research.

Intentions

You should explain how your viral image will reach its intended audience and how this will be targeted.

Pre-production

As this piece will probably be linked to work you are doing for a television advertisement, you should be able to make use of this material or have prepared specific scenes with the viral image in mind when producing the video. Refer back to the detailed scenarios for the television advertisement outlined on pages 186–89.

Production

The production criteria for this piece will be the same as for any video, but obviously need to be condensed. This means identifying key dramatic images, with ideas taken from the scenarios outlined earlier, and perhaps using the same slogan to create a uniformity of approach. It would make sense, and would save time and effort, to link this piece to the broadcast option rather than the print media option. The scenarios outlined for the broadcast option could then be reduced and adapted to suit the viral medium. Alternatively, you may wish to use a webcam approach for this task.

Evaluation

You should explain the links between the two production pieces and how they will work together in practice to reach the target audience. Remember also to discuss how the work could be adapted for the media platform you have not chosen.

3 Create three web pages of an internet site dealing with current affairs, aimed at women under the age of 30.

This task will involve identifying the interests of the target audience. Generally speaking, women are more likely to be interested in issues that affect them directly or have more of a human angle — so, for example, a story about the war in Iraq could emphasise the suffering of Iraqi civilians or the damage caused to families of military personnel, or describe the first-hand experiences of female members of the British armed forces.

Other current affairs topics could include issues relating to women's health, single mothers, child adoption, equal pay, crime against women, women's sports, women in politics, and women in business. The site needs to recognise feminist issues without being too obviously a 'feminist' site, as this might limit its appeal to potential audience members.

It is important to include a feedback element on the site, and invite visitors to comment on stories and add their own experiences. This can allow a 'blog' aspect to develop on the site, with visitors interacting closely with each other.

The design of the site needs to emphasise youth, energy, ambition and achievement for women against a background of current affairs.

Summary

It is difficult to cover the full range of production tasks you may encounter in this unit, but the principles for success are the same throughout:

- Assess your own skills and choose a task appropriately.
- Set yourself targets and deadlines for completing the various elements.
- Be clear about your intentions from the start.
- Establish the technology you need to complete your tasks.
- Research your target audience carefully and ensure that your product is tailored to meet its needs.
- Research your topic thoroughly and evaluate the materials you collect along the way.
- Plan the production process appropriately stage by stage.
- Refer to the assessment criteria and consider what you need to do to achieve a high grade.
- Spend time on your evaluation. Be honest and thorough — you have 1,500 words to explain your thought processes, your decisions, your level of success and your disappointments. Do not blame others for any delays or problems you may have encountered — remain objective throughout.

Advertising and marketing

The advertising industry

Advertising is the media-led promotion of goods or services for sale whereby audiences are brought to the market and encouraged or persuaded to consume. An **advertisement** is any paid-for communication designed to sell or publicise products or services.

Advertising is the key to financing many media products. Without advertising there would be no magazines, newspapers or commercial television stations. Without sponsorship there would be less money for blockbuster films and for major sports like football and Formula One motor racing.

Advertisers and sponsors know that gaining media exposure for their products in coverage of major sporting events is an effective way of identifying their products with sporting success and with personalities like David Beckham. Their objective is simple: to sell products by associating them with idealised and glamorous lifestyles. The cult of celebrity is therefore manufactured by advertising and marketing strategies.

Advertising platforms

The following are the main advertising platforms:
- **broadcast media** — television and radio
- **print media** — newspapers, magazines, flyers
- **ambient media** — e.g. computer mouse mats, beer mats, billboards, pens, T-shirts
- **e-media** — web advertising and viral marketing

Viral marketing, images and videos

The term **viral marketing** was coined by Professor Jeffrey F. Rayport of the Harvard Business School in 1996. It originally referred to marketing techniques that use pre-existing social networks to transmit messages by word of mouth. Today, the term is increasingly associated with the use of mobile phones and the internet. In viral marketing, people are encouraged to pass marketing messages on voluntarily.

Research suggests that a customer tells three people about a product he or she likes and 11 about a product he or she does not like. Advertisers aim to target individuals with a high social networking potential (SNP), i.e. those who have contact with many people. The classic example of early viral marketing is the 1999 film *The Blair Witch Project* (Daniel Myrick and Eduardo Sánchez), a low-budget horror movie that constructed an audience among young people entirely by word of mouth and the publication of viral videos on the internet.

A **viral video** gains popularity as a result of people sharing it through e-mail, blogs and websites. Amateur videos are shot on camera phones and distributed virally on the internet and by e-mail through Bluetooth technology. The phenomenon of video-sharing websites, the most famous one being YouTube, has encouraged the phenomenon of viral videos. The method is particularly popular with band and music promotion.

Ideas for discussion and development

The ethics of advertising

By the age of 12, girls in the UK have seen 77,500 ads. And does it make them happy? No, according to new research commissioned by Dove. So it has made an ad about it.

Two hundred girls in the UK and the US aged between 10 and 12 were surveyed to find out how they felt about their appearance. Seventy-seven percent of them felt fat, ugly and depressed when faced with pictures of beautiful models and celebrities. More than half described themselves in negative terms as 'disgusting' and 'ugly'. The cosmetics company Dove has produced a new viral video called *Onslaught*, which is designed to highlight the pressures placed on young girls by the beauty industry. This video is available on YouTube and in 4 days it received 380,000 hits.

The film starts with a smiling 7-year-old and then cuts to images of scantily clad models with promises of being 'younger, lighter, thinner, firmer', spoken by women over flashes of advertisements. It then moves to footage of cosmetic surgery and ends with a slogan across the screen: 'Talk to your daughters before the beauty industry does'.

(Continues)

The claim is that advertising images are responsible for creating low self-esteem in girls and can trigger damaging behaviour. There was a high proportion of physical and mental health problems among the girls surveyed. Ninety percent felt 'stressed and anxious' about their appearance, and 76% had eating disorders or were engaged in self-harming behaviour.

Dove is a manufacturer of beauty products. This video is part of its 'campaign for real beauty' which, of course, is designed to sell more Dove products. There seems to be no escape from the commercial world.

(Source: adapted from the *Independent on Sunday*, 7 October 2007)

Billboard featuring Dove 'real beauty' campaign

New Dove Firming. As tested on real curves.

- **Do you think that Dove is being hypocritical in criticising the ethics of advertising to girls when the company itself is trying to sell them what it calls 'real beauty' products?**

Advertising agencies

Advertising agencies are companies or firms engaged in the production of advertising and marketing materials in response to briefs developed with clients. In a sophisticated media environment, advertising agencies play an important role in assessing the attitudes, beliefs and values of audiences, and in relating advertising campaigns to current social, cultural and political moods and trends.

Skilled and creative professional teams ensure that powerful and lasting images of products and their place in contemporary life are projected on audiences, so that such images become part of their everyday cultural experience. The concept of a brand is crucial to successful advertising, and agencies concentrate on building brands in an increasingly competitive market.

Major worldwide advertising agencies include Ogilvy & Mather, J. Walter Thompson, McCann Erickson, BBDO Starcom, MediaVest, Midshare, OMD, Young & Rubicam Advertising, Bartle Bogle Hegarty, and Saatchi & Saatchi.

The control of advertising

The Advertising Association (AA)

This is a UK federation of 32 trade bodies representing the advertising, promotional and marketing industries. It acts as a pressure group and also develops and monitors standards within the industry through the process known as self-regulation. Members include the Cinema Advertising Association, the Institute of Practitioners in Advertising, ITV Network Ltd, the Royal Mail, the Market Research Society and the Newspaper Publishers Association.

The Advertising Standards Authority (ASA)

This is a body established by the Advertising Association in 1962 to oversee the self-regulation of the advertising industry. Its principal requirement is that advertisements should be 'legal, decent, honest and truthful'. The ASA publishes a monthly journal, passes judgement on issues relating to the context of advertisements and handles complaints brought to its attention by members of the public.

Ofcom

Ofcom regulates the content and frequency of advertising on independent television. This includes ITV, Channel 4, Five and satellite broadcasters such as Sky. Its Code of Advertising Standards and Practice works in conjunction with that of the ASA. Ofcom replaced the Independent Television Commission, the Broadcasting Standards Council, the Radio Authority and the Radio Communications Agency under the terms of the Communications Act 2003.

Ofcom's provisions include the requirement that advertisements should not:

- give misleading descriptions of products
- make unwarranted claims about products
- make claims that alcoholic drinks enhance social or sexual success
- contain **subliminal** messages

Key term

subliminal advertising: a form of advertising that works on a subconscious level by introducing barely perceptible messages into other media texts and therefore influencing consumers without their realising it. This can involve flashing images on a screen for a fraction of a second or inserting soundtrack messages in audio transmissions.

- be used for political purposes
- be confused with programmes
- encourage dangerous driving
- offend against good taste and decency

Marketing

Marketing is the transmission of information about a media text to a target audience in such a way as to maximise its appeal to that audience. Marketing is a process that is designed to ensure the commercial and financial success of a product and a healthy return on money invested. Successful marketing involves strategies based on a detailed knowledge of product and audience, and the use of a wide variety of methods to stimulate audience interest.

Lifestyle marketing is the presentation of goods for sale within the context of a total way of life. It is bound up with **consumerism** as part of the fabric of Western economic and social structures.

Key term

consumerism: the economic system and variation of capitalism based around the compulsive consumption of goods and services within a framework of lifestyle marketing and advertising. Happiness, personal fulfilment and self-actualisation are shown as being achievable through the constant acquisition and accumulation of wealth and possessions.

Critics of consumerism point to the waste of valuable natural resources by a society with a 'throw-away' mentality. They argue that consumerism is sustained and developed by the media and advertising industry's constructions and representations of an unobtainable ideal lifestyle.

For example, television house-makeover programmes like *House Doctor* (Five) generate dissatisfaction in the audience and a desire to change the décor of their homes. *House Doctor* is sponsored by tile company Topps Tiles, which has an interest in selling and improving houses.

Theories of lifestyle marketing

Anthony Giddens

Anthony Giddens is an important theorist in the field of 'late modernity', who has studied the democratisation of all aspects of life, together with globalisation and the changing role of the state. He argues that we are no longer given our identity through socialisation and inheritance. We constantly work on our 'self' and seek to express who we are through the adoption of lifestyles represented in the media. These representations play an important part in helping us structure and review our identity, and make personal decisions about ourselves, our relationships and the world around us.

Vance Packard

US cultural analyst Vance Packard (*The Hidden Persuaders*, 1957) expanded on Maslow's hierarchy of human needs (see page 100) to explore the ways in which advertisers exploited and manipulated human needs to sell their products. He identified eight 'hidden needs':

- the need for emotional security
- the need for ego gratification
- the need for reassurance of personal worth or value
- the need to give and receive love and affection
- the need to be creative
- the need for power and control
- the need to identify roots and origins
- the need to feel immortal

In analysing advertisements, you should be able to find some or even all of the above needs being exploited by the advertiser.

The four Cs

This term was coined in the 1980s by advertising agency Young and Rubicam to explain the changing pattern of consumer behaviour identified during this period. The four Cs, or categories of consumer, were defined as:

- **Achievers** — people who have achieved career and financial success and are at the top of their profession. They are high spenders on luxury and quality goods who expect the best of everything, from home furnishings to cars and food products. They do not feel the need to display their wealth and success too obviously as they are quietly confident of their achievements.
- **Aspirers** — people who are trying to improve themselves and who use consumer goods as status symbols to represent their aspirational status.
- **Mainstreamers** — people who need to feel that they are like others. They seek reassurance and reliability in household names and famous brands.
- **Reformers** — people who are usually confident and well-educated, often with careers in the social services or education. They are resistant to

consumer advertising, instead following their own instincts and often campaigning for social change or improvement.

It was argued that these consumer groups sought out and acquired products which reinforced their sense of identity and values.

Significance of four Cs approach

This approach to marketing indicated a growing awareness of the need to target individuals, their lifestyles and identities rather than viewing them as part of a mass market. It also represented a move away from the social classification approach represented by the ABC1 system (see page 49). Rather than relying on traditional social class and income bracketing of consumers, the four Cs approach recognised that lifestyle aspirations and the use of products to create a sense of personal identity were important in the lives of consumers.

Case study

The grey market is the advertising and marketing term for the over 50s and retired people, who are increasingly seen as a lucrative market for specific goods and services, and are consequently targeted by advertisers and the media.

The over 50s are currently 20 million strong and increasing. They hold 80% of the nation's wealth and show an increasing tendency to spend their money on holidays and leisure activities, rather than leaving it to their children.

However, predictions about the value of the grey market and the amount of wealth available to the over 50s are subject to changes in lifestyle. The traditional family pattern is the norm in only 30% of households, with the young more likely to return home after college, so imposing new financial burdens on parents. Men in their 50s can experience divorce, remarriage and the starting of new families, with consequent financial commitments.

Traditional grey market areas include holidays, gardening, leisure and antiques magazines, and second homes. However, with life seemingly becoming more cyclical and less linear, stereotypes of the over 50s can be misleading.

Lifestage

This is an advertising term used in lifestyle analysis, based on the idea that people have different tastes and aspirations at different stages of their lives. These can be categorised as follows:

- **dependents** — those dependent on other people's money, such as children and students dependent on parents
- **empty-nesters** — adults whose children have left home
- **pre-family** — young couples without children
- **DINKs** (dual income, no kids) — couples with no children and a large disposable income
- **grey market** — over 50s and retired people with significant financial assets and few financial commitments

Task

Discuss the ways in which the increasing economic importance of the 'grey market' has influenced the representation of the over 50s in advertisements.

The new man

This is a term used to describe a new type of masculinity identified and developed by advertising media in the 1980s, in line with lifestyle marketing strategies. The new man was said to be sensitive and caring, happy to share household responsibilities and in touch with his emotions. This new man was said to be more appealing to women than the sexist, macho male of the past. He was also a perfect target for those companies advertising aftershaves, clothes, shoes and consumer goods of all kinds, as well as traditional male consumer goods like watches, gadgets, cars and expensive toys.

Branding

Branding is a form of marketing that seeks to identify a product, idea or individual as having a unique and separate identity incorporating desirable qualities that are offered to consumers.

Brand identity can be associated with a range of products — for example, the Marlboro brand, with its trademark masculine, outdoor appeal, has been successfully transferred from the declining cigarette market to the flourishing fashion market. Fashion houses like Armani can also transfer their brand to sunglasses and perfumes. The Virgin brand created by Richard Branson began with records at the beginning of the 1970s and has since been applied to an airline, trains, mobile phones, digital, financial and motoring services, and a chain of music stores.

Celebrities and lifestyle

A **celebrity** is an individual who has become the focus of media attention and is therefore widely known and recognised by the public.

Celebrities are often associated with a particular career, lifestyle or activity. Increasingly, they can be ordinary individuals who become famous, and often wealthy, as a result of their lives and personalities being publicised by the media.

Although they usually have no real authority, the opinions and life choices of celebrities — including their consumption patterns — are highly influential and can be exploited by advertisers.

Celebrities are often presented as brands, associated with and endorsing a range of products. For example, David Beckham's brand of cool

Case study

Celebrity marketing — the David Beckham brand

When David Beckham joined Real Madrid in 2003 he brought with him marketing opportunities that helped improve the club's finances. He cost £25 million as a player but came with endorsements and revenue from Audi, Adidas and Siemens. He generated an increase in advertising income, and sales of products such as shirts increased by 60% to a total of £36 million. The club estimated that his presence was worth more than £300 million in marketing revenue.

Beckham's comment that 'People talk about selling shirts but I'm here to play football' may have been true for him, but the club probably took another view. In reality, the 'Beckham effect' meant that Real Madrid overtook Manchester United in 2006 to become the richest football club in the world.

(Source: *The Times*, 5 July 2007)

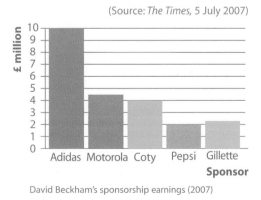

David Beckham's sponsorship earnings (2007)

masculinity can be associated with clothes, razors, trainers and mobile phones (see the case study on this page).

Remember that celebrities are involved in the construction of their own brand identity and that coverage of their activities — whether positive or negative — serves to endorse this identity.

Delivering audiences to advertisers

One of the main concerns of media producers is attracting advertising revenues. In order to do this, they must demonstrate that their products attract the audience sought by advertisers and sponsors. In effect, they aim to deliver audiences to advertisers.

For example, as discussed on page 102, the current most desirable target group is young and active women aged 25–44, who are seen as ideal for commercials and advertising.

Advertising and dissatisfaction

Imagine you are walking down the street feeling happy with yourself. You see an image of Kate Moss on a billboard looking glamorous and carrying a bag made by Dior. You are male and you wish you had a girlfriend like Kate Moss; you are female and you wish you had a figure like Kate Moss or a Dior bag. Either way, as an individual you have become dissatisfied with your present condition and wish for something more.

John Berger, an art critic, painter and author, produced a famous book and television series in 1972 called *Ways of Seeing*, which compared advertising images to images found in Renaissance painting. Berger argued that advertising (or 'publicity' as he called it) had become the new visual culture of a consumer society and was replacing traditional art forms. According to Berger,

'The purpose of publicity is to make the spectator marginally dissatisfied with his present way of life.' In advertising, 'The sum of everything is money, to get money is to overcome anxiety'.

Advertising and e-media

We have already considered viral marketing. Below are some examples of how big film studios have used small screens to market films:

- **Internet** — when Disney released *Pirates of the Caribbean: The Curse of the Black Pearl* (Gore Verbinski, 2003), it ran a competition on MySpace. The prize was to be the first to view a new trailer and send it to friends among the site's 74 million members.
- **Mobile phone** — the release of Paramount's *Mission: Impossible III* (J. J. Abrams, 2006) was marked by the distribution of ring tones of the familiar theme song and wallpaper images of star Tom Cruise.
- **BlackBerry** — when Columbia Pictures released *RV* (Barry Sonnenfeld, 2006) it launched a downloadable BlackBerry game, 'RV Pile-Up'.
- **Gaming** — Paramount made trailers for *Mission: Impossible III* (J. J. Abrams, 2006) and *Nacho Libre* (Jared Hess, 2006) downloadable for Xbox Live, a tactic also used by Sony via its PlayStation Portable (PSP).
- **Podcast material** — Disney makes all its movie trailers compatible with the video iPod. For the release of the Disney/Pixar film *Cars* (John Lasseter and John Ranft, 2006) it launched 15 iPod videos and created iTunes music playlists to reflect the characteristics of each of the film's vehicles.

Media theories

Theories about the mass media are mostly concerned with the impact and influence media products have on audiences, and how they can be used to further the interests of those with economic and political power in a society. This chapter deals with many theories already touched on elsewhere in the book, but in more depth and with A2 students in mind.

Media texts are social and cultural 'constructions' that are organised in particular ways to tell stories (narratives). Inscribed within them are particular meanings that go beyond simply providing information or entertainment. The media both represent and reproduce our social values and relations (ideology), and that is where theoretical issues and debates come in.

Media theories come in various guises, but they all sit somewhere between these two opposing hypotheses:

- **Reflection** — the media merely reflect the ideas and values of the external social world, providing a transparent 'window on the world'.
- **Representation** — the media control our reality, shaping and influencing social values according to the needs and demands of dominant elites.

Bill Schwarz (2006) suggests that media studies is bound by the 'necessity of understanding the media in order to understand contemporary life'. He warns that we need to see beyond a purely textual analysis approach to media studies. Looking at how representations of race, class or gender are 'constructed' in advertising is a valuable and stimulating exercise, but it is only a starting point. We also need to look beyond the ways in which texts are constructed and give greater consideration to the question of why.

Media studies at A2

Media studies at A2 requires us to consider the wider social, political, historical, technological and economic contexts that shape the construction and consumption of media texts.

Attempts to examine critically the media's role in contemporary life have produced many conflicting **theories**. Media theories are political in nature, and are determined by the social, economic and cultural backgrounds of those who propose them. For every theorist who sees the modern mass media as malign and manipulative, there is one who defends it as being an emancipatory and democratic force.

When watching a film, a Marxist, a feminist and a postcolonialist may be studying the same text but their interpretations of its effects and influence will invariably differ. With media theory there is no right or wrong answer but lots of fascinatingly different ones.

> ## Key term
>
> **theory:** an idea of or belief about something arrived at through speculation or conjecture; the body of rules, ideas, principles and techniques that applies to a particular subject, especially as seen as distinct from actual practice.

Use of media theories

It is important to be careful when using media theories. One of the most common errors students make is confusing theory and practice. Too often, students attempt to make an intrinsic link between the two. For example, a less able candidate may write:

> This advertisement uses Barthes' mythologies to sell a posh lifestyle.

This statement makes a sweeping generalisation. The producer of the text may not have consciously thought about mythologies. The advertiser in question may not even be familiar with the work of Barthes (it is impossible to know for sure). On the other hand, Barthes' theory about mythologies could be used as an investigative tool, to help us understand and analyse the text's values and meanings. Thus a more able candidate may write:

> We could say that the text uses a range of signifiers to connote, in Barthes' formulation, a mythology of bourgeois domesticity.

This is a far more conditional statement; it recognises that Barthes' theory — although quite relevant here — is only one of many theories that could be applied.

In this chapter we will look at the advantages and shortcomings of some of the main theoretical ideas and frameworks used in media studies. None of these should be studied in isolation, but at the same time you are not expected to learn all of them. It is important to develop a holistic approach to theory, and to be able to use a broad range of critical positions intelligently and appropriately.

Do:

- Use theories to help you understand and analyse media production and consumption.
- Exercise judgement and use appropriate theories.
- Engage with critical debates and use a range of conflicting theories to give your responses more intellectual depth. Be receptive to different ideas and opinions.

Do not:

- Look for theory as an integral part of the text.
- Expect all theories to fit all questions and contexts.
- Readily accept one particular theory as 'truth'.

Remember, 'practice' refers to the actual media text and 'theory' refers to the set of analytical tools we use for deconstruction and interpretation. Some tools are better for some jobs than others, but there is no one theory that can be applied to everything.

Analytical frameworks

Semiology

Semiology (or semiotics) has already been covered in Chapter 2. This chapter develops these ideas and concentrates on the extension of semiotic principles into other cultural forms. This extension is known as structuralism.

Structuralism and post-structuralism

Structuralism is the attempt to detect and analyse the underlying, universal rules that govern human communication, whether in linguistics or in media texts. Structuralist approaches were popular in British media and cultural studies in the 1970s, particularly in film studies. Although it now tends to be criticised for its 'totalising' approach, structuralism represents a good starting point for understanding how media texts are 'culturally' constructed. In this sense, structuralism is important to the formation of

media and cultural studies as serious academic disciplines. Structuralism regards the analysis of everyday **popular culture**, so often dismissed by elitist academics and critics as inauthentic or low-brow, as central to understanding the important role of culture in our social world.

The basic idea behind structuralism is that human language, values, symbols etc. are the product of culture, not nature. For example, we cannot adequately explain language as a purely biological function. We need words for reading, talking or listening, but our abilities to use words were not present at birth. We have acquired them culturally through our social relationships with parents, relatives, school and, of course, the media.

Ferdinand de Saussure and Roland Barthes

Structuralism was first developed by the Swiss linguist Ferdinand de Saussure (1857–1913) at the start of the twentieth century. Before Saussure, the study of language focused on philology — the evolutionary development of language — rather than its universal rules. Saussure's model is split between *langue* (universal structures) and *parole* (manifestations in different social and cultural contexts). According to Saussure, language does not refer directly to reality. For example, stones are natural but the names given to them (e.g. rocks, boulders, pebbles) are cultural. Language, then, has its own reality, mediating rather than directly reflecting. It is from Saussure that we get the key media terms 'signifier' and 'signified' — the 'object' and its associated, culturally generated 'meaning'. The relationship between the two is arbitrary.

The French academic Roland Barthes (1915–80) applied Saussure's structuralist ideas more immediately to popular culture. In his groundbreaking study *Mythologies* (1957), Barthes applied a structuralist semiotic approach to the texts and language of mass culture. Like Saussure, Barthes distinguished between two orders of signification: denotation (signifier) and connotation (signified).

Barthes took Saussure's work even further and came up with the idea that there is a third way we can read signs: ideology or myth. For Barthes, semiotic signs are 'arbitrary', i.e. there is no direct or natural link between the signifier (object) and its signified (meaning). Connotations are culturally specific — they belong to a particular time, place and people, and are representative of that society's shared ideas or values. Barthes calls those shared cultural meanings 'myths'. For a good example of how this works in practice, see the case study on Princess Diana as a cultural myth (page 20).

Remember not to fall into the trap of thinking that denotation and connotation are directly linked. Connotations are contextual — they mean different things to different people in different situations. An advertisement may denote a man in a smart suit and tie, connoting values of middle-class respectability. However, the same signifier in the context of a gangster film may connote ideas of style and deviance (see Gramsci's idea of 'common sense' on pages 227–28).

Claude Lévi-Strauss and Vladimir Propp

The French structural anthropologist Claude Lévi-Strauss (1908–) developed another structuralist interpretation of myth. His approach to anthropology was radically different from the traditional British idea of seeing primitive societies as 'childlike'. The British idea held that primitive societies had superstitious myths and legends, while the developed/industrialised countries had rational, scientific and philosophical explanations of the world. In his analysis of Indian myths, Lévi-Strauss suggested that these myths had, to a greater or lesser degree, the same underlying structures as our own modern narratives.

According to Lévi-Strauss, myths are the means by which cultures can attempt to resolve contradiction and explain the inexplicable. Central to Lévi-Strauss's theory is the idea that mythologies are structured around binary oppositions. In short, we understand the world by looking at relative differences between things, i.e. day and night, man and woman, war and peace. We understand things not just by what they are but also by what they are not.

Try to see connections between theories. For example, if we look at the idea of binary oppositions in relation to gender construction, we can begin to understand early feminist criticisms of media representations, which saw the construction of 'female' as the opposite of 'male':

Male	Female
Strong	Weak
Rational	Irrational/emotional
Self	Other

The same model can also be applied in a postcolonial context to the discourses of race and ethnicity.

Lévi-Strauss's concepts of mythology and binary opposition have been applied in film theory to the study of narrative structures (see pages 34–35). The structural driving force behind traditional film narratives is conflict. Most films begin by establishing a state of equilibrium; this is disrupted by the arrival of an opposing force, which must be defeated/resolved so that order can be restored. In the binary opposition between hero (good) and villain (evil) the audience is positioned, via the point of view of the hero, on the side of 'good'.

In early Western films, the 'goodies' and 'baddies' were indicated by hat colour — white and black respectively. More commonly though, film/television narratives are about conflicting loyalties or values rather than simplistic notions of good/bad.

This idea that modern media texts and pre-industrial folk stories share universal narrative structures can also be found in the work of Russian formalist writer and folklorist Vladimir Propp — see pages 35–36. Propp worked from the idea that narratives are central to human life, and argued that they provide us with a way of constructing and making sense of the world. In his study of Russian folk tales, Propp found that even though the stories differed in terms of characterisation, setting and plot, there was a set of basic character functions. Propp found that there were no more than eight character types, each with their own important narrative function.

Propp's ideas are a useful starting point for analysing narratives, but be wary of attempting to force narratives into Propp's structure. In many modern media narratives,

To what extent do Western films rely on ideas about 'goodies' and 'baddies'?

Case study

Life on Mars

In the BBC police-drama series *Life on Mars*, the 'politically correct' Sam Tyler travels back in time to 1973 and is united with the 'unreconstructed male chauvinist' Gene Hunt. However, in the two men's approach to policing we see an interesting binary opposition in play.

Hunt represents a more intuitive and uncompromising style of policing, where insulting people in terms of rank, gender, criminality or sexuality is 'all part of the job'. For Hunt, the end result — catching the criminal — is all that matters, regardless of the cost. Tyler, on the other hand, is schooled in the digital age of computer profiling, accountability and doing things by the book. The interesting thing is that it is Tyler who is forced to rethink and resolve his own value system.

We know that there is a social need for 'political correctness' but some people feel that it has gone 'too far'. In the case of contemporary law enforcement, we may feel that the police are hindered in their jobs by laws that seem to protect criminals. *Life on Mars* can be read as an attempt to resolve the opposing value systems of the 1970s with those of the early twenty-first century.

In what ways does a text such as *Life on Mars* represent contemporary views about political correctness and law and order?

particularly in films/television programmes, characters are ambiguous. For example, in Quentin Tarantino films, there may be no clear sense of which characters are the hero, villain etc.

Graeme Turner (1988) has demonstrated how Propp's eight character functions (below) fit neatly into the original *Star Wars* film:

The villain	Darth Vader
The donor	Obi-Wan Kenobi
The helper	Han Solo
The princess	Princess Leia
The dispatcher	R2-D2
The hero	Luke Skywalker
The false hero	Darth Vader

Ideas for discussion and development

Try applying Propp's character functions to a range of different film and television narratives.

• **Are they useful and are all characters always present? Have our storytelling techniques advanced at all since pre-industrial times?**

Turner has successfully applied Propp's function to *Star Wars* because, despite having a futuristic setting, the film has a very basic, almost fairytale narrative. Propp's ideas may not apply so readily to all media narratives, but they make an interesting structural connection between pre-industrial folk narratives and the supposedly more sophisticated narratives of the modern mass media.

Applying post-structuralism

Post-structuralism is notoriously difficult to define. Perhaps the easiest way to look at it is to say that it emerged out of a reaction to structuralist attempts to find a 'total' theory of 'universal' rules for all texts. Hence it is like postmoderism in that:

• it is made up of a plethora of other theories — including psychoanalysis, feminism, postcolonialism and structuralism itself (Roland Barthes, among other structuralists, has been associated with post-structuralism)

• it works against the scientific certainties of metanarratives — single over-arching theories like Marxism or Freudian psychoanalysis — which try to explain rationally how the social world works

• most of the academics/critics associated with post-structuralism deny both its existence and/or their involvement with it

This begs the question of how to apply a theory that is not really a theory. First, do not worry if you find it difficult to understand. Second, refer to it sparingly and only if you feel you can do so with confidence (manage this and you will certainly impress the examiner).

Let us look again at the structuralist idea of binary oppositions and character functions. This suggests that all texts operate within a structure of opposites — male/female, good/evil etc. Post-structuralism does not agree with the idea that 'binary oppositions' are an 'essential' part of the text, but are actively sought out by the reader. Similarly, think about the way we apply Propp's character functions to a film narrative. Does Propp's model fit perfectly for every film or do we sometimes have to shoe-horn characters into a specific role?

Structuralism is therefore as much a cultural text as the narratives it is used to analyse. 'Difference' is not a structural element of the narrative; it is something that the readers read into it. Post-structuralism argues that there are no guaranteed, universal structural elements in media texts, other than the ones which we, as media studies students, have been 'taught' to look for.

Modernism and postmodernism

Postmodernism, like postcolonialism and post-feminism, is an elusive and hotly debated subject. The only real definition of postmodernism is that it is a phenomenon that has no central or easy definition. To confuse matters even more, it is not solely confined to media (or cultural) studies but is associated with art, architecture, fashion, music and a whole host of academic disciplines.

The prefix 'post' denotes a historical break from modernism. On a connotative level, then, there is the implication that postmodernism represents a way of reading and representing the social world which is different from modernism.

Modernism can be defined as a philosophical and artistic movement that championed the 'high' culture of individual artists — like composer Schoenberg, writer James Joyce or painter Pablo Picasso — over mass-produced popular, or 'low', culture. The modernist era lasted from the mid-nineteenth century to the post-Second World War period. Modernism, moreover, is steeped in the Enlightenment notion of historical progess: this maintained that artistic and scientific knowledge would propel man towards absolute freedom (in this sense, Karl Marx is a modernist).

Modernism has been severely criticised by feminist and postcolonial writers for being elitist, patriarchal and Eurocentric — its thinkers were predominantly male and almost exclusively white and middle class. Questions of race and gender were at best ignored, and at worst treated with prejudice and scorn. In modernism, the thoughts of the white, male, middle-class European artist/intellectual are taken as being universal for all of humankind.

Postmodernism, on the other hand, is marked by an awareness of a multitude of identities along the lines of race, ethnicity, gender, sexuality, class, age etc. Just look at the number of different critical perspectives and debates in this section of the book.

The three main postmodern thinkers are Jean-François Lyotard, Frederic Jameson and Jean Baudrillard.

Key term

metanarrative (meta discourse): a postmodernist term used to describe all-embracing social theories, such as Marxism, which claim to provide a scientific framework for explaining how societies work. Postmodernists argue that in the fragmented postmodern world, dominated by media-generated realities or simulcra, such universal 'big stories' and 'big debates' no longer have validity in explaining the complex and often contradictory forces framing social, cultural and economic relationships.

Jean-François Lyotard: the end of big ideas

According to French philosopher Jean-François Lyotard (1984), the Second World War and the postwar period were pivotal in the collapse of modernism. He described the 'postmodern condition' as 'an incredulity towards **metanarratives**'. Contemporary society, Lyotard claimed, had lost faith in big ideas — or metanarratives — like technology, science or Marxism because they had failed to deliver their promises on a progressive society.

Modernists believed that Western society, in the post-Enlightenment age, had been following a linear path of history — moving towards a final goal of freedom and truth. However, after the Holocaust, the Hiroshima and Nagasaki bombings, the oppressive forces of European colonialism and the totalitarianism of Soviet Communism, the idea of civilised progress seemed far away.

Ideas for discussion and development

One of the main ideas to come out of Lyotard's work is the notion of 'fragmentation'.

- **How many different audience groups can you think of in terms of age, gender, class, ethnicity, educational background etc.?**
- **Do we still have single 'stereotypes' or have they also become fragmented? For example, think about how many different 'types' of grey market there are.**

Frederic Jameson: postmodernism or the cultural logic of late capitalism?

According to Frederic Jameson (1934–), the postmodern era is a postcolonial and postindustrial world of media-saturated global capitalism and consumerism. He sees the emergence of postmodern culture, in Marxist terms, as a result of a new era of social and economic life. He outlined three distinct periods of capitalism:

1 **Market capitalism** (roughly 1700–1850): an era of industrialisation in largely national markets.
2 **Monopoly capitalism** (1850s to the post-Second World War period): expansion of nation-states into a world market, organised around the imperialist exploitation of labour and resources from colonised countries (modernist period).
3 **Global capitalism** (post-Second World War period to the present day): growth of international corporations whose ownership and control transcends national boundaries (postmodern period).

Jameson's account of the mass-media culture seems to follow the Marxist model of base-superstructure (see page 226) — media industries create ideological smokescreens to hide real social and economic inequalities. However, he takes this idea further. Rather than seeing mass-media forms simply as distractions from/promotions of the economy, he argues that they have become economic products in their own right (see the section on the impact of new technology, pages 249–58):

> …everything in our social life — from economic value and state power to practices and to the very structure of the psyche itself — can be said to have become "cultural". (Jameson 1984)

Jameson's ideas about postmodern culture rely on the Marxist concept of reification (or alienation). According to Jameson, in the semiotic relationship of signs, the signifier and signified have, during the modern period, been moving further apart until the current postmodern era where, he suggests, signifier and signified are separated:

> …that pure and random play of signifiers which we call postmodernism [which] ceaselessly reshuffles the fragments of pre-existent texts, the building blocks of older cultural and social production, in some new and heightened bricolage.

In Jameson's view, postmodernism represents the erosion of the distinction between high art and popular culture. For him, postmodern culture

— including media texts — involves the random cutting and pasting of texts of all ages and styles. Think how many classic films have recently enjoyed Hollywood makeovers: *Psycho, Ocean's Eleven, Alfie, The Ladykillers, Cape Fear, Casino Royale* etc. For Jameson, postmodern culture lacks any kind of depth; it simply makes endless references to older cultural texts.

Jameson refers to this endless recycling of older texts as 'pastiche'. Modernist texts, by comparison, use parody — referencing older texts to make a political point. For example, James Joyce's novel *A Portrait of the Artist as a Young Man* (1914–15) reinterprets the myth of Icarus as an Enlightenment act of fleeing from the confines of family, nation and religion. According to Jameson, postmodern texts, such as the films of Quentin Taranatino, make intertextual references purely out of 'playfulness', 'knowing-ness' and fun (what is often referred to as postmodern irony).

> ### Task
> Use internet sites such as Wikipedia to find pastiche or homage references to *Psycho* in television, film and music texts.

Case study

There are many instances of the collision between high 'art' and popular culture. Football, for example, once the Saturday afternoon pursuit of working-class men, has now, in its live televised form, been driven to new cultural and commercial heights. Every televised UEFA Champions League match is accompanied by the 'Champions League' hymn, an arrangement by Tony Britten of Handel's 'Zadok the Priest' from the *Coronation Anthems*. The piece was performed by the Royal Philharmonic Orchestra and sung by the Academy of St Martin-in-the-Fields chorus in the three official languages used by UEFA: English, German and French.

Jean Baudrillard: hyperreality

Like Jameson, the French philosopher Jean Baudrillard believed that the postmodern world is one of media saturation involving endless recycling and reproduction of images. Baudrillard takes Walter Benjamin's point (see pages 254–55) — that technologies of mechanical reproduction have led to the creation of culture/artworks specifically because of their reproducibility — even further. For instance, we find out about politics, current affairs or celebrity gossip through media representations, but we have no way of knowing the truth of those representations (if, indeed, they truly exist). Baudrillard's point is that social and cultural processes, like politics or fame, are media events. For Baudrillard, the postmodern world has become so endlessly reproduced that the media is now our social reality. He calls this **hyperreality**:

The very definition of the real has become: that of which it is possible to give an equivalent reproduction… The real is not only what can be reproduced, but that which is already reproduced: that is, the hyperreal…which is entirely in simulation.

(Baudrillard 1983)

Baudrillard's ideas are difficult but they are applicable to A-level media studies. Think about the contemporary world of media celebrity. 'Famous' people used to appear in the media because they had a special skill (e.g. in entertainment or sport) in the external world; now they may be famous purely for being 'famous', with no life/skills beyond that of the simulated media world. The concept of 'reality television' is similar in that, although it is filmed in a documentary style, it has no reality outside the media (hyper) reality.

Ideas for discussion and development

Chantelle Vivien Houghton came to fame as the first 'non-celebrity' to feature in *Celebrity Big Brother* in 2006. As a twist to the show, she was instructed to convince the 10 'bona fide' celebrity housemates that she was a member of a fictional girl group, Kandy Floss, whose biggest hit was said to be 'I Want It Right Now'. She successfully fooled her housemates and proceeded to win the show.

In her *Big Brother* profile page, Chantelle portrayed herself as a 'bright, blonde bimbo'. She said, 'I look like Paris Hilton, not on purpose but it's just the way it turned out'. In the tabloid press, she has been given the more low-rent nickname of 'Paris Travelodge'.

• **Can you think of any other examples where the media manipulate the idea of celebrity?**

Chantelle Vivien Houghton

Political theory

Gender

When talking about **gender** we are referring to matters both masculine and feminine. However, a quick leaf through the index of most media books will reveal multiple feminist theory entries but few for 'masculinity'. Theories of masculinity have begun to emerge, but the issue of gender theory in media studies is a predominantly feminist affair.

Feminism comprises a number of social, cultural and political movements concerned with gender inequalities and discrimination against women in patriarchal societies. In today's world, we tend to take equal opportunities for granted. But it is worth remembering the gains made by the feminist movement in securing equality for women in the areas of law, education and employment and, more pertinently, in questioning and redefining the discourse of gendered subject identities in media representations.

Key terms

gender: psychological and cultural aspects of behaviour associated with masculinity and femininity acquired through socialisation, in accordance with the expectations of a particular society. Representations of gender increasingly challenge traditional concepts of masculinity and femininity.

gendered consumptions: the way that gender affects our consumption of media texts. Ann Gray (1992) suggested that women prefer open-ended narratives, such as soap operas, whereas men prefer closed narratives with a clear resolution, e.g. police dramas. The concept of 'women's fiction' (Christine Geraghty 1991) involves identifying characteristics in media texts that appeal to women, e.g. soap operas attracting large female audiences have strong female leads, deal with personal relationships in the domestic sphere and contain an element of escapism.

The term 'patriarchy' comes from two Greek words, *patēr* (father) and *archēs* (to rule), i.e. ruled by men. In Western capitalist societies, positions of influence and power in business, government, law, education and the media have traditionally been held by men. Men were seen as the organisers and providers; women, as naturally caring, passive and dependent. This gendered binarism has traditionally been represented as 'common sense' or natural in Western culture.

Sex and gender, while easily confused, are quite different. Sex is a biological given: men and women have a different physical and hormonal makeup. Gender, it is argued, is socially constructed, reproduced and 'naturalised' in cultural forms, such as media texts. It is, moreover, an ideological construction and by no means inevitable or permanent. The anthropologist Margaret Mead, in her classic study of tribal societies in New Guinea (1950), found that gender roles and sexual behaviour varied significantly from tribe to tribe. For example, in some cases she found that the women did the heavy physical work while the men reared the children and, among the Trobriand Islanders, the women were sexually aggressive and took the sexual initiative.

Feminist media theory is predicated on the notion that mass-media institutions operate within patriarchal discourses and, therefore, that media representations serve to reproduce and naturalise gender inequality. Feminist approaches to media studies are highly politicised because they challenge the media's reinforcement of dominant patriarchal ideologies. Like other political ideologies, feminism has its own history and its own debates and perspectives, which are beyond the scope of this book. For our purposes, we can roughly divide feminist media studies into three developmental stages:

- first wave feminism
- second wave feminism
- post-feminism

First wave feminism

This was a product of the political radicalism of the late 1960s/early 1970s. While feminists took many different theoretical approaches to analysing the media, they were united in the conviction that media forms (genres and narratives) and representations (stereotypes and subject positions) were a reflection of patriarchal society's view of women. Early analysis focused on such issues as narrative and representational objectification, and the ideological construction of femininity.

Objectification

Central to this early analysis was the idea that women were objectified in media texts, i.e. they were represented in advertising, cinema, newspapers etc. not as cognitive (thinking) subjects but as 'sexual' objects that existed merely to gratify male fantasies and desires. It could be argued that tabloid newspaper 'page three girls' are an example of this form of objectification.

However, the majority of work in this area was focused on film studies. A good example of the approach is Laura Mulvey's essay on the male gaze, 'Visual Pleasure and Narrative Cinema' (1975, see also pages 101–02). In it Mulvey argued that women's subject positioning in classical Hollywood film narratives replicates the same subordinate and sexually objectified status that they occupy in patriarchal society. The use of various film techniques, such as the point-of-view shot, makes audiences identify with the dominant male protagonist. Mulvey saw the practice of the camera lingering on women's bodies as evidence that women were being viewed as sex objects for the gratification of men. Women in the audience are also positioned by the narrative to identify with the male gaze, and, through the process of 'scopophilia' (the pleasure of looking), come to see the world through male eyes.

Case study

Some Like It Hot (Billy Wilder, 1959)

Wilder's screwball comedy, starring Marilyn Monroe, Tony Curtis and Jack Lemmon, is an ideal text to use for identifying and debating Mulvey's ideas. Monroe's body is pursued by the camera and held in the male gaze throughout the film. For example, the scene where Monroe's character first appears was as eroticised as 1950s

Marilyn Monroe in
Some Like It Hot

censorship laws would allow. Lemmon and Curtis abruptly stop talking, with the camera focused close up on their wide eyes and gaping mouths. The camera then cuts to their point of view: Monroe 'waggling' down the station platform, her hips and bottom filling the frame for a sustained period. The audience is therefore being invited to follow Curtis and Lemmon's point of view and enjoy their male gaze.

Interestingly, Curtis and Lemmon's characters are on the run from the mob, are disguised in drag and, as the narrative progresses, ironically become the object of the male gaze themselves.

Is a film like *Some Like It Hot* simply an example of sexist objectification of women or does it represent gender (masculinity and femininity) in more subtle ways?

Do these 'objectified' representations of women still exist in contemporary media texts?

Are similar 'objectified' representations of masculinity available?

Femininity

Charlotte Brunsdon (1991) suggests the terms 'femininity' and 'feminism' are opposites. She also notes that this distinction was crucial in early feminist analyses of 'feminine' media forms and genres, such as women's magazines and romantic fiction. According to critics like Brunsdon, Angela McRobbie (1978) and Judith Williamson (1978), women's magazines, while supposedly representing the issues, views and needs of their female readership, were in fact actively reproducing and reinforcing ideological positions of consumption, domesticity and sexual passivity/availability.

McRobbie (1978, 1991), focused on the narratives present in magazines for teenage girls. She found that one narrative structure (repeatedly referred to as 'love') occurred again and again: that emotional and financial success could be achieved by using idealised notions of 'femininity' — looking good, and being passive and submissive — to get the 'right' man, rather than in pursuing alternative paths of career, education etc. According to McRobbie, these magazines were complicit in validating and reproducing the dominant patriarchal ideology.

This first wave feminist movement created a number of important breakthroughs in the field of media studies:

- It was part of a wider political movement involved in the critique of gendered social inequality.
- It recognised the media's power and influence in representing and reproducing dominant ideologies of gender inequality.
- It spearheaded successful campaigns to have sexist imagery removed from the press and advertising.
- It put the issue of gender onto the media studies curriculum. McRobbie, for example, noted that British media and cultural studies courses in the 1970s focused on issues of class and male subcultures, and made little or no mention of gender politics.

However, these early feminist approaches can also be criticised in the following ways:

- They tended, through their reliance on structuralism and psychoanalysis, to see audiences as positioned in the text itself, and as such did not consider the complexities of the text–reader relationship that characterised later audience studies (see ethnographic audience studies on pages 239–40).
- Textual readings tended to assume the existence of a single dominant ideology at the expense of other possible meanings (such as oppositional or resistant).
- It can be argued that viewing capitalism and patriarchy as a joint universal system of male domination is too simplistic. Most feminist critics are from white, middle-class, academic backgrounds in Western countries. Their experiences of male oppression will be different from those of working-class women or, as postcolonial critics like Gayatri Chakravorty Spivak and Chandra Talpade Mohanty argue, from women in less developed countries.

Second wave feminism

This movement emerged in the 1980s and challenged the views of the earlier feminist media critics, who had effectively rebuked female audiences for passively accepting their subordination in patriarchal society.

It was noted that these earlier studies failed to consider the issue of pleasure when engaging with media texts. For example, Mulvey's essay does not mention the fact that women account for a sizeable proportion of cinema audiences. Why would women watch films or read magazines and romance novels simply to validate their subordinate identities? As McRobbie (1996) later put it, '…to dismiss so many millions of women as victims of ideology and therefore on the other side of feminism was both simplistic and demeaning to those ordinary women'.

Whereas early feminism battled for equality, and for women to be full 'subjects' like men, second-generation feminists — following the psycho-analytical insights of thinkers such as Luce Irigary — began thinking beyond such a simple concept of subjectivity. Sexuality and identity, they argued, are complex and never fully achieved.

We also need to remember that masculinity is not a fixed or 'natural' condition. As Andrew Tolson (1977) argued, men are as much subject to stereotyping and gender positioning as women are. They are raised to live up to a 'macho' image of strength and power, and must show themselves to be free of emotion and feeling. Images of such masculinity pervade media representations.

When looking at media representations of gender, we need to remind ourselves that they are not stable or uncontested. Media representations can be seen as a hegemonic attempt to anchor dominant notions of what it means to be male or female, but these are historically and culturally contingent. For example, images of males being interested in fashion and personal grooming were seen as deviant and 'cissy' in the 1970s. However, they have now gained hegemonic acceptance under the guise of 'metro-sexuality'.

The supposed binary opposition of 'feminine' and 'feminist' is more complex than was originally thought. Second-wave feminists argued that women could enjoy the pleasures of consuming feminine genres without mechanically accepting dominant patriarchal notions of femininity. For example, Janice Radway's ethnographic study of the romance genre (1984) showed that women read romantic novels as a way of evading domestic burdens, creating personal time and space away from domestic and familial duties — albeit in the escapist world of romance and sexual fantasy.

At this time, popular feminine genres like soap operas, romantic fiction and fashion magazines began to constitute a legitimate field of enquiry for feminist media and cultural studies. It was argued that, in despising popular feminine genres, early feminist critics were ironically very similar to elitist male academics and critics who traditionally dismiss such media products as culturally worthless.

Ideas for discussion and development

Look at the mid-week schedules in any television listings magazine or newspaper.

- **How do the reviews of popular 'female' genres compare to more traditionally 'male' genres, such as documentary or current affairs? Which is seen as an authored piece of work with a writer and/or director and judged on its aesthetic or social value? Which is described merely in terms of character or plot?**

Post-feminism

The term **post-feminism** first emerged in the 1990s. As with postmodernism, the prefix 'post' suggests a break or transformation from the past. There is much heated debate among feminist critics about what the term 'post-feminist' means, and how it differs from feminism and feminist issues of gender politics.

One of the basic ideas of post-feminism is that women can be both feminine/glamorous and enjoy equal economic and social power. A popular cultural manifestation of this ethos was voiced by the Spice Girls in the 1990s with their 'girl power' slogan. Whether the Spice Girls did strike a blow for women's rights or were merely cashing in on their own sexual objectification is a good point for discussion. Other texts worth examining in terms of post-feminist representations of women are *Sex and the City* and *Ugly Betty*.

There are perhaps two ways we can account for the emergence of post-feminism:

- The feminist campaigns of the 1970s/1980s have been successful in achieving gender equality and therefore feminism is no longer needed.
- The emergence of neo-conservative politics — particularly in the USA — has produced an ideological backlash against feminism.

There is evidence to support both accounts. As McRobbie (2006) points out, feminist issues, which had once been marginal and radical, had begun to fill the pages of mainstream women's magazines by the 1990s. The media, moreover, were full of stories about individual female success in business, sport, entertainment and politics. At the same time, there seems to have been a return to conservative notions of the nuclear family and traditional family values, particularly in politics and the popular press.

Marxism

Marxism is an ideology derived from the writings of the sociologist Karl Marx (1818–83). It provides us with a theoretical base for the critique of the economic, social and cultural conditions of capitalism. Marx's understanding of the workings of capitalism can be divided into three 'interlocking' models:

- **The economic model**, whose driving force is the creation and circulation of capital (money).
- **The social model**, in which the ruling class (the bourgeoisie) exploits the working class (the proletariat) for personal gain and profit.
- **The ideological model**, in which social forms, law, church, education, media etc. are used to reproduce and legitimise the exploitation of the proletariat and the resulting social inequality.

Before mass-production techniques were invented, individual workers controlled the whole production process. Under the capitalist mode of production — involving a division of labour — each worker is just a cog in the wheel, which leads them to become separated, or **alienated** in Marx's terms, from the fruits of their labours. Marx therefore saw capitalism as an unjust economic system in which the proletariat, as wage slaves, are pitted against their fellow human beings.

As a result of this situation, relationships between employer and employee are antagonistic and unequal, as the employer tries to maximise the profits from the workforce, paying as little as possible for the employee's labour while selling his or her output for the highest possible price.

From a cultural studies point of view, we could say that the emergence of the machine age and an urbanised mass workforce created the foundation for the modern mass media. Rural culture and pastimes either disappeared or were deemed unsuitable for urban living. Media and popular culture helped to fill the void, keeping the workforce entertained and, Marxists would argue, pacified.

Western media institutions, as discussed on pages 104–5, are profit-making commercial organisations that produce commodities for mass consumption. They are organised by the same principles of mass production and hierarchical control as any other industrialised capitalist business.

Note: do not confuse Marxism with communism. The theoretical tradition of Marxism in Europe (Western Marxism) has tended to be quite liberal, focusing more on the critiques of ideology and culture than the violent upheavals of revolutionary politics. Do not assume that Marx was opposed to the modern world. He welcomed the gains of science and technology, but thought that capitalism represented an alienating misappropriation of industry's true potential for human advancement.

Case study

Hollywood studio system

The basic business model for the classic Hollywood studio system is like any other mass-production industry:

- Division of labour — a film is not the product of a single person but involves many different people, from producer, director, cinematographer and editor to the set builders and props department.

- Chain of command — power is structured in a pyramid formation, with the least skilled/least powerful manual workers at the bottom significantly outnumbering the few powerful decision makers/financiers at the top.

- Mass production — films are made on a conveyor-belt process. At any one time, a studio can be working on a number of films, each at a different stage in the production process.

- Supply and demand — large-scale producers manage this by having controlling interests in distribution and exhibition, thus making it difficult for small-scale companies to gain a foothold in the industry.

The media are a commercial industry in that they mass-produce commodities for mass consumption. However, these commodities are also cultural texts that affect the way we see and think about the world in which we live. Media texts do not merely inform or entertain; they also provide particular 'ideological' representations of the social world.

From a Marxist perspective, media and cultural industries support the commercial and ideological needs of the ruling capitalist classes in the following ways:

- Mass production of cheap and easily accessible cultural forms — films, comics, television programmes, magazines etc. — destroys traditional forms of culture and diverts the working classes from seeing the inequities of their subordinate social status. Media products therefore provide an 'escapist' opiate for the masses. (Hollywood, interestingly, is popularly known as the 'dream factory'.)
- Media representations of the social order mask the underlying historic and economic conditions of class society, thus naturalising and reproducing these conditions.
- Media texts actively promote and reproduce dominant capitalist values and ideologies — e.g. private ownership, commercial success, individualism, class hierarchies and the patriarchal family — making them seem an obvious and inevitable result of human nature.

The basic Marxist model for analysing culture is known as the **base-superstructure model**:

Base = economic control/ownership of production
Superstructure = social, political and cultural forms

In this model, power is a one-way process. An example of the way it works is that the people who own the television company or newspaper have the means/power to promote their politics and ideas to a wider audience. Accordingly, media producers can impose their own values and ideology on the audience (see the section on Adorno and Horkheimer's critique of the 'culture industry', pages 255–56).

The base-superstructure model has met with strong opposition in media studies and is now generally thought of as being too inflexible, for the following reasons:

- Its reliance on economic determinism (i.e. economic ownership of production as the single dominant factor) leaves no room for other social, cultural and political factors that also affect values and ideology.
- The notion that media texts have a single underlying meaning makes no concession to the idea of 'active audiences'. Audiences are seen as passive 'dupes', taking on dominant ideology wholesale and without question

(for a critique of this view, see the sections on encoding/decoding on pages 238–39, and ethnographic audience studies on pages 239–40).

- It tends to see social conflict in purely class terms, with little consideration given to issues of race, gender or sexuality.
- By focusing on ideology and power, it fails to consider questions of pleasure or taste. Media texts are analysed solely for ideological meaning, and the idea that people might consume media texts purely for escape, pleasure or other gratifications is not considered.

Nonetheless, there are still good reasons why we should not dismiss Marxism out of hand. First, it recognises the media's powerful role in the reproduction and transformation of social relations. Second, it reminds us of the enormous institutional power of the media — which some populist audience studies, with their emphasis on multiple reader response and indeterminacy of meaning, have all but forgotten. (Remember, many of our ideas about the world come from the media.)

Gramsci and hegemony

The concept of **hegemony** was first developed by the Italian Marxist thinker Antonio Gramsci (1971). It represented an attempt to think beyond the economic determinism of the base-superstructure model. Politics, ideology and culture are not directly controlled by the economy but exist outside it. Gramsci suggested that ideological control does not come from economic ownership, but is filtered through various social institutions such as the law, the church, family, education and the media.

'Hegemony' is an ancient Greek word and refers to the dominance of one state (or class/social group) over another. Gramsci defined hegemony as '…moral and physical leadership, leadership which manages to win active consent of those over whom it rules'. Once a particular group has achieved hegemony, its viewpoint becomes accepted by public opinion as **common sense**, making it difficult for opposition groups to launch an effective challenge.

Identifying their interests with common sense is one of the means by which elites in a society can maintain their position of power. For example, between 1979 and 1997 the Conservative Party achieved hegemony with its policies for transforming the economy. Margaret Thatcher's phrase 'there is no alternative' expressed common sense views widely held at the time. Mainstream media texts are also seen as supporting dominant ideology and the common-sense consensus.

Gramsci saw the enormous influence and appeal of mass popular culture on workers in the industrial areas of northern Italy. This experience lead him to break with earlier Marxist ideas about audiences being duped into 'false consciousness', leading him instead to take a more humanist approach. Hegemonic power, according to Gramsci, has to be won through negotiation and is rarely, if ever, complete.

The concept of hegemony is extremely useful in media studies because:

- Seeing power as a dynamic two-way process allows the relationship between audience, text and institution to be seen as a complex one. Media audiences can be viewed as active consumers rather than a powerless mass being brainwashed by powerful institutions.
- Media representations of social forms such as race, sexuality or gender operate at the level of 'common sense' not because they are imposed from above, but because they work in concurrence with dominant social values and ideas.
- It allows us to envisage the idea that dominant ideologies are unsettled and always struggling with opposition from counter-hegemonic movements. For example, feminist campaigners have actively resisted 'common-sense' notions of femininity and have fought to redefine the terms of gender representations.

Nonetheless, hegemony, like any other theoretical framework, is not infallible:

- Some postmodern critics (see pages 214–17) have all but given up on metanarratives like Marxism and see no future for ideas of liberation or improvement.
- The fall of the Berlin Wall (1989) and the collapse of Soviet communism (1991) have led to a disenchantment with Marxism (which is often conflated with communism).

Liberal pluralism

Liberal pluralism can be explained as a symptom of globalisation and the collapse of national boundaries. As media production (and consequently consumption) happens on an increasingly global scale, it is difficult to pinpoint where the centre of political, social and economic power lies, or what its dominant ideology is. It can therefore be argued that classic models of media analysis (e.g. Marxism) based on the notion of the media being the mouthpiece of dominant national ideology are outdated. Instead, we see the emergence of a co-existence of many different theoretical positions.

pluralism: the view that where a society comprises a wide range of social and ethnic groups with different values, political and ideological beliefs, representations by the media will naturally reflect this diversity.

Pluralist models of the media suggest that, with a large number of organisations producing a wide variety of media texts, audiences and readers have total freedom of choice as to what they consume. This approach is challenged by the Marxist emphasis on economic determinism.

The liberal pluralist perspective can be summarised into three main ideas:

- **Reflection** — the mass media reflects rather than shapes social reality. It does not prescribe or transform social thought. In this sense, the media act merely as a messenger, carrying a message of pre-existing reality.
- **Autonomy** — the modern global media have a high degree of independence from state, government and politics. State ownership of the media and national models of public service broadcasting are on the wane and thus have a greatly diminished influence in contemporary social life. Similarly, media audiences are free to interpret texts according to their own individual needs and desires, and are not controlled or subjugated by dominant ideologies.
- **Consumer sovereignty** — competition within a global free market ensures that the media react to the needs, values and desires of the public. This means, for example, that the proliferation of fiction-based narratives and reality shows in our television schedules has occurred because these programmes are popular with audiences. The media simply give the public what it wants.

Audience research

Pluralist models developed as a response to narrower Marxist notions of the media audience as passive absorbers of dominant ideology. Pluralists such as Fiske (1987) argued that audiences 'actively' create their own meanings and pleasures. However, as Ang (1995) notes, Fiske's 'celebration of the semiotic power of audiences to create their own meanings' has been severely criticised for its 'connivance in free market ideologies of consumer sovereignty'.

From the pluralist point of view, media audiences are reduced to being 'consumers', in the sense that the consumption of media products is seen as no different from the consumption of other consumer goods. Global media corporations, such as Time Warner and Disney, subscribe to such a view, understandably, because it masks the ideological and economic power they hold.

The idea of plurality can be called into question by considering the idea of reflection. Audiences may actively create their own meanings, but they do not have the power to determine what aspects of society the media reflect upon. Postmodern globalisation may have led to a multiplicity of different identities and ideas among audiences, but this does not ensure that the media will always have a liberal, democratic agenda.

Global media corporations are powerful capitalist institutions with the economic, legal and political power to ensure that their particular reflections of society get produced, publicised, distributed and exhibited. The fact that these corporations operate within the structures of global consumer capitalism says much about the discourses they are inclined to promote. As Curran (1996) put it: '...if the media have so little effect, why study them?'

Ideas for discussion and development

- **Can you think of places, social groups and issues that are not routinely represented in the media?**
- **In our fragmented world, where political debate is no longer easily defined, it is said the media 'reflect' a plurality of voices. Is this the case or are more institutionally powerful discourses given greater representation?**

Colonialism and postcolonialism

Postcolonialism, like post-feminism and postmodernism, is a problematic concept. There are two spellings of the term: 'post-colonial' and 'postcolonial' (with and without the hyphen), the two having quite distinct meanings:

- In its hyphenated form, the term post-colonialism refers to the period after **colonialism** — the military, economic, political and cultural occupation of African, South American, Australasian and Asian territories by European countries from the sixteenth to the twentieth centuries. The system collapsed in the second half of the twentieth century, with liberation movements securing the independence, or decolonisation, of most former colonies.
- In its non-hyphenated form, postcolonialism refers to the lasting social and cultural legacy of colonial rule and, in many instances, oppression.

Postcolonial theory involves challenging the discourses of **cultural imperialism**. Colonial rule was not just about economic and political control; it also involved the cultural imposition of colonisers' language, discourses and subject identities. Postcolonial theory seeks to create a new language and identity for post-colonial subjects, rescuing them from the sense of disempowerment and cultural humiliation created through colonial discourses.

One of the first expressions of postcolonial theory can be seen in the work of Franz Fanon (1967, 1968). Working in the 1950s and 1960s as a psychiatrist in Algeria during its struggles for independence, Fanon was well placed to study the effects of colonialism on the minds of the colonised (see also Albert Memmi 1965 for a similarly located study).

According to Fanon, colonialism is so thoroughly internalised in the colonial mind that post-colonial rule simply mimics the operations of the coloniser. In this case, the colonised subject follows the oppressive lead of his or her former rulers, often expressing control through violence and force. In Fanon's view, escaping this predicament required a new postcolonial identity that would find expression through the development of positive representations in cultural practices, such as literature, drama and film/media. For example, the creation of a national cinema in India — known as Bollywood (based in Mumbai) — can be seen as a powerful means of challenging the cultural imperialism of Western media institutions.

Key term

cultural imperialism: the dominance of Western, particularly US, cultural values and ideology across the world. Cultural imperialism is a growing issue, with globalisation and the increasing domination of world media output by a few giant companies. This is combined with the tendency of the dominant culture to absorb texts generated by other cultures and to reproduce them in its own image. For example, the Spanish film *Open your Eyes* (Alejandro Amenábar, 1997) was remade with Tom Cruise in a US context as *Vanilla Sky* (Cameron Crowe, 2001); the Japanese horror film *Ring* (Hideo Nakata, 1998) was remade in the USA as *The Ring* by DreamWorks (Gore Verbinski, 2002).

Case study

Edward Said, *Orientalism* (1978)

Said's work on 'orientalism' is one of the key texts in postcolonial theory. Employing the ideas of French philosopher Michel Foucault on the relationship between power, knowledge and discourse, Said suggests that the Orient (the East) has been simultaneously constructed as both a geographical and imaginary space in Western (occidental) discourses.

By creating a discourse about the Orient in practices as varied as literature, anthropology, art and science, the West has been able to exercise power over its subaltern ('powerless' in Gramsci's terminology) 'other', the East. Said believed that such discourses were used to validate and legitimise the West's hegemonic control of the East. According to Said and other postcolonial theorists, the Western colonial project may be over in the geographical sense, but it is still a powerful discourse in cultural terms.

Do Western media representations of Eastern cultures — particularly Islam — focus on 'otherness' and difference (from the West)?

One of the main debates to come out of Said's work (see case study, above) is about what constitutes 'authentic' voices. Postcolonial theory is predominantly practised in Western academic institutions and thus operates within Western discourses of knowledge and power (even though many postcolonial theorists are from the less developed countries). In short, the Western institutions that helped to construct the colonial 'other' are now assuming the power to deconstruct and inscribe new cultural identities — a point that is picked up on in the work of the Indian post-colonial theorist Gayatri Chakravorty Spivak (1990).

Like many postmodern positions, postcolonial theory denies the existence of Eurocentric 'totalities'. Remember that the linear idea of history — e.g. pre-colonial, colonial, post-colonial — emerged out of the white, male-dominated European Enlightenment. Colonisation was not a single homogeneous event, and by the same token neither is postcolonialism. Its effects and legacies are felt quite differently by postcolonial subjects in, for instance, Ireland and Australia than they are in India or South Africa.

It is important to remember, as Stuart Hall (1995) suggested, that a film is not necessarily good just because it is made by a black film-maker. According to Hall, simply replacing the formerly 'negative' black stereotype with a new 'positive' stereotype is not a particularly useful exercise. Media representations of identity are ambiguous and complex, and are seldom reducable to simple ideas of negative or positive. *Do the Right Thing* (Spike Lee, 1989) and *Crash* (Paul Haggis, 2004) are two films that deal with the problematic nature of representing ethnicity.

Ideas for discussion and development

Postcolonial questions should be considered when discussing the effects of globalisation and the impact of new digital technologies:

- **There is perhaps a tendency to overstate the democratic potential of the internet, but do less developed countries enjoy the same access to digital communications technologies as people in the West do?**
- **Are Western cultural practices imperialist? Does the proliferation of Hollywood cinema, Western popular music and Western popular television represent a threat to the continuation of indigenous cultural practices?**
- **Are Western cultural texts simply better, or is it less expensive for many countries to buy them in than to produce home-grown texts?**
- **Is the global expansion of Western culture an inevitable consequence of free-market capitalism?**

Media consumption and production

Audience theory

There are two ways main ways of categorising media audiences:

- **Institutionally** as a quantifiable group, e.g. in terms of television viewing figures, cinema box office numbers or identifiable 'target audience' groups.
- **Discursively** as ways of theorising and interpreting the interplay of power and reading between media texts and media audiences.

The first is useful but limiting, falling more into the camp of opinion polls and market research. It may show statistically what is popular (or not) but does not explain how or why.

The second is a far more wide-reaching category and the source of endless debates in media and cultural studies. As we will see, there are several approaches to theorising about audiences, each with their own merits and limitations.

The traditional approach to audience theories and debates in A-level media studies tends to be limited to exploring the opposing camps of the effects model and the uses and gratifications model of audience research. This distinction is based on seeing audiences as either passive or active in response to media texts.

Passive audience theories

Passive audience theories are theories that see audiences as passive recipients of media output. Passive theories tend to see audience behaviour as directly affected by media content and theorists are concerned to measure these effects, particularly with regards to the effects of media portrayal of sex and violence.

Effects theory

Effects theory is concerned with the underlying 'message' of media texts. Audiences are viewed as an uncritical and undifferentiated mass who are in thrall to the powerful pleasures of media texts. The effects model thus focuses primarily on what effect the media have on people's thinking and behaviour. One of the best known is the **hypodermic** model, where there is an implication that meanings are literally injected into the audience's minds with no interpretative process occurring. This idea, moreover, has connotations of the media being addictive, destructive and manipulative.

One of the biggest criticisms of the effects model is that it focuses exclusively on the negative effects of the media. For example:

- **Social control** — the opiate powers of the media lull people into a state of 'false consciousness', preventing them from seeing the real conditions of their lives.
- **Copycat behaviour** — deviant behaviour seen in media texts (e.g. violence, drug-taking or sexual promiscuity) is mindlessly reproduced in real life, provoking moral panics (which are then reported in the media).

Key term

Bobo doll experiment: an experiment on social learning and the transmission of aggression carried out by Albert Bandura in 1961.

Bandura got children to watch a video where an actor aggressively attacked a plastic clown called a Bobo doll. The children were taken to a room where there were attractive toys they were not allowed to touch. They were then taken to another room with dolls similar to the ones seen in the video. Bandura observed that 88% of the children imitated the aggressive behaviour they had seen. Eight months later 40% of the children still reproduced the same violent behaviour.

The work is often used to justify the view that media violence encourages violence in television and film viewers, although there is no evidence in Bandura's work that aggressive behaviour towards a doll would be transferred to a person.

There are several problems with effects theory. First, objective evidence about the effects of media products on audiences is difficult to gather and assess. Critics like Guy Cumberbatch argue that studies are often devised in such a way as to justify the opinion of the researcher, and that there is a serious shortage of valid objective evidence. Second, the effects theory makes generalisations about 'weaker' social groups, such as children (e.g. all children are affected by television violence). The proponents of this model — academics, politicians and newspaper editors — tend to be middle-aged, middle-class and educated individuals who see themselves as existing outside the uncritical mass.

The effects theory has, ironically, created an alliance between critics from the conservative right and those from the anti-capitalist left who, while driven by very different agendas, share an affinity in their assumptions about the 'unconscious masses'. However, as Raymond Williams (1989) argued, 'there are in fact no "masses" but only ways of seeing people as "masses".' The media audience is as much an ideological construction as

the media text itself, which is imagined within discourses of prejudice and power.

Ideas for discussion and development

Moral panics

Take a recent moral panic based on negative effects theory — such as 'cyber bullying' — and look at the differences in age/gender/social position of those perceived to be 'at risk' compared to those discussing the risk.

- **What assumptions do the researchers or campaigners make about the 'at risk' group?**
- **Does the 'at risk' group have access to the same communications resources as the researchers/campaigners?**
- **Has there ever been a media moral panic about white, middle-class men? If not, why not?**

Cultivation theory

Cultivation theory comes under the same tradition as the effects model, with the emphasis shifting from immediate to slower, more ideological effects on audiences. It was begun by George Gerbner in the 1960s. Gerbner conducted research on how watching television affects people's views of the real world. Cultivation theorists argue that television has long-term effects, which are small, gradual, indirect, cumulative and ultimately significant. Television tends to reinforce values already present in a culture and to support the dominant ideology. Cultivation research also focuses on exposure to violence and sex and whether or not this can be said to influence viewers.

Cultural effects theory

Also known as the 'drip drip' theory, cultural effects theory argues that, in the absence of real substantial evidence of the direct relationship between media texts and people's behaviour, the effects of exposure to the media should be seen as long term and more subtle.

Constant exposure to particular messages can be seen as slowly affecting judgement and attitudes in the same way that the constant dripping of water from a tap wears away a stone. Cultural effects theory is associated with Stuart Hall and a Marxist approach to the part played by media content in reinforcing dominant ideology, in particular in relation to race and gender issues.

Media theories

In some cases, audiences may accept the preferred readings of **polysemic** media messages without challenging them, while other audiences may resist texts with oppositional readings. Negotiated readings, where audiences partially accept texts, represent a compromise between these positions.

Dependency theory

This theory is associated with researchers Sandra Ball-Rokeach and Melvin DeFleur, and focuses on the degree to which audiences become dependent on the media. Ball-Rokeach and DeFleur argued that the greater the uncertainty in a society, the more audiences will become dependent on media communication to form judgements and make sense of the world. Although it is obvious that most people depend on the media for knowledge of news and events outside their immediate experience, the approach probably underestimates the extent to which audience members will form negotiated or alternative readings of texts, other than those intended, in line with their own experience, attitudes, beliefs and values.

Does television directly affect children's behaviour?

Two-step flow

This theory sees media messages as reaching a mass audience in two stages. The model was devised by Elihu Katz and Paul Lazarsfeld in 1955 and was a move from the classic **stimulus response** principles, which had dominated audience theories during the 1940s.

The first of the two stages involves people called **opinion leaders** with influential status in society. In the second stage, these people pass on the message to the larger audience. The mass audience's willingness to accept the message is seen as being influenced by the status of the opinion leader.

Active audience theories

Active audience theories see the audience as active participants in the process of decoding and making sense of media texts. In active theories, the social and educational background, beliefs, values and life experiences audiences bring to a text are seen as influencing the way they accept, negotiate or challenge the preferred reading.

The uses and gratifications model

This model focuses on what people do with the media rather than what the media do to people. It argues that audiences have the power to choose their media consumption to gratify their own particular interests and desires, including the pursuit of entertainment, escape, diversion, and sexual or emotional stimulation. The approach is socio-psychological in nature, and gives more credence to the cognitive and emotional capacities of the audience. The media text and its underlying message is of little consequence.

The uses and gratifications model was developed in the USA by Jay Blumler and Elihu Katz in 1975, and was centred on the ever-expanding medium of television. Researchers sought to find out why people watch television and what pleasures they gain from it (e.g. education, emotional satisfaction, social identification or relaxation).

While this approach redresses the pessimism and prejudice of the effects tradition, it lacks a critical edge. By focusing solely on the audience, it sidesteps questions of influence and offers little or no critique of the power relations involved with the capitalist mass media. As Ang (1995) points out, the gratificationist formulation of the audience as powerful, active consumers with free choice equates this model with the triumphalist rhetoric of liberal pluralism (see pages 228–30). It could be argued that this model underestimates the power of the media in generating audience needs in the first place.

Ideas for discussion and development

Think about your own reasons for watching television.

- **Is it to gain knowledge or understanding about something? Or is it simply a means of relaxing after a hard day at school or college?**
- **How would you rather see yourself — as a passive victim of media effects or as an active reader with the freedom to choose your own media consumption?**

The encoding/decoding model

This model was devised by Stuart Hall in 1974, when he was director of the Centre for Contemporary Cultural Studies (CCCS) at the University of Birmingham. Under Hall's direction, the CCCS was highly influential in advancing the political and academic scope of British media and cultural studies, introducing ideas from anthropology, structuralism, semiotics and Marxist critical theory onto the agenda. Audience studies, particularly anthropological approaches, is one of its lasting legacies.

At its simplest, encoding/decoding is a synthesis of the effects and the uses and gratifications models. Hall believed that the liberal notion of consumer choice embedded in the uses and gratifications theory lacked any acknowledgement of institutional power. However, effects theory — particularly when framed in the Marxist base-superstructure notion of dominant ideology — was oppressive and coercive.

Hall argued that the battle for meaning was consensual and ongoing, and he came up with three different models of audience response:

- **Dominant** — broadly speaking, the recognition and acceptance of the 'preferred meaning/reading' or dominant ideology, for example those people who saw themselves as belonging to the 'nation in mourning' in the aftermath of the death of Princess Diana in 1997.
- **Oppositional** — the recognition, but simultaneous refusal, of the preferred reading, for example republicans or anti-monarchists who would not have given Princess Diana the same recognition.
- **Negotiated** — an ability to accept some of the preferred reading but to adapt it in the light on one's own beliefs, for example those who saw Diana's death as tragic but the public response to it as over the top.

Encoding/decoding was an important development because it attempted to resolve the text/context division in audience studies. Both text and audience are seen as operating within structures of power, where meaning is hegemonically contested in a two-way negotiation.

There are, however, some problems with this approach. First, it limits audience response to ideological meaning. As the research tended to focus on factual/news programmes, issues of pleasure — associated more with fictional narratives — were not considered. In addition, as befitted the broadly Marxist agenda of the CCCS in the 1970s, ideas of acceptance/opposition were defined more in terms of class rather than gender or ethnicity. Finally, the research conditions — which involved

people watching videotape in an academic environment — were somewhat artificial, making no allusion to the effects of a domestic context (as was focused on in later empirical audience studies).

Ethnographic audience studies

The most recent trend in audience research is to study audiences anthropologically in their domestic environment. Television, which accounts for the majority of domestic media consumption, constitutes the central focus of audience ethnographies. This method evolved from the Birmingham CCCS, so is commonly known as the **cultural studies approach**, **audience theory** or **reception theory**.

This active audience theory is associated with the work of John Fiske, Michel de Certeau and, in particular, David Morley. It sees the audience as actively engaging in the interpretation of media texts, rather than being simply passive consumers.

According to David Morley (1980), media studies tended to focus too much on the relationship between text and subject rather than text and context. Morley referred to structuralist and psychoanalytical approaches in 1970s film studies — or 'screen' theory, as it became known, after the British academic film journal, *Screen*, in which many of the articles appeared. In screen theory the audience is seen as a construction of the text. Film and television texts are studied for the ways in which they position or construct audience identification.

In his 1980 study, 'The *Nationwide* Audience' (*Nationwide* was an evening current affairs television programme that ran from 1969 to 1983), Morley found that audiences decoded media texts in ways related to their social and cultural circumstances and individual experience, which could be explored using the qualitative, ethnographic methods of group interviews and participant observation. He concluded that meaning is not found in the media text itself, but can change according to the different contexts in which audiences interpret it. Therefore, to understand audiences, the researcher must undertake empirical fieldwork and study audiences in their own contexts, namely the home.

In his *Nationwide* study, Morley showed that different groups interpreted the same texts differently depending on their own background and level of involvement with the subject matter. For example, a group of management trainees saw *Nationwide*'s items on trade unions as being biased towards the unions, whereas a group of workers saw the same items as being anti-union. Morley used the terms 'dominant', 'negotiated' and 'oppositional' readings (also associated with the work of Stuart Hall) to categorise responses.

Morley's approach is important because it combined semiological and sociological approaches. Semiological study involves the idea of directed preferred readings of media texts, and sociological study is concerned with how age, sex, race, class and gender may determine the reading of a text.

This approach was developed further in the 1990s through the work of David Buckingham. His research concluded that even by the age of 7, children have become skilled readers of media texts, and are able to interpret, challenge and reject media messages, including advertising. This research can be used to challenge earlier media effects models, which argue that audiences, particularly children, are affected negatively by media content.

Recent studies

Since the 1980s, a number of important audience ethnographies have been produced. For example, Ann Gray, studying the 'gendering of [domestic] leisure technology' (1987, 1992), found that the married women in her project watched popular television genres for 'escapist' reasons. Not for mindless escapism in the 'effects' sense, but for creating symbolic spaces of resistance — time on their own or with friends, away from the everyday demands of marriage and motherhood. Far from being unconscious of the media's role in reproducing gender inequality, the women in Gray's study were able both to identify with their media positionings and to struggle against them.

Marie Gillespie's work on 'Technology and tradition: audiovisual culture among South Asian families in West London' (1989) is another example of the ethnographic approach. Gillespie's cross-generational study looked at the complex relationship between British Asian families and the video player. Interestingly, she showed that media consumption and technology not only points to generational/cultural differences but also helps to sustain and strengthen older cultural traditions.

However, there are problems with the ethnographic approach:

- The presence of the researcher creates an artificial setting. People modify their behaviour when a stranger is present in their home, particularly when that stranger is a middle-class academic.
- In a number of disciplines — including anthropology, sociology and cultural studies — academic researchers have begun to cast doubt on

their own ability to represent the 'truth'. As a result, many studies — e.g. Valerie Walkerdine (1986) — have focused as much on introspective questions about the researchers' authority, role and influence as on simply representing the observed group.

- Observing people's domestic media consumption may be interesting in its own right, but the data themselves do not constitute an end point. There are many debates about what theoretical frameworks ought to be used to make sense of the data collected.

New communications technologies: interactive audiences

The audience research approaches we have looked at so far are all concerned with the traditional, one-to-many, model of media communications. For example, the transmission, or 'flow', of television is a one-way process from encoder to decoder, with no instant 'right to reply'. (The nominal presence of 'feedback' loops in terms of viewers' responses, typified by the BBC's *Points of View* programme, or phoning in to complain, were always limited and therefore unsatisfactory.)

However, recent developments in communications technologies have resulted in a different kind of active audience. Audiences can now be more closely engaged in dialogue with media producers through blogs and posted comments, and they can even generate media texts of their own. Audience theory now needs to address this new generation of active and interactive audiences.

Case study

Television feedback

In the 1960s and 1970s, the pro-censorship pressure group the National Viewers and Listeners Association (NVLA), founded and led by 'ordinary housewife' Mary Whitehouse (1910–2001), achieved some success in influencing BBC programme decisions by orchestrating mass phone-ins to complain about programmes it found offensive.

The NVLA exploited the fact that the BBC, at the time, regarded a few hundred complaints about a programme as a significant number and sufficient to take seriously the views of this relatively small and insignificant pressure group. By giving the

NVLA television coverage and discussing its agenda of 'cleaning up television' seriously, the BBC gave the group 'the oxygen of publicity' and, with it, credibility. Television interviews helped to turn Whitehouse herself into a television personality — in today's terms, a 'celebrity'. She later claimed to having never watched the programmes and films she wanted censored.

How do minority interest pressure groups use their media skills to attract a disproportionate amount of media coverage for their views and agendas, in order to try and influence governments?

Genre theory

Genre theory was introduced briefly in Chapter 3. What follows is a more detailed explanation of aspects of genre studies, appropriate for A2 work.

Genre is a French term meaning 'type' or 'kind' In media studies, it is used primarily as a means of classification. When you rent a film from your local video shop you do not find films set out on the shelves alphabetically (by title or director) or chronologically (by release date). Such a system, given the thousands of film titles available, would be unworkable. Rather, you will find that they have been set out alphabetically but within smaller sub-categories or genres.

Genre parameters can be both wide and narrow. For example, Hollywood cinema can be seen as a single genre if we compare it to European (arthouse) cinema, in that both have recognisably different generic features:

Hollywood	European cinema
Big budget	Low budget
High production values	Lower production values
Big 'stars'	Actors rather than 'stars'
High degree of narrative closure	Low degree of narrative closure
Multiplex exhibition	Art house exhibition

Hollywood's cinematic output can then be further divided into genres (such as horror or comedy), sub-genres (psychological horror or slapstick comedy) and hybrid genres (teen-horror or romantic-comedy). While genres, in all their forms and sub-forms, have recognisable conventions/features, they undergo constant evolution.

Nonetheless, genre goes beyond a simple means of classification, as genre production and consumption is governed by the complex needs of both institutions and audiences:

- **Institutional** — modern media institutions are commercial organisations in the business of creating mass-produced commodities for mass consumption. Successful formulas are repeated, as they equate to lower production costs and represent more of a guarantee of commercial success. 'Originality' would, in a business context, represent an expensive gamble. Genre production allows for the creation of specific marketing discourses. For example, the launching of a new film product is surrounded by a vast array of posters, souvenirs, press releases, trailers and 'hype', all aimed specifically at target audiences.
- **Audience** — media consumption is likewise measurable in terms of investment (both economic and personal). With a proliferation of media

and entertainment choices, audiences are becoming increasingly discerning. Genres allow audiences to develop narrative expectations and to hypothesise (speculate as to how the film or programme will end) or identify with the work of specific writers, directors or actors. Audiences make consumer choices according to their own particular social, personal and emotional needs and expectations. In this way, target audiences for genres vary across gender, age, occupation and background. The horror genre, for example, has always been popular with teenage audiences and the romance genre with women.

Nonetheless, as Steve Neale (1990) points out, genres are simultaneously conservative and innovative. While institutions and audiences share a set of practices and expectations, genres are not static. Genres are socially, technologically and culturally specific practices that evolve over time and sometimes disappear altogether. Repetition of successful formulas may satisfy expectations of familiarity, but audiences also expect change and innovation. Media institutions operating within competitive market economies and striving to stay ahead of their rivals must therefore respond to consumer demands for innovation and change.

The best way to think about genre is to see it as a tripartite relationship between industry, text and audience. Genres are driven by institutional economic imperatives and sociocultural consumer expectations, but both categories are affected and transformed by economic, technological and cultural (aesthetic and ideological) change. As Neale (1990) puts it, genre conventions 'are always in play rather than simply being *re*-played'.

'Genre', as Graeme Turner (1988) reminds us, is a term appropriated from literary studies, used to describe how groups of narrative conventions — like plot, character and setting — become organised into recognisable narrative forms (adventure, gothic etc). The term now more commonly refers to commodified mass culture, particularly popular film and television texts. As we have seen in Marxist and audience approaches, 'genre' has developed negative connotations — mass (re)production being equated with generic texts lacking any artistic innovation on behalf of the producer and not requiring any intelligence on the part of the audience.

From this standpoint, genre is a straightforward concept. However, as already mentioned, there are several reasons why we should see it as dynamic. Any given film or television text may adhere to a defined set of codes and conventions but it will, to a greater or lesser degree, evince transformation from the 'generic norm' and may possibly make inter-textual reference to other media forms.

Genre theory, according to Turner (1988), evolved from 1960s *auteur* film theory (associated with the French film journal *Cahiers du Cinéma*, and the work of directors and critics like François Truffaut and André Bazin). *Auteur* theorists resisted the dismissive notion that Hollywood films were predictable with the argument that individual directors were struggling beyond the confines of generic codes and conventions to produce their own signature films. Genre films — like thrillers, Westerns and gangster films — were now accorded critical status. Directors such as Alfred Hitchcock and John Ford were elevated to 'artist' or 'author' (hence *auteur*) status.

The 'canonisation' of directors/key films brought film studies close to literary studies and preoccupations with artistic style (arguably very difficult in a 'factory'-produced text involving hundreds of different people). However, the *auterist* tradition recognised that generic codes and conventions could be identified by director and audience alike. Directors (and, in the case of television, writers) seeking to challenge generic conventions are constrained by audience values and expectations. Fans of horror films, for instance, may expect innovation but will still anticipate seeing something that resembles a 'horror' film.

Case study

The Blair Witch Project (Daniel Myrick and Eduardo Sánchez, 1999)

This independent film used innovative production and marketing techniques. The plot follows three film students shooting a documentary film about the legend of a local witch. Haunted by an unseen presence, the students disappear one by one, leaving us with only the unseen videotapes.

The film, breaking with the special effects and high production values associated with the genre, looks and feels like a low-budget documentary. This illusion of realism was enhanced by a clever internet publicity campaign that suggested the events in the film were real.

However, *The Blair Witch Project* makes many intertextual references to the horror genre. The protagonists are 'vulnerable' teenagers cut adrift in a hostile and isolated rural setting. Mise-en-scène is used to create a high degree of tension and suspense. For example, point-of-view shots are used to suggest that 'the antagonist' is watching/stalking the teenagers. The antagonist as an all-but-physically absent presence is a technique borrowed from psychological horrors and thrillers like *The Shining*, *Psycho* and *Jaws*.

The Blair Witch Project grossed over $200 million worldwide and successfully transformed the horror genre, by harnessing the technologies and audiences of the internet while simultaneously employing generic horror codes and conventions. It also made intertextual references to other horror films, to psychological thrillers and to the generic codes of documentary. It is a truly postmodern text.

Who has the greater power in terms of genre production: institution or audience? Is originality possible in genre production, or is it always about new twists on old themes?

Ideology, social and cultural concerns

Discussion of the audience–producer dynamic inevitably brings us into the field of ideology. While it is important to remember that genres are shaped by the economic demands of capitalist media industries, we can, following Leo Bauldry, suggest that genres represent a way of measuring the social and cultural concerns of media audiences. Hence genre production is not a guarantee of critical or commercial success; some films or television texts are unsuccessful because they either fail to meet genre conventions or because they are out of touch with contemporary social and cultural tastes and values. For example, if we look at social representations across the history of any film or television genre, we can identify hegemonic processes at work.

Structuralist accounts of genre stress the operation of binary oppositions as an organising narrative code. For example, in gangster genre narratives this may point to the operation of a dichotomous virgin/whore female subject position. If we look at texts as varied as *The Public Enemy* (William A. Wellman, 1931), *The Godfather* (Francis Ford Coppola, 1972), *Goodfellas* (Martin Scorsese, 1990) and *The Sopranos* (David Chase/HBO Network, 1999–2007), we can detect the presence of this binarism, but we can also see that the representation of female subject positions has altered over time. A similar phenomenon can be detected in the James Bond films.

Structuralism has, of course, been highly influential in the development of genre theory. As Turner (1988) points out, while structuralism 'accepts that films are produced by film makers […] it also reminds us that film makers are themselves "produced" by culture'.

Ideas for discussion and development

Christian Metz argued that film genres go through structured stages of development, from a classic stage, to a self-parody of the classics, to a period when films contest the proposition that they are part of a genre, and finally to a critique of the genre itself.

- **How far do you agree with Metz's assertions?**
- **Is it possible for a genre to remain in any one stage (e.g. at the classic stage)?**
- **What social, economic or political factors effect genre transformation?**
- **What does the future hold for classic genres?**

Cross-media debates

This chapter examines some of the current debates about the media's place in our lives. In particular, it explores in detail the far-reaching technological developments that are transforming our relationship with the media.

Ownership and control

The concentration of media ownership in the hands of a few powerful multinational corporations seems to have been accepted, in spite of fears that editorial independence cannot always be guaranteed in such a context. For example, despite the controversy aroused by the US/UK decision to invade Iraq in 2003, all the newspapers owned by the News Corporation (whose proprietor is Rupert Murdoch) on three continents ran broadly similar editorials supporting the war. Many people believe that, in this concentration of media ownership, alternative views of world events and the way society is run are excluded from the general debate.

Six media corporations control the US media:

- **News Corporation** (Fox News, HarperCollins, the *New York Post*, 35 television stations)
- **General Electric** (NBC, CNBC, Telemundo, Bravo, Universal Pictures, 28 television stations)
- **Time Warner** (AOL, CNN, Warner Bros, 130 magazines)
- **Disney** (Disney-ABC Television Group, ESPN, 10 television stations, 72 radio stations)
- **Viacom** (CBS, MTV, Nickleodeon, Paramount Pictures, Simon and Schuster, 183 radio stations)
- **Bertelsmann** (Random House with 120 imprints worldwide, Gruner + Jahr with 110 magazines in 10 countries)

Copyright and the music industry

Copyright is the protection by law of the author and publisher of a media text from unauthorised reproduction of that text. The downloading of free music from the internet through websites like Napster (see page 264) has created problems for the music industry and raises issues of copyright violation.

Legal challenges have been brought by media organisations seeking to defend their products against copyright violation. Corporations feel that new media technologies, which allow free unlimited access to their music and moving image products, will destroy the economic basis of their production.

Censorship

Censorship is the practice, exercised by elite groups in authority, of monitoring and controlling media content by removing, suppressing or classifying elements deemed offensive or subversive for moral, political, economic, social or religious reasons.

Relaxation of censorship has been a feature of Western-style pluralist democracies in recent years, although the protection of children is still cited as justification for the classification of films, videos and DVDs into categories restricted by age group. In the UK, this is carried out by the **British Board of Film Classification**. Systems devised to restrict access to the internet and to television channels are available to protect children from sexually explicit or violent images.

Censorship is still practised in fundamentalist or politically oppressive societies. The Taliban, when in power in Afghanistan between 1996 and 2001, forbade the playing of music tapes and destroyed any that they found. Google's recent deal with the Chinese government involved acceptance of the heavy censorship of the internet operating in that country.

Key term

British Board of Film Classification (BBFC): the organisation responsible for classifying and certificating films, DVDs and videos for public showing and — in the case of videos and DVDs — also for private viewing. The BBFC replaced the British Board of Film Censors in 1985 following the wider remit required under the Video Recordings Act 1984, which included the classification of videos for home viewing. The BBFC sees its role as classification within acceptable guidelines, rather than censorship. It has been involved in liberalising restrictions on visual material directed at adult audiences.

Censorship issues: the internet

The internet, from its founding, has been free from censorship (except in countries such as Iran or China, where political or religious censorship is

Case study

The communications potential of the internet was first demonstrated during the San Fransisco earthquake of January 1994, when it was used by private individuals to send out news about the disaster, beating CNN, Reuters and all of the other international news organisations to the 'scoop'.

standard practice). However, in recent years, pornography (especially child pornography) has caused widespread concern. Terrorism and terrorist websites have also become an issue.

Governments around the world are becoming more eager to control internet content. It could also be argued that corporate interests are increasingly taking over the internet and are structuring it in ways that maximise their profits.

Ethical issues: the press

'Chequebook journalism'

'Chequebook journalism' involves the payment of large sums of money for sensational or topical first-hand accounts or exclusive photographs. Although newspapers deny using this system, in practice they continue to buy such photographs/stories to attract readers. Criminals, victims, celebrities and eyewitnesses of spectacular or sensational events are the most likely beneficiaries. For example, Princess Diana's former butler Paul Burrell was paid a large sum for his memoirs.

One aspect of 'chequebook journalism' is the so-called **kiss and tell**, a popular term for the practice whereby attractive young women actively seek out sexual relationships with male celebrities in order to sell their story to newspapers or magazines for large sums of money. The practice becomes even more suspect when newspapers pay individuals to set up relationships with celebrities and then later to expose them.

Invasion of privacy versus public interest

Newspapers often claim that their intrusion into people's private lives is in the public interest, especially where the behaviour and morals of celebrities and public figures is concerned. Individuals have little recourse other than to the Press Complaints Commission or the libel laws if they feel that their privacy has been violated or that they have been misrepresented. Libel actions are expensive and usually undertaken only by extremely wealthy individuals.

Those who have complaints upheld by the Press Complaints Commission are often disappointed by the limited coverage newspapers give to an apology, compared to the size of the original story.

Ideas for discussion and development

Royal Navy — hostages of the Iranians

In the spring of 2007, 15 Royal Navy personnel, including one woman, Faye Turney, were captured by the Iranian navy while carrying out a search for weapons on ships in international waters in the Persian Gulf under United Nations authority. The Iranians claimed that the British unit was in Iranian waters and held the group for 12 days. Throughout the affair and afterwards, the UK government denied emphatically that its forces had crossed into Iranian territory.

The British personnel did not resist capture and were soon appearing on Iranian television admitting their guilt. Faye Turney was shown wearing a headscarf in accordance with Iranian law and apologising for the incursion. Much was made of the fact that she was a mother with a young child. Other members of the crew were also shown on British television. When their release was finally obtained, the sailors were shown wearing fake Hugo Boss suits, clutching a bag of presents containing nuts, books, handicrafts, vases and CDs, and waving to the cameras.

Once they arrived back in the UK, two crew members (including Faye Turney, who it is claimed received £100,000) sold their stories to the press, admitting their fears and concerns — one man said he wept when his iPod was taken by the Iranians.

The incident was regarded as a triumph for Iranian propaganda and a public relations disaster for the UK and the Royal Navy, which was seen as an object of derision. It led to serious criticism of the government and the Royal Navy for their incompetence in handling the media and for allowing the sailors to make money selling their stories. However, an inquiry found that no particular individual was responsible for the fiasco.

- **Why were the sailors so unprepared for what was a likely eventuality?**
- **Why had they not been briefed about how to handle such a situation so as not to aid Iranian propaganda?**
- **Why did the British media aid Iranian propaganda by screening Iranian television interviews with the sailors?**
- **Why were the sailors treated like celebrities by the media on their return, and why were they allowed to sell their stories to the press?**

The impact of new technology: print and film

The fact that digital media now occupies a central role on the revised AQA A-level specification is evidence of its increasing importance in the contemporary media world. The revolution in media largely took place in the 1980s and 1990s with the shift from analogue to digital technologies, and from mechanical hardware — such as the typewriter and printing press — to the computerised software of the word processor and e-publishing.

Indeed, technology is a problematic area in media studies, not least because of the danger of being seduced by the novelty of 'new technologies'. We risk making the false assumption that if newer (bigger/faster) automatically equals 'better', then we should disregard everything that has gone before. To understand the implications and debates surrounding new/digital media, we need to think about the issue of media technology within a wider historical context.

Technological determinism

When talking about a 'determinism' — like technological determinism — we are referring to the way that people look at that factor in isolation, as though it is not affected by other social factors like politics, culture or the economy. Digital media technologies have not just appeared; they have emerged out of enormous and expensive research and development, as much to address the cultural needs of global audiences as to create them.

Technology has always been central to media production, distribution and exhibition, meeting a continuing need to find the ideal means to represent our social world. Media producers have thus endeavoured to develop the technological means to better achieve this goal. The history of the mass media is itself a story of technological development, with each new advance having profound social consequences. Each technological stage of development — from the early printing press to the World Wide Web — has had its supporters and detractors: the former rejoicing in the potentially democratic and liberating possibilities brought about by new communications networks, and the latter predicting the demise of existing social communities.

Karl Marx, who is most famous for his critiques of the dehumanising and divisive nature of modern industrialised capitalism, was equally aware that within the same alienating technology there lay the potential for social progress. He welcomed the industrial age, declaring that it had helped to free mankind from reliance on nature. More controversially, Marx also argued that scientific progress and technological innovation had helped Europe to rid itself of the stigma of 'rural idiocy'. This inherent contradiction between utopian and dystopian views informs our ideas, attitudes and debates about the impact and social implications of media technology.

Each new technological revolution has been hailed, in more or less equal measure, for its potential either to liberate or constrain society. Two classic examples (discussed on the following pages) are the impact of the printing press and reactions to film/photography.

Newspapers coming out of a rotary press

The printing press

Johannes Gutenberg invented the first moveable type printing press in Germany around 1450, and it was introduced to England by William Caxton in 1476. It was responsible for the much wider dissemination of ideas, allowing challenges to the dogmas of the Church as well as standardising spelling, grammar and vocabulary to create what we now know as Standard English.

The rotary printing press, developed in the nineteenth century, represented a significant technological development in that it allowed, for the first time in human history, mass publication and hence mass communication to take place. Thousands of copies of national newspapers could be printed at speed and distributed by rail around the country overnight, so that everyone had access to a standard version of a newspaper each morning. Previously, printing had been slow and the number of copies was limited. With the new developments, huge circulations were possible and the idea of a mass audience was conceived.

In 1815, for example, it had taken news of the British victory at Waterloo an entire month to reach parts of Scotland. By the end of the nineteenth century, such news would take only a few hours to travel this distance. The printing press and the introduction of mass-circulation daily newspapers allowed a revolutionary communication process to emerge, which was fast and efficient.

With each technological innovation comes profound social and cultural change. According to the historian Benedict Anderson (1983) the printing press and the mass-circulation daily newspaper were vital in the formation of modern political 'nation-states'. By engaging in the daily habit of reading the same newspapers containing the same news and at more or less the same time, readers separated by distance are united into what Anderson calls 'imagined communities'. He sees print media as providing a symbolic resource with which readers supposedly 'imagine' the nation into existence each day, creating a 'confidence of community in anonymity':

> The significance of this mass ceremony…is paradoxical. It is performed in silent privacy… Yet each communicant is well aware that the ceremony he performs is being replicated simultaneously by thousands (or millions) of others of whose existence he is confident… This ceremony is incessantly repeated at daily or half-daily intervals throughout the calendar. What more vivid figure for the secular, historically clocked, imagined community can be envisioned? (Anderson 1983)

Anderson's point is that we cannot personally know or meet everyone in the country, but we feel connected to them because we share the same daily news and the same national calendar of events. Would annual sporting events, such as the Grand National, the University Boat Race or the FA Cup Final have assumed such ritualistic significance in British popular culture without the means of the popular press?

Ideas for discussion and development

- **Do radio and television, particularly the BBC, provide a similar 'national' function?**
- **Will digital/satellite media, which allow us to access events/ information from around the globe, lead to the end of the 'national' broadcasting culture?**

Before the emergence of mass-circulation newspapers, the majority of people got their ideas from word of mouth, pamphlets, local news sheets or, traditionally, the church pulpit. A significant outcome of mass publishing in the nineteenth century was the growth of mass literacy. Newspapers, and to an extent books and journals, offered the potential for education and improvement. With wider dissemination of new and diverse ideas, people's cultural horizons were arguably extended beyond superstition or religious dogma.

Nonetheless, it is important to remember that the contemporary press are complex and powerful commercial institutions. As explained earlier in this chapter, issues of ownership, control, regulation and censorship limit how much freedom the press may have. Yet it would cost, as a conservative estimate, somewhere in the region of £25 million to establish a new daily newspaper. As James Curran (1996) points out, this 'high cost excludes talent with limited resources'. He goes on to note that over half of the existing UK daily papers were launched before 1920, and the remainder were either launched or acquired by those existing institutions. Attempts to found new newspapers in the 1980s failed — examples being the *News on Sunday* (1987), the *Sunday Correspondent* (1989–90) and *Today* (1986–95). Therefore, although technology may hold democratic potential, the issue of who owns and controls the application of that technology has important cultural implications.

Film and photography

The visual media of film (and, to a slightly lesser extent, photography) have also been perceived as both progressive and regressive forces of technological change. In media studies, technology (or hardware) in itself is not particularly important compared to the social, cultural and economic effects of new technologies — the newspaper headlines that have shaped history or the films that have broken box-office records. We are more interested in the processes of media production and consumption.

People have always sought to create a visual document or representation of their social world and practices. The technology available to Stone Age people may have been simple but it was sufficient for their means of expression, and the cave paintings they created were loaded with magical, religious and cultural significance. Fixing images and then making them seem to move were achievements of the nineteenth century, and the moving image has transformed the representation of our world. Imagine how our idea of history would change if we had moving image records of events such as the Battle of Hastings.

Media communications are symbolic 'constructions', representative of our desires, fears, hopes, dreams and wishes. It is therefore important always to try to see a connection between technological, social and cultural change, and not to lose sight of issues to do with economic/institutional ownership and control.

Ideas for discussion and development

- **Would popular cultural forms, such as newspapers, magazines, advertising or film, have been developed if there had not been mass audiences of industrial workers to consume them?**
- **Does technology help to facilitate social change? For example, Anderson believed that the daily newspaper was central to the creation of modern 'imagined' national identities.**
- **Do digital technologies like the internet have the potential to create transnational or global communities (imagined international communities)?**
- **Will the liberating potential of any new communications technology be constrained by issues of institutional ownership and control?**

The following accounts of cinema come from German-Jewish critics, all of whom were associated with the Frankfurt School of cultural criticism. They are loosely Marxist in their approach but are different in their readings of cinema's social potential and/or effects. Walter Benjamin's ideas were based on Soviet propaganda cinema and European avant-garde, whereas Theodor Adorno and Max Horkheimer based their ideas on the highly commercialised business models of Hollywood cinema and the US advertising industry.

Walter Benjamin

From a photographic negative, for example, one can make any number of prints...to ask for the original makes no sense [...] for the first time in world history, mechanical reproduction emancipates the work of art from its parasitical dependency on ritual [and] it begins to be based on another practice: politics.   (written in 1973)

In his famous 1936 essay on film and photography, 'The work of art in the age of mechanical reproduction', Walter Benjamin discusses the social and cultural effects/possibilities of 'mechanical reproduction'. He argued that:

- Before film and photography, works of art were normally single artefacts with their own unique authenticity or, as Benjamin put it, 'aura'. As such, they would only have been viewed by minority/privileged audiences.
- When artworks are continuously reproduced, originality — or aura — is worn away, bringing them closer to the mass audience and making them more accessible.
- Reversibility develops: the work of art being reproduced leads to the work of art being designed for reproducibility. For example, few of us have ever seen the original *Mona Lisa*, but we have seen countless reproductions on posters, postcards, in books and even on coffee mugs. (Benjamin's ideas come very close to what we now, 70 years later, term postmodernism.)
- As well as seeing the democratic potential of mechanical reproduction, Benjamin took a radical approach towards its aesthetic possibilities (particularly for film). First, film audiences can have an active role in the viewing of a film. Second, that film can change our field of perception. Unlike theatre, where the audience identifies with the actor, when watching a film the audience is directed by the point of view of the camera. The camera, with its use of close-ups and extreme close-ups, allows us to see aspects of our environment that had previously been hidden.
- Benjamin takes film as his model of political communication, arguing that its collective production and reception represents a concerted attack on the essentially private and contemplative experience of high culture — e.g. reading a novel or studying a painting — thus making it suitable for revolutionary/educative purposes.

Benjamin was perhaps guilty of overstating the potential of film and photography. Rather than devaluing the original artwork, mass reproduction tends to make the original copy all the more unique and hence valuable. He also did not give much consideration to economic control — particularly with regard to capitalist media institutions. Benjamin's ideas were based around the overtly politicised texts of Soviet film-makers such as Dziga Vertov and Sergei Eisenstein, and did not give any real account of commercial media institutions.

Theodor Adorno and Max Horkheimer

German-Jewish Marxist academics Adorno and Horkheimer wrote their highly influential essay 'The culture industry: enlightenment as mass deception' in the mid-1940s, soon after fleeing to the USA from Nazi

Germany. After witnessing the 'brainwashing' of the German people through Nazi propaganda and then arriving in a country where advertising and cinema were dominant media forms, they conceived their idea of mass media as an economically and ideologically powerful social force. They agreed with Benjamin's theory of the political potential of mass media culture, but were pessimistic about the political ideologies of the US capitalist media.

For Adorno and Horkheimer, the modern media are produced by capitalist industries along capitalist lines, with embedded messages that endorse capitalist values and offer consumers a false sense of identity, to help them 'escape' the realities and inequalities of everyday modern life.

Their theory on the 'culture industry' can be summarised as follows:

- Media texts are produced in the same way as other goods and services in a capitalist economy. Production is marked by standardisation, with assembly-line characteristics and a rigidly enforced division of labour. In short, media production is subject to the same 'rationalised' organisational procedures as those that exist in, for example, car manufacturing plants.
- Media texts, as a consequence, are inauthentic and repetitive, and communicate at the level of the lowest common denominator. They are designed to be empty and unintelligent so that the largest number of people (the masses) can consume them.
- Media texts are loaded with dominant ideology, which is subconsciously included by the producers. This dominant ideology can be defined as an interlinking chain of myths, values and cultural representations that work to 'naturalise' social differences — of class, race and gender — and to legitimise the value of capitalism. These appear so 'common-sensical' that they deny the existence of inequalities or prejudices that capitalism (re)produces (see the section about Gramsci on pages 227–28).
- Media texts produce a mass, passive and obedient audience of consumers who are lulled into accepting the dreams and hopes offered by the cultural industries.
- Hollywood, in particular, has replaced the notion of uniqueness, or aura, through the 'cult of movie stars'.

These are just two accounts of the impact of film. Every new technology carries with it the potential for social and cultural change. What we need to ask is whether those changes are progressive or not. Is it inevitable that economically powerful institutions will eventually monopolise the use and distribution of new communications technologies?

Dystopian images

Social fears and anxieties about the dehumanising or alienating consequences of technology have been shown in a number of dystopian filmic
representations:

- Fritz Lang's *Metropolis* (1927) and Charlie Chaplin's more comedic
  Modern Times (1936) both comment on the unemployment and
  desperate economic conditions faced by workers in the modern era as a
  result of mechanised/rationalised industrialisation.
- In Jacques Tati's *Mon Oncle* (1958), the bumbling, childlike Monsieur
  Hulot (the original Mr Bean) struggles with postwar France's mindless
  obsession with modernity and US-style consumerism.
- Numerous science-fiction films have represented dystopian visions of
  futuristic virtual realities, including *Blade Runner* (Ridley Scott, 1982),
  The Terminator (James Cameron, 1984) and *The Matrix* series (Wachowski
  brothers, 1999–2003).

Recent years have also witnessed films depicting the darker side of modern
media culture. David Cronenberg's *Videodrome* (1983) depicts a disturbing
world of media domination and manipulation. *The Truman Show* (Peter
Weir, 1998) chronicles the nightmarish life of a man existing in the
constructed hyperreality of a television soap opera.

The impact of new technology: new media

Life can only be understood backwards, but it must be lived forwards.

(Søren Kierkegaard, Danish philosopher)

As we have seen, the history of the mass media is one of technological
advances which have brought about profound social consequences and
implications at every developmental stage. There is, however, evidence to
suggest that our contemporary mass media in particular is in the process
of dramatic technologically-driven change, bringing in its wake a distinctive new era in the culture of global capitalism.

The twenty-first century technological revolution can be characterised by
the shift from analogue to digital technology. The vast majority of students
whose schooling began after the mid-1980s will have had continuous
access to computer technology. Students today download music and listen

to it on their MP3 players or iPods. Yet there are many people belonging to older generations who struggle to compose a Word document or send an e-mail, and who despair that young people today have no idea what an LP is. The change has been both enormous and rapid. This is, moreover, an era characterised by media interactivity, accessibility and diversity, with 'new' freedoms for the audience. As Manuel Castells argues:

> Increasingly, the use of the internet provides an appropriate material support for the diffusion of networked individualism […] New technological developments seem to enhance the chances for the networked individualism to become the dominant form of sociability…cell telephony fits a social pattern organised around…individualised interaction, based on the selection of time, place and partners of the interaction.   (2001)

Castells may be correct in his assertion, but we need to be careful about how we respond. The internet is not owned by any state or multinational corporation, and hence no state or company can fully control its use. By the same token, however, there are virtually no controls over the content of web pages.

It is impossible to know for certain how the democratic possibilities of the digitalised world will play out. There were many predictions in the 1990s about the bright new world of e-commerce, but we know now how spectacularly the 'dot-com' bubble burst. Predicting the future is always a risky endeavour, but one thing is guaranteed — the process of change in our media world is dramatic, and we will be required to respond critically to those changes, whether they are cultural, economic, political, social or technological.

Media debates

There a number of topics, issues and debates that A-level media studies students are expected to study and be able to respond to critically. These include:
- the interactive consumer
- social networking
- the internet and World Wide Web
- blogs and podcasts
- the changing contemporary media landscape
- the changing role of distributor and exhibitor
- new technologies and the audience

Analysing the topics in this list will allow us to apply some of the issues and debates we looked at with the press and cinema: issues such as ownership and control, and the effects of the digital revolution on production and exhibition.

We may also consider how new technologies will affect the way audiences consume media products and therefore have an impact on the ways that media products are produced, distributed and exhibited. Consequently, we need to think more carefully about applying media theories which, for the most part, were developed in response to conventional media forms. The AQA specification requires that you are able to:

- consider how new/digital technology affects the construction of media products (media analysis)
- consider the effects so far, and possible future effects, on media production (media institutions)
- consider the role of the interactive audience (media audiences)
- consider the political and social implications of new technologies and the methods of their consumption (media theories)

Analogue to digital

The contemporary rate of technological change is unprecedented. The introduction of new digital technologies is occurring at a rapid speed and on a huge scale. Communications industries are now among the biggest industries in the world. Where traditional capitalist industries used to produce commodities such as cars, there are now many more people employed in the production of information and entertainment. In the postmodern world, culture is an industry.

Interactivity and accessibility are the embodiments of the new information and communication technologies:

- Older media technologies operate on a one (institution) to many (consumers) model of communication — a one-way process from encoder to decoder.
- New digital media have opened up the possibilities of one-to-one communications, allowing for the possibilities of multi-user groups and two-way exchange between audience and institution.
- Interactivity opens up the possibility of the audience as producer.

For these reasons, it is easy to see the appeal of the new information and communication technologies, with their increased active consumer choice and participation. The internet, however, is virtually unregulated and while we may bask in its new-found freedoms, it has also provided an outlet for the darker side of human expression. Many critics, academics and politicians have raised concern about the internet as a site for pornography and violence.

Internet and interactive communities

Websites are dynamic forms of communication that allow for audience interaction and freedom of navigation. User-friendliness and ease of access to information are key factors involved in the production and design of websites. In short, the internet allows consumers to navigate their way along multiple pathways to gain access to information, entertainment and interactive communication on a global scale.

Conventional media forms, such as television, operate on a one-to-many model of communication, with the content and scheduling of programmes being controlled by the broadcast institution. The internet, on the other hand, has broken down the barriers of time and space that have traditionally constrained human communication. Many people see the internet and new media as the final realisation of Marshall McLuhan's concept of the 'global village'.

In the early 1960s, McLuhan wrote that the visual, print culture would soon be brought to an end by what he called 'electronic interdependence'. McLuhan's ideas were extremely pessimistic — he saw these 'electronic' communities as 'tribes' that would destroy individualism. The term 'global village' is now often used in a positive way to describe internet communities, and the original meaning has largely been lost by its popularisers.

Peer-to-peer social networking: effects on media institutions

Much of traditional media studies has focused on how media forms affect audience ideas and behaviour. With the explosion of digital technologies and the internet, the question has been reversed. We are now arguably more interested in what effect digital technologies, and their more empowered interactive audiences, are having on traditional media forms.

Peer-to-peer (P2P) networks are often held up as proof positive of the democratising effects of the internet. These are computer networks that allow individual internet users to communicate directly, bypassing the need to go via a central server-based network. Essentially, P2Ps are file-sharing networks where people can share news, information, music and videos, or set up 'communities' for everything, from simply chatting to political protest.

Ideas for discussion and development

In 2007, the social networking site Facebook took internet communication to a new level when a group of graduates got together to campaign against the HSBC bank's 'unfair charges' on student loans. Their 'viral campaign' — as Patrick Collinson and Tony Levene called it (*Guardian*, 25 August 2007) — was able to gather enormous support over a short period of time. The group's 'wall' received over 2,500 'postings' in a 2-week period, causing the bank to back down and review its policy. Seen in this way, sites like Facebook represent an outlet for individuals quickly and efficiently to make their voices heard.

- **Would traditional media institutions have been interested in this story? They have, like the *Guardian*, taken up the story retrospectively but would they have risked running it as a leading story?**

Unlike traditional forms of media communications, internet forms like P2Ps bypass any restrictions of time and space. As discussed earlier, daily newspapers were part of a shared time-based ritual, whereby most working people followed similar daily routines. In terms of distribution, daily newspapers were only really available within a limited geographical space — usually a national one. A similar model can be seen in television news, with main bulletins being broadcast at particular points in the day. With digital media and the internet, these restrictions no longer apply. Instead of 'imagined communities', Hills (2001) prefers to see social network users as 'communities of imagination'. In multi-user domains (MUDs), people log on at different times so the 'mass ceremony' is not so synchronic. Quite simply, you can access or relay media/information from anywhere and at any time.

Newspapers and terrestrial television companies have responded to these changes by creating their own websites and making audience interactivity a

Ideas for discussion and development

- **What effect does the fact that we can tune into television news at any time have on the content and quality of news broadcasts (think about CNN, Sky News or BBC News 24)?**
- **How have news broadcasts been transformed by digital/satellite communications — rolling news, picture values, tabloid style headlines etc.?**

Cross-media debates

Task

Look at the *Spooks* page on the BBC website. List all the interactive features you can find on this page.

Ideas for discussion and development

- **In the highly competitive market of global media communications, can media institutions afford to dictate style/content to audiences?**

key element of their ethos. Many television programmes in various genres — from sport to soap operas — have their own interactive websites, where audiences can review or preview episodes, post blogs or podcasts, watch or use downloads, or play interactive games.

In short, these new media technologies take the idea of active audiences to a whole new level. Audiences are no longer just consumers but are now, arguably, producers. By interacting with their favourite media texts they are able to make their voices heard. Audiences have always had the choice of switching something on or off, but now they have the forum for voicing the reasons behind those decisions. In terms of power relations, where does this leave us in considering the relationship between audience and producer?

YouTube

YouTube was founded in February 2005 by two friends, Chad Hurley and Steve Chen. In November 2005 it received funding from Sequoia Capital, and in November 2006 it was purchased by Google inc. for $1.65 billion. It struck partnership deals with a host of large media institutions including CBS, BBC, Universal Music Group, Sony Music Group and a range of corporate advertisers.

YouTube accounts for approximately 10% of all traffic on the internet, with 75 billion e-mails being sent through the site each day. One hundred million video clips are downloaded on YouTube every day.

Its institutional ethos is as follows:

> We want to entertain, inform and empower the world through video [...] our goal is to have YouTube on every screen — to take it from the PC to the living room and the mobile phone.
>
> (Chad Hurley in BBC news interview, 20 June 2007)

> Everyone can watch videos on YouTube [...] YouTube is empowering them [the audience] to become the broadcasters of tomorrow.
>
> (Company statement on YouTube homepage)

From a technological point of view, YouTube relies on accessibility — videos can be created using inexpensive camcorders or phones and easy-to-use software. Socially, YouTube works as a social networking site resulting in internet 'communities', where people create and share information together.

It could be argued that YouTube is symbolic of fragmentary postmodern culture. Older ideas of institutional 'top-down' culture are rejected in favour of a plurality of views and positions. The fact that much of the footage it contains is amateur and raw/unedited seems to add to the notion of 'authenticity' as opposed to the biased/'constructed' world of traditional media institutions.

The interactive audience

Looking at the number of people who use the site, it is not difficult to see why YouTube is held up as the epitome of new media start-up (or 'upstart') companies. It is also a social phenomenon, the 'YouTube generation' being synonymous with contemporary youth internet culture in the way that MTV defined the cable and satellite television revolution of the 1980s and 1990s.

In terms of its ideology, YouTube has a clear, liberal pluralist discourse of active audiences and consumer choice. The maxim of 'educate, inform and entertain' created by John Reith (the first director general of the BBC) — the ideological touchstone for public service broadcasting — has been reinterpreted and reversed to read 'entertain, inform and empower'. 'Empowerment' has fewer didactic (socially improving and moralistic) connotations than 'education', giving the audience a voice rather than imposing one on them.

Many commentators suggest that YouTube's success is reducable to two simple, audience-friendly premises:

- It is easy to use — if you are able to send an e-mail with an attachment then you will be able to upload a clip on YouTube. Downloading and viewing clips is even simpler.
- It does not tell you what to do. With the exception of pornography and some 18 ratings on viewing there is no overt censorship on content. The audience chooses what to watch and when to watch it.

YouTube has 12 video categories and millions of clips, ranging from the mundane to the outrageous, amateur to professional. Unlike the output of traditional broadcast institutions, the clips are short — up to a maximum of 10 minutes long. Content varies from hobbies, sports, stunts, advertisements, promotions to **blogs**. **Blogging** is an important aspect of YouTube in terms of content and audience.

Key terms

blogs/blogging: many blogs provide commentary or news on a particular subject, such as food, politics or local news, while others function as more personal online diaries. The ability for readers to leave comments in an interactive format is an important part of blogging.

Entries are usually shown in reverse chronological order. The term is a contraction of 'weblogging'.

Many of the clips form videostream responses to other clips, some are of 'wacky' amateur footage, while others are composed, in the spirit of postmodern pastiche, from a bricolage of existing media texts.

Copyright

Copyright is a contentious issue on file-sharing social networking sites such as YouTube. Like the music-sharing site Napster before it, YouTube has generated a great deal of controversy among mainstream media institutions.

Napster is an interesting case, as it was one of the first successful P2P file sharing sites and also one of the first to come up against the institutional might of existing media players. In 2000 the record label of heavy-metal band Metallica filed a lawsuit against Napster for uploading and sharing their unreleased single 'I Disappear'. A month later, Metallica were joined in litigation by the rap artist Dr Dre. Napster lost the case and would subsequently have gone out of business if it had not been taken over by a more powerful media institution.

Institutional context or contest?

In 2007 there was a great deal of discussion about large media corporations suing YouTube for breach of copyright and failure to pay royalties. However, when Google took over YouTube, far from being hounded into court, it was able to seduce other large media corporations into partnership deals. As a recent report on BBC News website stated:

> YouTube may have started life as an online repository for wacky home videos but has quickly grown up to become a professional media platform that has transformed the way global broadcasters look at content and audiences. (BBC News website, 20 June 2007)

A similar scenario can be seen with other internet start-up companies. The social-networking chat-room site MySpace was bought by Rupert Murdoch's News Corporation, and Napster is now controlled by Roxio.

Far from being overly concerned about the threat of new digital media, traditional media institutions seem to be embracing it. Web-campaign movie promotions are now a key feature on video-sharing sites, as are branding and advertising campaigns in general. A pessimistic Marxist analysis of the situation may predict that these powerful media institutions will simply buy up fledgling P2P file-sharing sites and in the process will destroy the competition, impose regulation and standardisation, and resume monopolistic business as usual.

It may, however, be more fruitful to see the power struggle between digital networking sites and traditional institutions as a hegemonic process of negotiation and exchange. 'Ground-up' popular (sub)cultural forms and movements — like youth fashion and independent music — are engaged in a perennial hegemonic contest with mainstream media institutions. It could therefore be argued that mainstream media institutions recognise that social networking sites like YouTube provide both a breeding ground for new popular cultural creativity and an ideal forum for reaching lucrative sections of the consumer market.

Interestingly, when Google took over YouTube it had not made any significant profit. The takeover price of $1.65 billion then seems all the more surprising — unless, of course, we see it as a major investment in contemporary media culture. YouTube originally hit upon the winning formula of combining the technologies of the internet, cheap camcorders and user-friendly video software with the cultural needs of a generation disenchanted with mainstream media, but those self-same institutions are not similarly disenchanted with social-networking audiences. Part of YouTube's stated goal is to expand its output to every screen, including mobile phones and television. Is that the rhetoric of free-market capitalism? Or will YouTube be able to hold onto its initial aim of empowering the audience/community?

YouTube and moral panics

YouTube has received a great deal of attention from traditional media institutions, particularly the press. Indeed, it has provoked something of a moral panic, with tabloid headlines warning that the site is promoting, among other things, violence, bullying, racism, homophobia and 'dangerous/life-threatening pranks and stunts'. The *Sun*, for example, carried 248 stories relating to YouTube in less than 10 months in 2007 (source: *Sun* online archive).

Consider this headline from the *Observer* (29 July 2007), relating to videos uploaded by schoolchildren.

Teachers call for YouTube ban over 'cyber-bullying'

Association claims website ignored pleas to remove violent clips

The report does not actually concern teachers en masse, but relates to a group called the Professional Association of Teachers. This association accused YouTube of 'encouraging cyber-bullying' — both student-on-student and student-on-teacher — by refusing to take down inappropriate clips.

Another example is an edition of the BBC's current affairs programme *Panorama*, 'Teenage Fight Club', 29 July 2007, which discussed the issue of teenagers staging fights purely for the benefit of the camera and to upload onto sites like YouTube.

YouTube insisted that such clips make up only a 'tiny minority' of the site's content, but it is under pressure from teaching and parenting associations to introduce stricter censorship controls and to 'flag up' inappropriate material. In the *Observer* article, a spokesperson for YouTube claimed that the site strictly 'prohibits content like pornography or gratuitous violence', and that in a bid to put parents' minds at rest it has 'joined a cyber-bullying taskforce set up by the government'.

Policing a global network like the internet is obviously difficult, but as Thomas Craig and Julian Petley (2001) point out, 'a number of measures have been put into place in recent years'. Craig and Petley go on to show that government and police legislation to protect people against violence, and particularly pornography, on the internet have been introduced. This article predates the arrival of YouTube and focuses more on the 'cyber-cultural' phenomenon of video games, such as *Carmageddon 2*, *Grand Theft Auto* and *Resident Evil*. Interestingly, the newspaper/television headlines and worries surrounding video games are strikingly similar to those circulating about sites like YouTube. In terms of discourse, they fall directly into the 'effects' tradition of audience analysis. It is always the young (i.e. vulnerable/impressionable) who are at risk:

Internet crazes that are killing our kids

(The *Sun*, 26 June 2007)

YouTube 'cashes in on footage of beaten children'

(*Daily Mail*, 29 July 2007)

This type of negative reporting raises a number of questions:

- Do traditional media institutions feel 'threatened' by new technology? If we look at the *Sun* we see a curious contradiction. The *Sun* was one of the first newspapers to move away from traditional hot-press printing technology to embrace digital/electronic print culture. In addition, the *Sun's* global parent company, News Corporation, owns the social networking site MySpace, and the newspaper itself is available online and via mobile downloads.

- Are traditional media institutions merely reflecting the views of their readership? There is certainly a generation gap between traditional newspaper readers or television viewers and the internet's online communities. From the press reaction, it seems that many parents are concerned about what their children are exposed to on social networking sites. But to what extent are these views representative of all parents?

- Do sensational stories of teenagers and sex/violence fit existing discourses? In the 1980s and 1990s the press ran moral panic stories about the effects of 'video nasties' and video games. It is currently doing the same with P2P sites (presenting them as grooming sites for paedophiles) and the morally reprehensible antics of some YouTube contributors. Interestingly, the *Sun* is much more upbeat about YouTube when covering another of its favourite topics: sex. Many of the *Sun's* YouTube headlines are about videos of beautiful and glamorous young women, with viewer/reader polls to select 'the hottest babes'.

Ideas for discussion and development

A significant proportion of the video clips on YouTube are stunts and gimmicks.

- **Do you think there is a long-term market for such content?**
- **Is it inevitable that when a site like YouTube attains the status of a popular cultural phenomenon it will attract the attention of more economically powerful institutions?**
- **How much of YouTube's content is now taken up with professional, promotional material compared to amateur/individual uploads?**
- **Do you agree that sites like YouTube need to be controlled and censored? If so, who decides on how or where to set the limits of what is acceptable and appropriate?**
- **Do you think YouTube will remain an online culture or is it destined to be appropriated into mainstream broadcast media?**
- **Will it become nonsensical to talk about different media platforms, like television, internet or radio? With entertainment 'hubs', everything could be available in one hardware package.**

Digital utopia or dystopia?

There is considerable speculation about the potential positive social effects of digital media technologies:

- The global village — the internet can be seen as a benign virtual community, which is accessible to anyone, anywhere and at any time.
- Empowered media audiences — the rise of blogging and file-sharing exchanges through P2P social networks have given consumers access to a greater variety of information sources.
- The source and distribution of information had previously been the domain of powerful media institutions but now, in the context of inter-activity, consumers can also be producers.
- Increased competition on a global scale and across media platforms has made existing media corporations sit up and take notice, and create more opportunities for audience participation and exchange.
- Digital communications provide a symbolic resource for groups displaced within the global economy to keep in touch with their 'local' cultures.

However, many people see digital media technologies in a more negative way:

- Isolation — the internet is the latest in a long line of 'dehumanising' technological developments, producing a population of computer 'nerds' who are unable to communicate with 'real' people.
- Pastiche — the endless recycling and recirculation of images in cyber-space has arguably led to the death of original artworks.
- Hyperreality — media culture is taking over every aspect of our lives, to the point where it has become our only 'reality' and no longer needs to make any reference to the 'external' social world.
- Globalisation — many of the so-called 'democratic' social networking websites are already owned by multinational corporations, which are more interested in the advertising/marketing potential of a new breed of consumers than in creating 'empowered' audiences.
- Cultural imperialism — dominant cultural forms will destroy local/minority cultures. Many less developed countries do not have the resources to compete or resist this process on a global scale.

Regardless of the consequences, it is obvious that the internet and e-media as a whole will be a dominating cultural force in the twenty-first century. The important thing, as always, is to try to ensure the account-ability of the powerful agencies involved and the maximum democratisa-tion of the new services, so that they are available for the benefit of all.

Cover of *Metro*

Text 1 — reference for the following questions

Article from the *Daily Mail*

Text 2 — reference for the following questions

Daily Mail, Wednesday, May 23, 2007

Why this gang of young yobs must now be called a 'group'

By **Steve Doughty**
Social Affairs Correspondent

ANYONE who has been a victim of their contempt for the law or menacing behaviour might find it a little difficult to swallow.

But on the orders of a government agency, gangs of teenage criminals should no longer be called 'gangs' because it might offend them.

Instead they should be referred to as 'groups' and their crimes described as 'group-related'.

The instruction comes from the Youth Justice Board, which organises probation, training and detention for under 18s.

It echoes the decision by the Metropolitan Police three years ago to drop the phrase 'gang rape' and replace it with 'group rape'.

Officers reasoned then that the word gang can wrongly suggest clearly-defined membership.

The YJB sets out its case in a 200-page report on 'gangs' and how teenagers are drawn into them. It

'Dislike being labelled'

states: 'Many young people interviewed for this study resented the way in which the term had come to be used to describe any group of young people involved in anti-social behaviour. They

Watch your language: Teenagers resent the word 'gang'

Posed by models

Daily Mail

felt adults attached the label to them simply on the basis that they were young and met in a group, assuming that crime was their main purpose for meeting.

'In fact, the label conjured up an image with which they might not want to be associated, even where they were involved in offending – not least because in some cases they knew from their own local experience what real gangs were and several of the young women in particular had suffered at their hands.'

The report said that some youngsters could find the idea of a gang seductive because of crime films and TV programmes and black 'gangsta' music.

It added: 'There has been a noticeable trend toward referring to groups of young people indiscriminately as gangs.

'This is not appropriate and it could exacerbate the extent and seriousness of group-related offending or create problems where none previously existed.

'Juvenile gangs do exist in some urban areas, but most young people involved in group offending do not belong to gangs – even if others label them in this way.'

Examining the broader issues behind youth crime, the agency said that chaotic family lives and the lack of role models were frequently to blame.

It found that youngsters drawn into gangs overwhelmingly come from family backgrounds characterised by disruption, conflict and single parenthood.

Young men follow brothers or more distant adult relatives into crime as they look for someone to emulate.

For many from the worst backgrounds, a gang provides a home life better than their 'chaotic and unstable' families, it added.

The findings are further evidence linking broken family life with crime.

Children of single parents are far more likely to do badly at school and drift towards vandalism and crime. In particular, boys who grow up without fathers are at risk of falling into criminal behaviour.

The report said: 'Teenagers could gravitate toward gangs and group violence as a result of poor family relationships, exclusion from school, absence of positive role models and a lack of youth facilities.'

It found that among 25 girl gang members interviewed, only two lived with both parents.

■ The Oxford English Dictionary says a gang is 'any band or company of persons who go about together or act in concert (chiefly in a bad or deprecatory sense, or associated with criminal societies)'.

s.doughty@dailymail.co.uk

This unit is split into two sections:
- **Section A** (AO1) = 32 marks or 40% of the total.
- **Section B** (AO2) = 48 marks or 60% of the total.

Section A

The assessment objective (AO1) requires you to demonstrate knowledge and understanding of media concepts, contexts and critical debates.

This section comprises **three compulsory** responses to two 'seen' stimulus texts. You should spend:
- **15 minutes** studying the texts and making notes
- **45 minutes** answering the three questions

Question 1

Compare and contrast text 1 and text 2 (pages 269–70), with particular reference to the representation of teenagers. (8 marks)

Student answer A

Both texts refer to stereotyped representations of British teenagers. Text one, the *Metro* front page, carries the headline of 'The YouTube gangsters', immediately connoting an image of troublemakers and the idea that teenagers have abused the potentials of internet technology. The signifier 'gangsters' connotes a sense of fear, and ideas about organised crime and social problems. The teenager is the modern-day criminal.

The story is based around a very small minority of video clips on YouTube — which contains millions of clips. However, the article makes sweeping generalisations. It says 'The Metropolitan Police say they are aware of gangs using YouTube and MySpace.' This suggests a widespread problem. Also, the article does not include any quotes from teenagers, showing how powerless they are in terms of self-representation. YouTube allows teenagers to represent themselves but the mainstream media pick on the worst elements of this.

The images shown are blurred and cropped to appear more enigmatic, connoting a threatening or shady character. The character is anonymous and unidentified, like a real gangster. You could also say that because he is not named/identified he could represent any teenager.

The *Daily Mail* article, however, represents the same ideas of 'teenage gang recruitment' but in a better way. It shows why teenagers end up in gangs, such as 'youngsters drawn into gangs overwhelmingly come from family backgrounds characterised by disruption.' On the other hand, the image again is a typical media representation of teenagers with a group of 'hoodies', huddled together, drinking canned lager within an urban, graffiti-scrawled mise-en-scène. The shot is staged and looks deliberately set up. The article appears in the *Daily Mail,* which is a well-respected institution and this more balanced view represents this.

Grade and examiner's comment

Level 3 — 6 marks

The candidate has made a sound analysis of both texts and has shown a good awareness of the differences between the two representations. It is a well-written response, with good use of media terminology and understanding of concepts. The analysis of the *Metro* front-page image is particularly good.

To gain a high level 3, the response needs to cover much more about the concept of representation and the context in which both texts were produced. It could have given some explanation of the social role and effects of media representations — particularly common sense, myths and stereotypes.

The final paragraph on institutional context could have been developed further — the *Daily Mail* is a middle-brow tabloid with a predominantly lower-middle-class, middle-aged readership holding key 'conservative' values of patriotism, family and law and order.

Student answer B

Both texts are from middle-brow tabloid newspapers whose readership of conservative 'middle-Englanders' share the institutions' ideology of family values and law and order. In terms of representation, both texts use stereotypical discourses of 'the teenager' as a homogeneous, vulnerable and impressionable group who, if not controlled by the dominant majority, poses a threat to 'national' cohesion.

Text 1 gives a more sensationalist representation than text 2's more developed 'comment'. This is understandable, as text 1 has all the generic conventions of a tabloid front page: picture values, emotive headlines and shocking 'exclusive' strapline. Text 2, an article from the *Daily Mail*, provides a more balanced account. Yet both texts occupy the same ideological ground, sharing binary oppositions of 'menacing', 'violent thugs' on one side and innocent 'victims' on the other.

Text 1 expresses a 'moral panic', not only about 'teenage gangsters', but also about the perceived lawlessness of internet social-networking sites like YouTube and MySpace. The editorial line is within the 'effects' tradition. It looks at what certain media texts do to vulnerable groups — in this case, 'recruiting' them as armed 'teenage thugs'. This idea of 'recruitment' and the word 'gangsters' in the striking white-on-black headline connotes a world away from hanging around street corners to a more systematic, militaristic and organised world of criminality and lawlessness. The revolver image further signifies this, as does the cropped, blurred image of the armed black youth, connoting a shady and threatening character. His anonymity compounds the worrying connotation of 'any' teenager. The signifier of ethnicity perhaps anchors the representation within a more urban, inner-city context.

Text 2 works firmly within the *Daily Mail*'s editorial line on, or more precisely distaste for, political correctness. The headline, which is deliberately provocative, juxtaposes the binarism of 'gang of yobs' and 'group' — 'group' being in inverted commas to signify further its ridiculousness in this context. Although the article sets out to take a balanced look at issues surrounding youth criminality, its underlying bias is quite apparent. The article begins by speaking on behalf of the 'victims' of youth crime and sees the government's politically correct linguistic directives as 'orders' and 'instructions'. This connotes the idea that the government is directly telling us — the average British taxpayer — what to think, which goes against the grain in a free-speaking, democratic country.

Text 2 represents teenage crime not as a problem of dominant British society but as a result of 'single parent' and 'disrupt[ed]' families. The fall of the nuclear family and family values are seen as being responsible. Again, as in text 1, the 'teenager' is seen as vulnerable and a victim. The posed picture, with signifiers of sportswear and hoody-wearing youths, drinking canned beer against a mise-en-scène of graffiti-strewn brick/concrete walls connotes the sense that the problem is urban, council-estate and predominantly working class.

Both texts represent teenagers as a source of antisocial behaviour. They try to show that if they are not protected within the confines of 'normal family values', teenagers will be drawn into criminal worlds and thus pose a threat to the dominant society.

Grade and examiner's comment

Level 4 — 8 marks

This is an insightful and articulate response with a clear, fluent comparative structure and confident use of media terminology throughout. The candidate is able to analyse the subtle difference in the two representations and makes detailed reference to wider concepts and contexts. The discussion of institutional and social/cultural contexts is particularly strong.

Question 2

Consider the view that the current press treatment of teenagers is simply another 'moral panic'. (12 marks)

Student answer A

The media have always created 'moral panics', whether about mods and rockers, football hooligans, muggers or binge-drinking hoodies. This exaggeration of a relatively small problem — amplified into an enormous social problem to sell newspapers — could certainly be applied to the current press treatment of teenagers.

The *Metro* article is a good example of this, as the story reports on a small minority of teenagers who are getting into gangs through internet recruitment. But instead of concentrating on explaining the reasons for or solutions to these problems, the article leads with the headline 'The YouTube gangsters'. This is provocative and emotive, suggesting that these teenagers are modern-day gangsters, in order to shift more copies off the news-stand.

Teenagers fit the criteria for a new 'moral panic' group perfectly because they are a highly visible group — they spend lots of time in public — and have little influence on their representation in the media. They are a vulnerable group who are not the audience for big newspapers. Teenagers do not usually buy newspapers and get their ideas more from the internet. Maybe newspapers feel threatened by this. This is reflected in the *Metro* article, which makes generalisations about teenagers but has no teenage voice.

One of the reasons why teenagers are the 'folk devils' is that they are a minority group. They are powerless to fight back against the power of large media institutions. There will always be crime and teenagers will break the rules, but constantly giving all the blame to us for society's problems encourages everyone else to turn their backs on the real problems instead of facing up to them.

Grade and examiner's comment

Level 2 — 6 marks

This is a reasonably well written and presented response. It makes a number of engaged and interesting points, and generally sticks to the demands of the question. The candidate shows a sound awareness of the concept of 'moral panics' and is able to give some evaluation. However, the response is generally lacking in examples and analysis.

To gain a level 3 mark, the candidate needs to develop the interesting points made with more concrete media examples and more developed analysis.

The candidate should also move beyond the simplistic idea that all media texts exist simply to make profit (sell copies), by looking at the complex social/cultural relationship between institution, text and audience.

The candidate could have given a clearer explanation of the concept of 'moral panic' and used media terminology/concepts more thoroughly.

Student answer B

Geoffrey Pearson has traced press concern about teenage 'hooligans' as far back as the Victorian press. Every decade of the modern era is underscored by 'moral panics' about youth subcultures — for example, 1950s teddy boys, 1960s mods and rockers or 1970s punks. There is, moreover, nothing simple about 'moral panics' when a particular social group is vilified as perennial 'folk devils'. So why, then, are teenagers perceived as the 'moral' threat?

According to Stanley Cohen, 'moral panics' provide cohesion for dominant social groups by uniting them against a minority threat. Teenagers represent the paradigmatic object of moral panics, since they are highly visible, naturally rebellious and do not have the same 'representational' powers as mainstream media institutions. Cohen suggests moral panics work by taking reports of social problems and amplifying them — focusing on representations of similar narratives at the expense of other news. This gives the impression of a much bigger problem.

The current 'moral panic' about internet social networking and youth gangs is a good case in point. The revolution in digital technologies has been enormous and rapid. Teenagers have quickly adapted to the democratic communications potentials of the new networking platforms. So why have the mainstream press focused on the negative behaviour of a minority? First, it provides sensationalist copy, which sells. Second, we have the complex relationship between media, culture and society. A 'daily' newspaper provides a symbolic resource for playing out the fears and anxieties of its readership. For a conservative 'blue-top' readership, the breakneck pace of modern digital life is perhaps alarming. The moral panic may then be seen as part of a wider campaign to introduce control on an otherwise 'unregulated' communications platform.

Over the years, we have witnessed similar 'moral panics' about technology, adhering pretty much to the 'effects' tradition of audience studies. From 'video nasties' to mobile-phone 'happy slapping', modern communications technologies are perceived as a dangerous and corrupting influence when in the wrong hands — the wrong hands belonging inexorably to the impressionable, vulnerable and easily corruptible teenager. The teenager is represented in terms of peer pressure and copycat behaviour — as though they lack the same sophisticated reading skills as any other media reader.

Moral panics can be further understood within the Gramscian concept of hegemony. The mainstream press acts as a conduit of 'common sense', manufacturing the consent of what Stuart Hall refers to as two-thirds society — the moral majority. Teenagers fall within the one-third minority and thus are perceived as an antisocial force. Hall's studies of mugging and football hooligans in the 1970s are reminiscent of contemporary press discourses about chavs, asbos and cyber-bullying. Hall, for example, found that the 'moral panic' about muggers was part of a wider social process of bringing in the New Right law and order values of the Thatcher government. Law and order continues to be an issue that contributes to parties winning or losing elections.

From the 'social problem' films of the 1950s to modern-day soap operas, teenagers have been represented as 'problems'. The new norms, practices and ideas that the younger generation have need to be negotiated (and in extreme cases of violence and crime, coerced) within dominant ideology.

So, in one sense, representation of teenage 'thugs', 'gangs' and 'yobs' can be seen as a sensationalist way of filling tabloid front pages with dramatic headlines and pictures and thus selling newspapers. However, if we consider that the media has a cultural function, shaping people's consciousness, then this representation is more problematic. The practices and values of the younger/next generation will always find discord with the conservative norms of dominant society and thus will lead to less than positive representations.

Grade and examiner's comment

Level 4 — 12 marks

This is a highly articulate and clearly organised response, which shows a conceptualised understanding of the complexities of the question. The candidate has personally engaged with the question and has produced a sophisticated and thought-provoking response.

A good balance is struck between media theories/ideas and reference to relevant examples. Media terminology is used throughout with confidence.

Question 3

There are always concerns about new technology. In your view, what are the possible benefits and problems attached to social networking, particularly on the internet? (12 marks)

Student answer A

It can be argued that social networking has had both positive and negative effects on today's society. Whether these effects are positive or negative, social networking is playing a huge role in today's society. This has recently been acknowledged by Google, which spent $1.68 billion on buying YouTube, and Microsoft, which recently spent $168 million on a less than 2% share of Facebook. Microsoft valued the Facebook site as a whole at $15 billion.

The advantages of social networking are obvious. It has become increasingly easy to communicate with people from anywhere in the world, regardless of age, sex, race or background. Social networking is highly diplomatic because it allows the world to unite, free from discrimination. These sites are also a database of information. Recently, a British university student was murdered in Italy and within hours the police were able to construct an accurate timetable of events leading up to her death.

However, social-networking sites could just as easily be a negative story. Identity fraud could happen. Grooming by paedophiles is worrying and people are no longer developing face-to-face communication skills. They are talking to a computer screen, not a real human being.

I believe social networking is more beneficial than negative as it is uniting the world, at little cost.

Grade and examiner's comment

Level 2 — 4 marks

This is a reasonably well-presented response, but many points are left undeveloped and the links between points are not always clear. The candidate gives a basic analysis and evaluation of the 'social networking' part of the question but disregards the concept of 'new technology'.

To gain a level 3 mark, the candidate needs to cover all aspects of the question. The candidate should also develop clearer lines of argument and use evidence and analysis/evaluation more carefully. For example, the purchases of YouTube and Facebook by global media institutions is an excellent contextual example, but it is not really developed within the framework of advantage/disadvantage. The same applies to the point about the student murder case in Italy.

Finally, the candidate needs to bring in the concepts of audience and institution and discuss issues of control, power and democracy (which was confused with 'diplomacy').

Student answer B

Technology is the difference between modern and pre-modern communications. Mass communications are industrialised mediums. Throughout media history there has been mixed reaction to new technologies. The printing press advanced mass literacy and Protestantism, thus falling foul of the dominant Catholic Church. Popular cinema, television, radio and music have all been seen as socially liberating forces. Like the press, however, they have been criticised and accused of corrupting the innocent and 'dumbing down' cultural standards.

The revolution in digital technologies and the internet is arguably no different from the advent of printing or cinema. However, the cyber revolution has occurred on a much larger scale and at an unprecedented speed. This has been highly advantageous to media audiences and to new, start-up media institutions. The internet, for instance, is not yet as institutionalised in terms of ownership and regulation as cinema and television are.

Media production and consumption are radically different in the digital age. One main advantage lies with opportunities for audience interactivity. Traditional mass media forms work on a one-to-many model: one institution to many consumers, with obvious implications of power and responsibility. Internet technology permits a more one-to-one model of communication, with the consumer being able to interact with other consumers and, crucially, with institutions.

Social-networking sites like Facebook are advantageous to consumers because they create what Castells refers to as systems of 'networked individualism'. The internet has collapsed time and space to allow individuals — regardless of age, gender, race etc. — to interact instantaneously and globally. It is a truly liberating/democratic phenomenon (if you have computer access). YouTube, for example, allows consumers to be producers — to upload/download each other's video productions rather than relying only on global corporate productions. Facebook and MySpace have also allowed consumers to create 'communities' through forums, podcasts and blogs, allowing individuals a political and cultural voice and a means of self-representation. For example, a viral campaign was recently and successfully generated by graduates on Facebook against the bank charges policy of HSBC.

Media audiences have more choice about where/when they consume media products. When you can download texts at any time from the internet or your mobile phone, it makes less sense to be governed by institutionally controlled scheduling.

However, before we get carried away, we need to consider the reactions of traditional media institutions. Google, for example, paid over $1 billion for YouTube, and Microsoft has recently paid a similar sum for a small share in Facebook. If global companies are paying vast amounts of money for control of free/interactive sites then we have to ask why. First, social-networking sites deliver a generation of consumers — no longer traditional television viewers — to advertisers. Many of the videos and links on YouTube, for example, are sponsored links, such as Hollywood film trailers. Second, social-networking sites give excellent marketing indications, allowing global media institutions to see what is popular and how to tailor their future productions. So the threat to the existing institutional hegemony is arguably not so profound.

Another disadvantage is the liberal idea of 'networked individualism'. Are these real communities or, in Baudrillard's words, 'hyperreal'? If we consider the names, many are prefixed with individualist, consumerist names: 'YOU' tube, 'MY' space and 'I' pod/phone. There is nothing suggestive of 'community' here — just materialistic acquisition.

The final disadvantage of social-networking sites concerns this mass of individual voices. This appears democratic, but what about social responsibility? There is much content on the internet that represents the darker side of human nature, including pornography, neo-Nazi politics and cyber-crime/cyber-bullying. The internet's biggest advantage — its freedom — is also its biggest disadvantage. Do we introduce tighter control and regulations? If so, who decides what is appropriate and what is inappropriate? A lot of things, like paedophilia, fall within 'common sense', but who is to say that the same forces of 'institutional self-censorship' and control that defined Hollywood cinema will not eventually be imposed on social networking sites?

Grade and examiner's comment

Level 4 — 12 marks

This is a highly articulate and clearly organised response, which shows a conceptualised understanding of the complexities of the question. The candidate discusses both advantages and disadvantages with confidence and is able to illustrate this discussion with evaluation and analysis of carefully selected examples.

Section B

The assessment objective (AO2) requires you to apply knowledge and understanding when analysing media products and processes to show how meanings and responses are created.

In this section you will have studied a pre-set topic in class. The questions are designed to assess your ability to apply your knowledge and understanding of media products and processes.

It is important to remember that examiners will be looking out for evidence of 'independent study' and 'critical autonomy'. You should not limit your studies (and by implication your examination responses) only to those texts/ideas studied in class. Individual examiners tend to mark *all* the papers from a school or college, so will be able to spot the input of the teacher(s) in your responses. Therefore, responses from the most able candidates — those who can demonstrate that they have carried out their own textual examinations and have read widely around the subject area — will easily stand out from the crowd.

Remember that quality of written communication will be on the examiner's tick-list of requirements. So plan your work and read it through afterwards.

In this section, there are two areas of study: representations in the media and the impact of new/digital media. Each section has a choice of two questions. You only need to have studied **one** of the two case-studies and you only need to answer **one** question. You are advised to spend **1 hour** on your answer.

You will be rewarded for making detailed reference to specific media texts and to your own case study.

Questions

Question 1 — Representations in the media

(a) It has been said that media representations often reflect the social and political concerns of the age in which they are created. Discuss.

(48 marks)

OR

(b) 'Media representations favour those with power at the expense of those without.' To what extent do you think this statement is true?

(48 marks)

Question 2 — The impact of new/digital media

(a) 'Digital media have, in many ways, changed how we consume media products.' Who do you think benefits most — audiences or producers?

(48 marks)

OR

(b) 'Media institutions are right to feel threatened by new/digital media.' Consider this statement and show how media institutions are reacting to technological developments. (48 marks)

Question 1: Representations in the media

(a) It has been said that media representations often reflect the social and political concerns of the age in which they are created. Discuss.

(48 marks)

Student answer

The above statement arguably adheres to the liberal pluralist idea of media reflection. Representation is, however, conceptually abstract; dissimilar to mimetic reflection. According to Richard Dyer, media representations are reality re-told; mediation over verisimilitude. Moreover, media institutions are increasingly global, commercial concerns that have the power to influence cultural values and ideology. Yet dominant media representations can be challenged by external social and political forces. For example, representations of gender in contemporary Hollywood cinema are unlike those of the 1940/50s. The political intervention of feminism has rendered objectified discourses of 'femininity' inappropriate. So can institutions define representations, or can audiences resist? Gramsci's concept of 'hegemony' — the two-way contesting of power between institution and audience — provides a useful model for trying to understand the complexities of representation.

When considering the representation of a place like Manchester, we must begin by asking what is 'Manchester'? Geographically, it is a city in the northwest of England. Socially, historically and culturally, 'Manchester' is more difficult to locate. According to Benedict Anderson, modern communities are 'imagined'. Many British people have never actually been to Manchester, but through exposure to various media representations have an 'imagined' sense of Manchester/Mancunians.

Representations of Manchester tend to fall within discourses of working-class realism, urban gang crime, subcultural hedonism or sport. From the new wave films of the 1950s, such as *Taste of Honey*, and four decades of the popular soap opera *Coronation Street* to the sitcoms *Early Doors* and *The Royle Family*, Manchester exists through an iconographic mise-en-scène of terraced rows, pubs, cobbled streets, factory chimneys, and of course rain. The working classes — feisty, straight-talking pub frequenters — are 'represented' as paradigmatic Mancunians.

Nowadays, however, much has changed. Politically, Manchester has moved away from its hard-left, working-class socialist identity. Economically, it relies on service economies rather than heavy industries; it is more of a cultural centre than a manufacturing one. This change in media representations of Manchester was 'reflected' in a number of 'Manchester' texts. *Cutting It*, *Cold Feet, Queer as Folk* and *24 Hour Party People* were all texts that subverted the grim, working-class, social-realist paradigm of 'Manchester'. These texts represented a more upbeat, metropolitan, cosmopolitan and metrosexual image of Manchester, where people worked in cultural industries or service jobs, and where night-life and entertainment moved beyond 'Rovers Return' style locals.

However, these representations of the 1990s and early 2000s have been replaced by a return to a more prosaic Manchester — albeit without the industry. (The exception to this is *Coronation Street*, where the last vestiges of the 'factory-girl' cling on in the face of global manufacturing practices.) A classic example of a text that harks back to an earlier vision of 'Manchester' is *Life on Mars*, a police drama in which the lead character, played by John Simm, is transported back to 1973. Produced by an independent company, Kudos, for the BBC, the text can be seen to be addressing a number of contemporary social issues. Central to the interplay between contemporary police officer, Simm, and his 1970s counterparts is the conflict between political correctness and unreconstructed male chauvinism. Interestingly, the viewer is hailed more by the straight-talking values of the 1970s than by the overtly procedural/bureaucratic policing of the early twenty-first century. Simm's character, Sam Tyler, has to resolve for us the binary oppositions of pre- and post-political correctness and in doing so he plays out a contemporary concern. Political correctness is now seen by many as an inhibiting and repressive force that often protects the criminal more than the law enforcer. In this way, *Life on Mars* is certainly 'reflective' of changing social and political concerns.

Yet in terms of its representation of 'Manchester', *Life on Mars* denies cultural regeneration. The programme takes us back to a time before punk, Factory Records, The Haçienda or 'Madchester', employing a northern stereotype as a nostalgic signifier for a more 'honest' age. We have a contradiction here in that this text 'represents' one contemporary social/political concern at the expense of another. On another level, however, *Life on Mars* can be read as a postmodern pastiche, self-consciously using random signifiers of 1970s — cars, clothes and attitudes — in an 'ironic' parody of police dramas like *The Sweeney*.

Other popular television texts that perpetuate the Lowry-esque representation of cobbled, terraced streets are *The Royle Family* and *Early Doors*. Both are excellent television sitcoms that give a working-class representation of a paradigmatically 'northern' city, but avoid the regenerated version. However, Channel 4's *Shameless*, written by Paul Abbot, who was once a scriptwriter for *Coronation Street*, takes the Manchester stereotype and subverts it. In *Shameless* the representation is more about the underclass than the working-class and gives a more positive representative voice to a much-maligned social group.

In the Jimmy McGovern-inspired *The Street*, made for the BBC by ITV productions, the opening titles take us from the regenerated city centre, via various iconic landmarks to a drama set in a terraced row in Salford. *The Street* is recognisably *Coronation Street* in its physical form, but in its representation of characters and community it is significantly different. Each episode deals with a different character and a different social concern: sexuality, family, unemployment etc. When tragedy strikes, the community is seen as a group of onlookers, leaving the protagonist to deal with the situation alone. The representation here is neither nostalgic nor shallow. It shows us the two 'Manchesters' and leaves us with the concern that regenerated cities may look great on the surface but hide a multitude of social inequities.

A similar point is raised in the BBC4 documentary *Factory Records: Manchester, from Joy Division to Happy Mondays,* which gives a well-researched and balanced account of Manchester's transformation from working class to middle class and from industry to culture. The documentary gives a broad contextualised account of why Manchester has changed and in what ways. Here too, however, is the underlying sense that the regenerated cultural centre lacks even the community spirit of the punk and post-punk Factory years.

Grade and examiner's comment

Level 4 — 48 marks

This is an articulate and stimulating response written by a candidate who has the confidence to understand that 'discuss' invites a more open-ended response. Ideas are clearly structured and fluently expressed.

The idea of 'representation' is approached both conceptually and contextually, and a wide variety of textual examples are used for analytical exemplification. Detailed reference is made to a number of different media debates and ideas. This candidate has shown clear signs of independent research and 'critical autonomy'.

Simplified mark schemes

When marking examination papers for this unit, examiners are encouraged to look for evidence of 'independent study' and 'critical autonomy' — in other words, thinking for yourself. Unit 3 is a 'synoptic' unit, where case-study material from a range of different media platforms is studied. It is inevitable that when the examiner is marking responses there will be many similar responses from each centre. After all, students will have analysed the same texts, had the same tutors and took down more or less the same class notes.

How do you go about showing the examiner that you are an 'independent student' with 'critical autonomy'? Try to do the following:

- Study a wider range of texts than you have time to look at in class. Remember, your tutor will have chosen a range of texts about a specific subject, concept or genre. There will, however, be many more similar texts that you could look at outside class.
- Study a wider range of media theories and debates than those covered in class time. Remember that class lessons are time-dependent and your tutor will not be able to cover everything.
- Be prepared to voice your own opinion, as long as it is backed up with relevant textual evidence and relevant media theories. AQA specifically instructs its examiners to 'expect the unexpected'.
- Back up *everything* you write in your exam response with detailed evidence and analysis.

Section A

Level 4	7–8 marks	• Analyses and evaluates both texts in a fluent, articulate and detailed response.
		• Shows a wide knowledge and understanding of media concepts and ideas.
		• Backs up every point with detailed references to the text(s).
		• Shows a very good understanding of the contextual factors that affect the production of media texts — particularly when comparing texts from different institutions, and for different target audiences.
Level 3	5–6 marks	• A well-written, fluent response that shows a good knowledge and understanding of media concepts and ideas.
		• Backs up most points with detailed reference to the text(s).
		• Shows a good understanding of the contextual factors that affect the production of media texts — particularly when comparing texts from different institutions, and for different target audiences.
Level 2	3–4 marks	• Gives an adequate response to the question with some evidence and analysis/evaluation from both texts.
		• Makes reference to some media concepts and ideas, and shows an awareness of some of the contextual factors that shape media texts.
		• Writes a reasonably clear response.

Unit Focus 3 Critical perspectives

Level 1	1–2 marks	• A basic response with limited knowledge and understanding of media concepts.
		• Little in the way of evidence or analysis, and written expression is generally weak.
Level 0	0 marks	• Nothing written.
		• Nothing relevant written.
		• Nothing suitable written.

Section B

Questions 1(a) and 1(b) Representations in the media

Level 4	37–48 marks	• A confident answer that responds to the question with appropriate, detailed discussion and analysis.
		• Thorough knowledge and understanding of media ideas, debates and theories, backed up with a wide range of detailed textual evidence and analysis.
		• Excellent understanding that media representations 'reflect' the complexity of social, political and cultural ideas.
		• An engaged and sophisticated personal response, which is clear, well written and well structured, and clearly demonstrates evidence of independent study and critical autonomy.
		• Answers that are articulate, stimulating and interesting, and have clear evidence of wider personal study, will move towards the top end of this level.
Level 3	25–36 marks	• A proficient answer that responds to the question in an appropriate, detailed and analytical manner.
		• Very good understanding of media ideas, debates and theories, backed up with a range of detailed textual evidence and analysis.
		• Very good understanding that media representations 'reflect' the complexity of social, political and cultural ideas.
		• An engaged and interesting personal response, which is clear and well written, and demonstrates some evidence of independent study and critical autonomy.
		• Answers that are interesting and have a strong line of argument will move towards the top end of this level.

Level 2	13–24 marks	• A sound response to the question, with some appropriate discussion and evaluation.
		• Adequate understanding of media ideas, debates and theories, with some use of textual evidence to back up points. Ideas, debates and theories are backed up with a range of detailed textual evidence and analysis.
		• Awareness and some understanding that media representations 'reflect' social, political and cultural ideas.
		• Generally easy to read but not always fluently structured.
Level 1	1–12 marks	• A basic response with limited knowledge and understanding of media concepts.
		• A very basic awareness that media representations 'reflect' social, political and cultural ideas.
		• Little in the way of evidence or analysis, and written expression is generally weak.
Level 0	0 marks	• Nothing written.
		• Nothing relevant written.
		• Nothing suitable written.

Question 2 (a) The impact of new/digital media

Level 4	37–48 marks	• A confident answer that responds to the question with appropriate, detailed discussion and analysis.
		• Thorough knowledge and understanding of media ideas, debates and theories about the advantages and disadvantages of digital media, backed up with a wide range of detailed textual evidence and analysis.
		• An engaged and sophisticated personal response that is clear, well written and well structured, and clearly demonstrates evidence of independent study and critical autonomy.
		• Answers that are articulate, stimulating and interesting, and have clear evidence of wider personal study, will move towards the top end of this level.
Level 3	25–36 marks	• A proficient answer that responds to the question in an appropriate, detailed and analytical manner.
		• Very good understanding of media ideas, debates and theories about the advantages and disadvantages of digital media, backed up with a range of detailed textual evidence and analysis.

- An engaged and interesting personal response, which is clear and well written, and demonstrates some evidence of independent study and critical autonomy.
- Answers that are interesting and have a strong line of argument will move towards the top end of this level.

Level 2	13–24 marks	• A sound response to the question, with some appropriate discussion and evaluation of the question.
		• Adequate understanding of media ideas, debates and theories about the advantages and disadvantages of digital media, backed up with some textual evidence and analysis.
		• Generally easy to read but not always fluently structured.
Level 1	1–12 marks	• A basic response with limited knowledge and understanding of ideas, debates and theories about the advantages and disadvantages of digital media.
		• Little in the way of evidence or analysis, and written expression is generally weak.
Level 0	0 marks	• Nothing written.
		• Nothing relevant written.
		• Nothing suitable written.

Question 2(b) The impact of new/digital media

Level 4	37–48 marks	• A confident answer that responds to the question with appropriate, detailed discussion and analysis.
		• Thorough knowledge and understanding of media ideas, debates and theories about the changes in production, distribution and consumption of media texts, backed up with a wide range of detailed textual evidence and analysis.
		• An engaged and sophisticated personal response that is clear, well written and well structured, and clearly demonstrates evidence of independent study and critical autonomy.
		• Answers that are articulate, stimulating and interesting, and have clear evidence of wider personal study, will move towards the top end of this level.
Level 3	25–36 marks	• A proficient answer that responds to the question in an appropriate, detailed and analytical manner.
		• Very good understanding of media ideas, debates and theories about the changes in production, distribution

and consumption of media texts, backed up with a range of detailed textual evidence and analysis.

- An engaged and interesting personal response, which is clear and well written, and demonstrates some evidence of independent study and critical autonomy.

- Answers that are interesting and have a strong line of argument will move towards the top end of this level.

Level 2	13–24 marks	• A sound response to the question, with some appropriate discussion and evaluation of the question. • Adequate understanding of media ideas, debates and theories about the changes in production, distribution and consumption of media texts, backed up with a range of detailed textual evidence and analysis. • Generally easy to read but not always fluently structured.
Level 1	1–12 marks	• A basic response with limited knowledge and understanding of ideas, debates and theories about the changes in production, distribution and consumption of media texts. • Little in the way of evidence or analysis, and written expression is generally weak.
Level 0	0 marks	• Nothing written. • Nothing relevant written. • Nothing suitable written.

Unit Focus 4
Media research and production

In this unit, you are required to produce two pieces of work:
- a critical investigation of a range of media forms (48 marks)
- a linked production piece (realised media artefact) (32 marks)

The critical investigation gives you an opportunity to investigate a media text of your choice and to demonstrate your understanding of the link between media research and practical production work. You should be able to demonstrate the links between the two elements for assessment purposes. As this is A2 work and you will have already completed a production piece at AS, it is expected that this production piece will demonstrate greater use of media technology and also be of a higher standard than the piece submitted previously.

You should explore in depth a text, issue, debate or theme forming part of the contemporary media world, and use the information gathered to develop the production piece. 'Contemporary', for the purposes of this unit, is specified as meaning 'within 5 years of the commencement of the study of the A2 units'. Older pieces may make contemporary contextualisation difficult. For further guidance, the examination board can advise on the suitability of material.

Candidates working together may produce similar research work or can each focus on different texts, issues, debates or themes relevant to their study area. (Group work is dealt with more specifically later in this chapter.)

Critical investigation

The critical investigation should be around 2,000 words, not including supporting materials, captions, footnotes, references or quotations.

The title of the investigation should be clearly focused. The work should be textually based and researched, with appropriate evidence collected and evaluated, and with conclusions based on the evidence assembled.

The work should include a bibliography and a source list, including both the texts studied and the sources accessed. Film review websites are not recommended by AQA, as they rarely discuss issues in the appropriate depth. However, articles in *Sight and Sound* magazine may be of use here.

The investigation work should be word-processed. The focus of the critical investigation is on content not format, and no marks are awarded for presentation.

Assessment

Top-level work will take the form of a fluent and analytical investigation. It will make good use of AS and A2 learning, and will explore the topic from a critical perspective. It will be well presented with a detailed bibliography. The work will be clearly placed in the context of contemporary media, and clear links will be made between the investigation and the production piece.

Production piece

The production piece should be a fully realised media artefact. Storyboards and other mock-up or preparatory materials are not acceptable. Moving image work does not need to be longer than 5 minutes. Although longer work will not be penalised, its length may detract from its quality. Productions can be shorter — animated work, for example, can be no longer than 30 seconds.

Print productions should be at least 3 pages in length for each candidate and should contain a high proportion of original images. Found images are generally not acceptable at A2.

Work can be submitted in any of the following formats:
- video
- print
- DVD
- website submitted on a CD-ROM
- MP3/podcast
- CD-ROM

The format you choose will depend on your own skills, the availability of appropriate facilities and the advice given to you at your centre.

Assessment

Top-level work will be a creatively and aesthetically successful product that has high production values and demonstrates highly competent use of technology. The best work will have high production values approaching professional standards.

Group work

Candidates may work in groups of no more than four individuals, and individual roles and contributions should be clearly identified for ease of assessment.

A print or website production might be more suited to individual or paired work, rather than a larger group, to allow for a sufficiently substantial individual contribution to be assessed.

Think carefully before you begin group work, particularly as a member of a large group (i.e. a group of four). You must be comfortable with the other members of your group and have a clear idea of what your own particular contribution will be. Working in pairs is generally much easier — the work can be divided simply and you will only have to deal with one other person. If you feel uncomfortable with the size, membership or division of tasks in your group, you should discuss these matters with your teacher before you start work on the production.

Planning media research

Research methods

The quality of your research and production pieces will depend largely on how successful your research is, so it is important to approach this in a methodical and structured way.

All the research you undertake for your critical investigation is valuable, even though the final submission is only 2,000 words. You will need to include a thorough bibliography, which should list all your sources, and all the textbooks, magazines, films and other materials you have referred

to, so it is a good idea to make a note of everything you consult as you go along. The examiner will look through your bibliography to see how you have gathered your materials together, so you need to record the various elements systematically.

Research is usually classified as being either *primary* or *secondary*.

Primary research

Primary research is any research you have undertaken yourself. It could include your own reading and evaluation of media texts, together with content analysis. For example, you might watch an evening's television advertisements to see how women or ethnic minorities are represented. In this case, you would need to log your viewing and record your findings systematically. Remember to include all the details in your bibliography or source list.

Secondary research

Secondary research is where you make use of research done by other theorists and academics. You will need to make organised notes on your readings, identifying sources, works and authors, and evaluating the material.

Where to find the information you need

Textbooks, libraries and resource centres

Textbooks, libraries and resource centres are the obvious first point of call, although most course textbooks will not cover your topic in sufficient detail to be useful on their own. (You cannot just reference your core course textbook.) Libraries are full of under-used specialist texts, so make use of them and ask for assistance if you need it.

You may find that your school or college library does not stock the particular text that you require, but if you know the title, author and publisher, or the ISBN, they will be able to order it for you through the inter-library loan system. Magazines, newspapers and other publications may be available on the internet.

Examiners often comment on how little use students make of established academic texts and theories in any field of study. With lengthy academic texts, do not try to read every word — you can read introductions, skim through chapters and read conclusions to see what points are being made.

Before you start, it is a good idea to make an outline plan of the various sources you think will be useful and where you will be able to find them. You should find out how recent these sources are by looking at publication dates and the examples and case studies they use. For example, the subject of women and cinema is well covered and you will find many sociology and film, media and cultural studies textbooks covering this ground. However, some of these studies may be 20 years old and you must take this into consideration when applying them to contemporary texts.

You are also expected to introduce media perspectives and theory when analysing your key texts. This involves more than just inserting theoretical extracts and definitions; instead, you should look at your text and topic from a theoretical point of view.

Back copies of newspapers and periodicals are invaluable, and library or resource centre staff will often be able to locate materials for you far more quickly than you could on your own. *Benn's Media* and the *Guardian Media Guide* are useful reference works for information about all aspects of media institution ownership, audience and regulation. *Sight and Sound* magazine is essential for film study, and back issues contain vital reviews and analysis. (To help you find direction in your study, a bibliography of some key research texts is provided at the end of this book.)

The internet

Most of the information you need for your research will probably be available on the internet. In particular, newspapers and magazines have sites with back issues of their publications. The Audit Bureau of Circulations and the BBFC have valuable websites. Your challenge is to sift through such sites and decide what is really useful to you. Think carefully about your search criteria: use the names of authors and try to be as precise as possible.

When you download material, be prepared to spend some time going through it and remember that all source material must be acknowledged — do not be tempted to plagiarise. Much of the material on the internet is of dubious quality and you should be selective about downloading and using it. You should avoid media studies sites offering you instant answers to essay questions. Your critical investigation must be entirely your own work.

E-mail

You can try e-mailing companies and publishers for advertising materials or articles. They are often overwhelmed with such requests but you might

be lucky. Remember to follow up your enquiry and do not let yourself be easily discouraged.

Advertising agencies

With the right approach, agencies can sometimes be persuaded to part with useful campaign information, with plenty of glossy exemplary materials.

Audience surveys and questionnaires

As this is an academic text-based study, questionnaires, focus groups and audience attitude surveys are not appropriate research methods and should not be used.

Making progress

Working through academic textbooks, magazines and other materials can be a trying experience. However, you need to make systematic notes on your progress so that you can report back to your tutor when asked to do so.

Research work involves developing skills that are important in higher education, where you will be expected to work mainly on your own. Think about the way you are reading these texts and always try to make the best use of your time.

The critical investigation gives you the opportunity to develop your skills of research and analysis. The limit of 2,000 words means that it is quality and analysis, not quantity, that is being looked for, and the quality of your research will directly affect the quality of the final product.

Link to the text

The critical investigation involves textual analysis, so your background research should be used to support this. Remember not to give a narrative or descriptive account of the text in question. You should reference selected elements to illustrate and explain the arguments you are making, rather than just telling the story or providing character sketches.

Link to the production piece

There should be a clear and obvious link between your critical investigation and your practical work (see the following examples). The production piece should follow on from the investigation.

Example titles

The following subjects for critical investigations and linked production pieces are suitable for A2 work.

Contemporary men's lifestyle magazines

Titles could be:

- How do contemporary men's lifestyle magazines represent the values of the 'new man'?
- How do contemporary men's lifestyle magazines create and retain their target audience?
- An investigation of the view that contemporary men's lifestyle magazines do no more than deliver audiences to advertisers.
- An investigation into the reasons why men read lifestyle magazines.
- *Zoo Weekly* describes itself as offering: 'Girls, sport, videos and funny stuff'. How does this mix appeal to its male readers?

Production piece: mock-up of the first edition of a new men's lifestyle magazine.

Gender representation in soap operas

Titles could be:

- Is *Hollyoaks* guilty of sexism in its representation of women as 'babes' and men as 'hunks'?
- In what ways does *Hollyoaks* both reflect and shape the attitudes, beliefs and values of its youth audience?

Production piece: opening sequence of a new soap opera illustrating gender representation.

Viral marketing techniques

Titles could be:

- An analysis of whether companies are using viral marketing techniques simply to exploit social networking, in order to achieve cheap publicity.
- What are the strengths and weaknesses of using viral marketing techniques to launch a product?

Production piece: viral video marketing a new product.

Japanese animé

Titles could be:

- How significant has the influence of Japanese animé been on mainstream directors and films?
- What is the appeal of an essentially Japanese art-form to Western audiences?

Production piece: opening sequence of an animé production.

'Shock jocks' and local commercial radio stations

Titles could be:

- An analysis of the view that radio stations use 'shock jocks' to gain publicity for themselves, through shocking audiences and creating controversy.
- An investigation into the opinion that 'shock jocks' create controversy by pushing the limits of what is acceptable to say on radio, by using sexually offensive innuendo and thinly veiled racism.

Production piece: audio sequence of a 'shock jock' in action, illustrating the techniques used.

Hints on practical work

Although the content of your practical work is more important than the presentation of it, you should endeavour to produce work to the highest possible standard. What you can achieve in terms of professional presentation depends to some extent on your centre's resources or on other resources that may be available to you.

Print work

Much print work can be done using Microsoft Publisher, which should be available at your school or college, although you may need some advice on how to get the best out of the program.

You will need an A3 colour printing facility to achieve a mock-up tabloid newspaper, but a magazine is obviously closer to A4 size. If you do not have access to A3 printing, you could tape two A4 sheets together to produce an acceptable mock-up.

The specification emphasises that the contents of the practical are more important than the presentation, and explanations of the limitations of what is available to you at your school or college will help explain the quality of the work you submit.

Video work

Your centre should be able to supply you with appropriate video cameras and editing facilities. Editing software is usually Adobe Premier, but you may have access to Apple iMovie or other packages. You should think about your own skill level and aptitude in using edit suite technology before choosing your topic. If you are determined to do a video project, then you need to be committed to mastering the necessary skills. Friends who have these skills can help you to acquire them, so do not be afraid to ask.

Access to hardware and technical support will vary from centre to centre, so you should check out the available facilities before embarking on a complex project.

When attempting to reproduce known genres like soap operas, news programmes, crime dramas or movie trailers, you must take note of the conventions of the genre, as these will affect audience expectations and the credibility of your production. Within the limits of the resources available to you, your completed work must be credible and realistic for the purpose for which it is intended.

Final advice about practical work

Practical work at this level can be the most rewarding part of your course, and the opportunity to produce a media artefact may well have influenced your original choice to do media studies at A-level. On completing it, you will find that you have learned far more than you expected and if all goes well, you will have produced an artefact, either on your own or as part of a team, of which you can feel proud.

Practical work is difficult, demanding and can be frustrating. You will have to overcome disappointments, failures and sometimes being let down by people you have relied on. However, your media artefact is one you can become really involved with. It is hoped that the outcome will leave you with a positive and thorough understanding of all the media principles involved, and will bring your whole media studies A-level to a successful conclusion.

Bibliography

Media theory

Adorno, T. and Horkheimer, M. (1973) 'The culture industry: enlightenment as mass deception', in T. Adorno, *Negative Dialectics*, The Seabury Press.

Ang, I. (1995) *Living Room Wars: Rethinking Media Audiences for a Postmodern World*, Routledge.

Barthes, R. (1957) *Mythologies*, French and European Publications.

Baudrillard, J. (1983) *Simulations*, Semiotext(e).

Berger, J. (1972) *Ways of Seeing*, BBC Publications.

Brunsdon, C. (1991) 'Pedagogies of the feminine: feminist teaching and women's genres', *Screen*, Vol. 32, pp. 364–82.

Bruzzi, S. (2006) *New Documentary*, Routledge.

Curran, J. (1996) 'Rethinking mass communications', in J. Curran et al. (eds) *Cultural Studies and Communications*, Arnold.

Dyer, R. (1992) *Only Entertainment*, Routledge.

Fanon, F. (1967) *Black Skins: White Masks*, Grove Press.

Fanon, F. (1968) *The Wretched of the Earth*, Grove Press.

Fiske, J. (1987) *Television Culture*, Methuen.

Geraghty, C. (1991) *Women and Soap Operas: Study of Prime-Time Soaps*, Polity Press.

Gillespie, M. (1989) 'Technology and tradition: audio-visual culture among South Asian Families in West London', *Cultural Studies*, Vol. 3, No. 2, pp. 226–39.

Gramsci, A. (1971) *Selections from the Prison Notebooks*, New Left Books.

Gray, A. (1987) 'Behind closed doors: video recorders in the home', in H. Baehr and G. Dyer (eds) *Boxed In: Women and Television*, Pandora Press.

Gray, A. (1992) *Video Playtime: The Gendering of a Leisure Technology*, Routledge.

Hall, S. (1980) 'Encoding/decoding', in S. Hall et al. (eds) *Culture, Media, Language*, Hutchinson.

Hall, S. (1995) 'New ethnicities', in B. Ashcroft et al. (eds) *The Post-Colonial Studies Reader*, Routledge.

Bibliography

Hall, S. and Jefferson, T. (1976) *Resistance through Rituals: Youth Subcultures in Post-War Britain*, HarperCollins.

Hebdige, D. (1979) *Subculture: The Meaning of Style*, Routledge.

Jameson, F. (1984) 'Postmodernism and consumer culture', in H. Foster (ed.) *Postmodern Culture*, Pluto.

Jameson, F. (1991) *Postmodernism: Or, the Cultural Logic of Late Capitalism*, Verso.

Katz, E. and Blumler, J. G. (1975) *The Uses of Mass Communications: Current Perspectives on Gratification Research*, Sage.

Katz, E. and Lazarsfeld, P. F. (1955) *Personal Influence: The Part Played by People in the Flow of Mass Communications*, The Free Press.

Lyotard, J. F. (1984) *The Postmodern Condition: A Report on Knowledge*, Manchester University Press.

McRobbie, A. (1978) *Jackie: Ideology of Adolescent Femininity*, University of Birmingham.

McRobbie, A. (1991) *Feminism and Youth Culture: From Jackie to Just Seventeen*, Macmillan.

McRobbie, A. (1996) 'More: new sexualities in girls' and women's magazines', in D. Morley et al. (eds) *Cultural Studies and Communications*, Arnold.

McRobbie, A. (2006) 'Post-feminism and popular culture: Bridget Jones and the new gender regime', in J. Curran and D. Morley (eds) *Media and Cultural Theory*, Routledge.

Mead, M. (1950) *Male and Female: A Study of the Sexes in a Changing World*, Penguin.

Memmi, A. (1965) *The Colonizer and the Colonized*, Beacon Press.

Mohanty, C. T. (2003) *Feminism without Borders: Decolonizing Theory, Practising Solidarity*, Duke University Press.

Moores, S. (2005) *Media/Theory: Thinking about Media and Communications*, Routledge.

Mulvey, L. (1975) 'Visual Pleasure and Narrative Cinema', *Screen*, Vol. 16, No. 3, pp. 6–18.

Neale, S. (1990) 'Questions of genre', *Screen*, Vol. 31, No. 1.

Packard, V. (1957) *The Hidden Persuaders*, Random House.

Radway, J. (1984) *Reading the Romance: Women, Patriarchy and Popular Literature*, University of North Carolina Press.

Said, E. (1978) *Orientalism*, Penguin.

Schwarz, B. (2006) 'The "poetics" of communication', in J. Curran and D. Morley (eds) *Media and Cultural Theory*, Routledge.

Spivak, G. C. (1990) *The Post-Colonial Critic: Interviews, Strategies, Dialogues*, Routledge.

Tolson, A. (1977) *The Limits of Masculinity: Identity and the Liberated Woman*, Harper & Row.

Turner, G. (1988) *Film as Social Practice*, Routledge.

Walkerdine, V. (1986) 'Video replay: families, films and fantasy', in V. Burgin et al. (eds) *Formations of Fantasy*, Methuen.

Williams, R. (1989) 'Culture is ordinary', *Resources of Hope*, Verso.

Williamson, J. (1978) *Decoding Advertisements: Ideology and Meaning in Advertising*, Marion Boyars.

Winston, B. (2000) *Lies, Dam Lies and Documentaries*, BFI Publishing.

New technology

Adorno, T. and Horkheimer, M. (1991) 'The culture industry: enlightenment as mass deception', in *Selected Essays on Mass Culture*, Routledge.

Benjamin, W. (1936) 'The work of art in the age of mechanical reproduction', in H. Arendt (ed.) *Illuminations*, Fontana.

Castells, M. (2001) *The Internet Galaxy: Reflections on the Internet, Business and Society*, Oxford University Press.

Craig, T. and Petley, J. (2001) 'Invasion of the Internet abusers: marketing fears about the internet superhighway' in M. Baker and J. Petley (eds) *Ill Effects: The Media/Violence Debate*, Routledge.

Curran, J. (1996) 'Rethinking mass communications', in J. Curran et al. (eds) *Cultural Studies and Communications*, Arnold.

Friedman, D. (2006) 'Internet transformations: "old" media resilience in the "new" media revolution', in J. Curran and D. Morley (eds) *Media and Cultural Theory*, Routledge.

Hills, M. (2001) 'Virtually out there: strategies, tactics and affective spaces in online fandom', in S. Munt (ed.) *Technospaces: Inside the New Media*, Continuum.

McLuhan, M. (1964) *Understanding Media: The Extensions of Man*, Routledge and Kegan Paul.

Miller, D. and Slater, D. (2000) *The Internet: An Ethnographic Approach*, Berg.

Morley, D. (1980) *The 'Nationwide' Audience: Structure and Decoding*, BFI Publishing.

Morley, D. and Robins, K. (1995) *Spaces of Identity: Global Media, Electronic Landscapes and Cultural Boundaries*, Routledge.

Scannell, P. (1992) 'Public service broadcasting and modern public life', in P. Scannell et al. (eds) *Broadcast Talk*, Sage.

Sport

Anderson, B. (1983) *Imagined Communities: Reflections on the Origin and Spread of Nationalism*, Verso.

Barnett, S. (1990) *Games and Sets: The Changing Face of Sport on Television*, BFI publishing.

Blain, N. and Boyle, R. (1998) 'Sport as real life: media, sport and culture', in A. Briggs and P. Cobley (eds) *The Media: An Introduction*, Longman.

Carmichael-Aitchison, C. (ed) (2006) *Sport and Gender Identities: Masculinities, Femininities and Sexualities*, Routledge.

Hargreaves, J. (1994) *Sporting Females: Critical Issues in the History and Sociology of Women's Sports*, Routledge.

Whannel, G. (1992) *Fields in Vision: Television Sport and Cultural Transformation*, Routledge.

Further reading

Bignell, J. (1997) *Media Semiotics: An Introduction*, Manchester University Press.

Branston, G. and Stafford, R. (2003) *The Media Student's Book* (3rd edn), Routledge.

Chaney, D. (2002) *Cultural Change and Everyday Life*, Palgrave.

Fiske, J. (1989) *Reading the Popular*, Routledge.

Gauntlett, D. (2002) *Media, Gender and Identity: An Introduction*, Routledge.

Hawkes, T. (1977) *Structuralism and Semiotics*, Routledge.

McGuigan, J. (1999) *Modernity and Postmodern Culture*, Open University Press.

Neale, S. and Smith, M. (1998) *Contemporary Hollywood Cinema*, Routledge.

Strinati, D. (1995) *An Introduction to Theories of Popular Culture*, Routledge.

Strinati, D. and Wagg, S. (eds) (1992) *Come on Down? Popular Media Culture in Post-War Britain*, Routledge.

Thwaites, T. et al. (2002) *Introducing Cultural and Media Studies: A Semiotic Approach*, Palgrave.

Wasko, J. (1994) *Hollywood in the Information Age: Beyond the Silver Screen*, Polity Press.

Index

Bold page numbers indicate definitions of key terms

Index

Index

Index